'Headhunter' Hiring Secrets

The Rules of the Hiring Game
Have Changed . . . Forever!

SKIP FREEMAN

Learn How to Position Yourself
as a TOP Candidate
in ANY Job Market—and GET HIRED!

DEDICATION

This book is dedicated to the men and women worldwide who have valiantly struggled through the worst job market since the Great Depression of the 1930s. If this book helps just one person regain employment, or helps someone pursue the job or career of his or her dreams and desires, then I will consider it to be a tremendous success!

More Praise
for *'Headhunter' Hiring Secrets*

"I'm the author of **Guerrilla Marketing for Job hunters 2.0** and the *Wall Street Journal* labeled me the 'Rogue Recruiter' because of my unconventional tactics. Well unconventional is now the new NORMAL so step up. I am an industry 'insider' and I'm telling you Skip's book nailed it.

"Skip tells you in hard-hitting, straight-to-the-point language, how to position yourself to win this new game.

"As a 'headhunter' who's completed more than 1,000 assignments for every position from entry level to CEO, I know what it takes in 2010 to get a candidate placed. Skip does too. This is not another 'me too' book. It contains the relatively unknown techniques we use as headhunters every day to place people, and Skip clearly tells you how to employ them for yourself.

"*'Headhunter' Hiring Secrets* is a MUST read. Ignore it at your career peril!"

David Perry, Co-Author, *Guerrilla Marketing for Job Hunters 2.0*

****

"Skip has expertly identified that a *quantum shift in the rules of the hiring game occurred* in 2009. Play by the old rules and be penalized. Play by the new rules and get hired. Adding the three-point shot to basketball in the '86-'87 season changed the game forever. *The same thing happened in 2009 for getting hired.*"

Pat Scopelliti, Consultant to the Executive Search Industry, Awarded Best in Class Consultant 2009 by MRI Network

****

"A high-octane, must read for *every* job seeker."

Dale Collie, President and CEO, *Courage Builders*

****

"An extremely practical **handbook that will empower you for the life of your career!** Most of us will be looking for a job at some point in our careers. Everyone needs to get a copy and keep it as a handy reference manual."

Brent Darnell, President & CEO, Brent Darnell International, author of *The People-Profit Connection: How Emotional Intelligence Can Maximize People Skills & Maximize Your Profits*

"Skip's ideas are impressive, backed by years of experience and clearly not commonly practiced. This book will not only open your eyes, it will also change your whole perspective on your job search."

Shelly Rosenberg – "To the Point" Editing, Proofreading and Resume Services

****

"Skip's book provides an abundance of real-world experience and perspective that both new college graduates, as well as all job seekers, really need. I highly recommend it!"

Ellen Cross, Senior Lecturer, Department of Management and Entrepreneurship, Coles College of Business, Kennesaw State University (Georgia)

****

"Most people now change jobs every three to five years. Having excellent job change skills can make the difference between success in life and financial ruin. *'Headhunter' Hiring Secrets* is an outstanding guide to the 'inside game' of the new world of job search success."

Mike Seagraves, Creator of the award winning "Mastering Executive Job Change" workshop series

****

"I just finished reading *'Headhunter' Hiring Secrets* for the second time. It contains powerful guidelines for navigating the new hiring landscape. In this new decade you never know when you will need it."

Bob Hayllar, Co-founder www.jobchangecenter.com and www.jobnetworkingcenter.com

A Special Thanks

This book involved the efforts of a great number of people. Many people gave selflessly and freely of their time and made the effort to provide invaluable input and remarkable insight regarding the published product. The suggestions they made for improvements, clarifications where needed, as well as a whole host of other extremely helpful, valuable information added immeasurably to this book. I want to thank each and every one of them for their assistance.

Everything we do in life is, in essence, sales. I want to thank my good friend and colleague, **Paul Jensen (CEO, HALO Maritime Defense Systems)**, for his influence in encouraging me to go into the profession of sales. Job hunting is sales, and as Paul emphasizes, "Hope is not a strategy!" **One must learn, follow and implement a successful process.** His strong influence and powerful input into this book will help all job seekers in this or any economy.

Caroline Taylor Player and **Tiffany Norman (Career Services, Georgia Tech Alumni Association)**, spent valuable time providing relevant input that will certainly increase the probability of job seekers more strongly positioning themselves as top candidates for consideration by a hiring company when they apply the concepts. **Ellen Cross (Senior Lecturer and Professor, College of Business, Kennesaw State University - Georgia)**, provided validation that the "real world" examples and guidance in the book will help new college graduates immeasurably. Caroline, Tiffany and Ellen give unselfishly everyday to dozens and dozens of students and alumni and I want to especially thank them for their selfless service.

George Thornton (a recent job seeker) provided inspiration to publish the book when he told me in an unsolicited email, "Skip, you don't know me but I just got the job I wanted and I have you to thank in many ways. I bought your eBook, followed the principles and scripts throughout your book, and was able to find the right answers when I needed them most. Very cool! Thanks again." **Shelly Rosenberg (To the Point, Editing, Proofreading and Resume Services)**, who has helped a number of our candidates craft resumes with impact and stand out from the crowd, stated after her review, "I work with job seekers every single day and I am here to tell you, most of these concepts are not commonly practiced. You need to get this book out there sooner rather than later in order to get this information into the hands of as many people as possible." George and Shelly, thanks for the inspiration.

Human Resources is involved in all corporate hiring at some point in the process. Both **Tim Schira (VP of HR, MetoKote Corporation)** and **Buddy Key (VP of Talent Acquisition, major engineering firm)** are involved in hiring people almost every day. I want to thank both of them for their powerful suggestions that were incorporated into the final product. Their suggestions will help the readers of this book to more effectively apply the secrets to truly differentiate themselves from other job seekers, a critical factor in successfully landing a new opportunity today.

Tom Koentop (a colleague with Lee Hecht Harrison, a Worldwide provider of outplacement services) has been involved in successfully coaching candidates every single day for the past seventeen years. Tom's review confirmed that this is a guidebook that will add value to the marketplace and not be just another "me too" book. Tom helped us refine some points and affirmed that the materials contained within provide a solid guide to today's job seeker in this vastly different hiring environment. Thanks, Tom, for your help for today's job seeker.

Recruiters work with candidates and clients all day every day. Two exceptional coaches and trainers to the recruiting industry, **Scott Love (President & CEO, Great Recruiter Training, High Stakes Achievement and game theory expert)** and **Pat Scopelliti (sixteen-year consultant and coach to the recruiting industry),** provided powerful suggestions for further refining how a recruiter's techniques can be directly and effectively modified by job seekers to position themselves as TOP candidates; in other words, *how job seekers can become their own "headhunter."* Today, many job seekers, either directly or indirectly, owe their success to Scott and Pat and we all thank you.

Hillary O'Keefe of www.indeed.com took valuable time to provide additional tips and information relevant to all job seekers, enabling them to differentiate and separate themselves from the pack. Her recommendations have already proven to be invaluable to many job seekers we work with. Thank you, Hillary.

Dale Collie (President & CEO, Courage Builders) is somebody everyone should get to know and you can get to know him by signing up for his "Courageous Leadership Tips" newsletter at www.couragebuilders.com. Whether you are employed or unemployed, today's world is stressful. His book, *Winning under Fire,* teaches all of us how to turn stress into success. Dale shared some very compelling thoughts with me as he reviewed the book and we wove them into the text. We feel these will indeed help you "win under fire." Dale, you are a true inspiration. Thank you.

"All things being equal, the people who excel in the workplace and beyond are the ones with higher levels of emotional intelligence." Colleague **Brent Darnell (President & CEO, Brent Darnell International)** has had a profound influence on the direction of our book. Looking for a new job/career opportunity is not only stressful, but emotional. Brent's work in the field of emotional intelligence weaves itself into the very fabric of networking and a successful job search campaign. Brent, thank you for your input and for the help it will bring to many job seekers.

Mike Seagraves, creator of the award-winning "Mastering Executive Job Change" workshop series, and **Bob Hayllar, Co-creator of www.jobchangecenter.com,** offered their many years of experience in job change success to help us not only bring this information together in its final form, but to get it in front of as many people as possible who can use this information. Bob and Mike, thank you for your ongoing support.

And a very special thanks to my Princess who gives me inspiration.

FIRST EDITION

Also available as an **eBook** at http://www.headhunterhiringsecrets.com

ISBN: 978-0-615-34621-2

Printed and published in the United State of America.

Library of Congress registration pending.

Edited and designed by **Michael Garee**

Cover design by **Michael Little**, University of Alabama

All photographs and illustrations used in this book, including the cover photograph, are licensed for use by www.istockphoto.com.

The "Rag Man" drawing © **Syd Yeager** and used by permission.

CONTENTS

PHASE FOUR • CLOSING THE DEAL

INTRODUCTION & OVERVIEW

THE RULES OF THE HIRING GAME CHANGED IN 2009 . . . FOREVER!

A virtual tsunami of change has occurred in the job market since the Great Recession officially began in December 2007. In the United States alone over seven and one-half *million* jobs have simply disappeared into thin air, and over four million of these jobs were lost in 2009. Worldwide, of course, many more millions of jobs have also simply evaporated during this same period.

In addition to the fact that many of these jobs simply will not be coming back, the **"rules" of the "hiring game" changed forever in 2009.** (And, yes, that is the way you must look at finding a new career opportunity . . . as a "game," a very serious game in which there are many players and only one winner per job.)

Thus, as we enter the new decade, there actually are TWO sets of rules being used to play the game:

➢ The *old* rules most candidates *think* hiring companies still play by; and,

➢ The *NEW* rules that the hiring companies are *actually* playing by.

Just as adding the three-point shot to NCAA basketball in the 1986-1987 season changed the rules of the game of basketball forever, the new hiring rules instituted in the "2009 job season" have changed the hiring game forever. And, just as is the case with the three-pointer, the rules won't change back.

So, which set of rules are you going to play by? If you pick up, read and play by the *old, wrong* set of rules, your chances of being a top candidate under consideration for a position in the new decade will be *significantly* reduced. It doesn't necessarily mean you won't win the game and get hired playing by the old rules. What it's likely to mean, however, is that you will have to play the game longer *and* harder in order to win.

THE 'TOP TEN' NEW RULES OF THE HIRING GAME

What, then, are the NEW rules of the hiring game? What are the implications of these NEW rules for job seekers of today *and* tomorrow? And, most importantly, what are the strategies and tactics needed to successfully play by the new rules? The three-point addition in NCAA basketball was in and of itself rather simple. However, the strategies and tactics necessary to make it an offensive weapon, as well as to fashion effective defenses against this change, weren't simple at all. This same principle holds true for the NEW hiring game rules!

With all of this in mind, then, here are the "Top Ten" NEW rules of the hiring game:

—NEW Rule Number ONE—

Today's unemployment situation is *not* merely part of a "normal" job cycle. Many, if not most, lost jobs simply are NOT going to return.

IMPLICATIONS FOR JOB SEEKERS

In the new decade, job seekers who will GET HIRED will only be those who are powerfully and exceptionally skilled at differentiating themselves within an ever-increasing pool of available candidates for an ever-decreasing number of jobs.

—NEW Rule Number TWO—

Recent worker productivity *increases* necessitated by *decreasing* numbers of employees is *not* a temporary phenomenon.

The workload carried by today's—and tomorrow's—employees has become the new "norm," the new expectation. Thus, many of the lost jobs over the last couple of years will *never* come back, simply because employers no longer see the need to replace them.

IMPLICATIONS FOR JOB SEEKERS

Effectively communicating and proving beyond any reasonable doubt your business worth and profit-enhancing relevance to a company has become, and will remain, more critical than ever.

—NEW RULE NUMBER THREE—

The economic landscape has already changed *significantly*, and that change can only be expected to continue, with substantial, long-term implications for future job seekers.

Among many other things, the altered economic landscape means that many of the skill sets that currently are or recently were "in supply," unfortunately, are no longer "in demand."

IMPLICATIONS FOR JOB SEEKERS

Repositioning oneself in the job market is no longer a luxury; it has become, and will remain, a fundamental requirement.

—NEW RULE NUMBER FOUR—

Job seekers who continue to rely exclusively, or nearly exclusively, upon the Internet for job leads will no longer be seeing the "whole picture."

IMPLICATIONS FOR JOB SEEKERS

Since most job seekers only apply to positions online, they are missing out on being considered for close to one-half of all available jobs. Tomorrow's job seekers MUST effectively market themselves like a "headhunter" would market them, in order to have MAXIMUM exposure to all positions.

—NEW RULE NUMBER FIVE—

It is *substantially* more difficult today to get one's résumé in front of a hiring manager/company, and it can only be expected to become even more difficult to do that in the future.

Because the majority of job seekers apply to positions online, companies have set up extremely effective "screening" software and other mechanisms that quickly *exclude* the majority of candidates—without them ever getting a chance to have their credentials reviewed.

IMPLICATIONS FOR JOB SEEKERS

Only those job seekers who learn about and apply the adaptive techniques for avoiding exclusion from the available pool of candidates will get HIRED today and in the future. Those job seekers who insist on continuing to play by the "old" rules, which involved trying to figure out how to be included in the pool, will likely not even be considered.

—NEW RULE NUMBER SIX—

The interview process is taking TWO to THREE times longer today than ever before.

Gone forever are the days when just one, or perhaps even two or three, interview sessions were sufficient for landing a new job.

IMPLICATIONS FOR JOB SEEKERS

New skills, better preparation and considerable patience and planning are required from today's job seeker, in order to effectively manage the lengthy and often grueling process of actually getting HIRED!

—NEW Rule Number SEVEN—

More so than ever before, hiring managers today are constantly "under the gun" and are growing increasingly fearful of making hiring "mistakes."

Because of the continued threat to their own jobs, hiring managers today (and for the foreseeable future) are going to go to great lengths to avoid making hiring mistakes. As a result, they tend to hire the "safest" candidates, not necessarily the "best" candidates.

IMPLICATIONS FOR JOB SEEKERS

Job seekers who will get HIRED in the new decade will only be those who take into consideration, and then learn how to effectively deal with, the substantial pressures hiring managers are under. That is, the successful job seeker will understand, and then take measures to eliminate, any and all things that may cast "shadows on the wall" (unreasonable or perceived fears) for the hiring manager and get them summarily excluded from further consideration.

—NEW Rule Number EIGHT—

Due to economic business pressures and downsizing, many hiring managers and Human Resources professionals are now essentially doing the work of 1.3 people.

This overworked, and some might say, under-appreciated, group of people literally has a job seeker's career in their hands. Yet many either don't have the training and/or expertise to effectively interview candidates. Or worse, they simply can't (or don't) take the time to conduct an effective interview.

IMPLICATIONS FOR JOB SEEKERS

The successful job seeker in the future will learn, and then effectively employ, techniques such as "leading the witness." That is, he or she will learn how to proactively answer the FOUR basic questions all hiring managers want answered but may not know to ask: Can you do the job? Do you want to do the job? Will you do the job? Are you a good cultural fit?

—NEW Rule Number NINE—

Get used to the current economic upheaval because it is here to stay, at least through much of the decade ahead.

Former CEO of Intel Corporation Andy Grove is quoted as saying, "Only the paranoid survive." That would seem to be a particularly apt quote considering today's economic climate.

IMPLICATIONS FOR JOB SEEKERS

In the old days, there was a person known as "the rag man." This person was called in whenever a death in the family occurred and he took away clothing and other personal effects of the deceased so that the family wouldn't have to deal with those details. Then, the "rag man" went from town to town around a circuit hawking, "Rags for sale. Get your rags." People of course flocked to the "rag man," not necessarily to purchase the rags he offered (although some did), but more importantly, to learn the "news" from other towns the "rag man" traveled through on his rounds. In other words, he became a valued source of information, a person considered by most to be "in the know."

The effective job seeker of the future must become a modern day "rag man," i.e., a person "in the know" within his/her industry.

—NEW Rule Number TEN—

In order to be effective in the hiring game over the next decade, job seekers must STOP playing by the "old" set of rules.

The days of putting together a *generic* résumé, along with a "one-size-fits-all" cover letter, and firing off hundreds (thousands!?) to jobs posted on the Internet are a significant part of the "old" rules. They have, in every sense of the word, been supplanted by the NEW rules!

IMPLICATIONS FOR JOB SEEKERS

Those job seekers in the next decade who will be successful in landing a new job or pursuing a new career will consist of those who take the time and make the effort to learn the NEW rules of the hiring game. What's more, they will diligently and relentlessly implement and practice these NEW rules, in order to WIN and get HIRED!

'HEADHUNTER' HIRING 'SECRETS' AND 'THE NEW RULES'

The "headhunter" hiring "secrets" comprising the individual chapters of this book have been carefully selected for, and are intended to provide assistance to, today's (and tomorrow's) job seekers in the *significantly* changed job market. All "secrets" are fashioned to recognize the impact, significance and substantial influence of the NEW hiring rules, and then to offer job seekers concrete, specific tactics and strategies for *effectively* competing in current and future job markets.

Some of these "secrets" are not new. Many "headhunters," hiring managers and Human Resources professionals are already aware of them, at least instinctively. Unfortunately, however, the same can't be said for the majority of job seekers. They either aren't aware of many of the "secrets" at all, or have chosen simply to ignore them altogether, waiting for the "good times" to return once again to the job market. Job seekers falling into one of these categories and continuing to take a laissez-faire attitude toward the current and future job markets will do so at their own considerable peril.

However, some of these "secrets" are, without equivocation, certainly new. For example, I have read many "career" and "job seeking" books and I have never seen one where job seekers were taught how to telephonically market themselves like a "headhunter" would market them. That idea might be out there, but it is clearly not in the mainstream.

THE 'EXCLUSIONARY' HIRING PRINCIPLE[1]

A consistent thread running throughout this book involves this basic principle: No longer is the hiring process one of inclusion. Today, it is one of *exclusion*. That is, hiring managers and hiring companies, during each and every step of the *entire* hiring process, are *not* trying to identify job applicants they can include in their "hiring pool." Instead, they are trying to determine, as quickly and as efficiently as possible, how many applicants they can *exclude* from that "pool"!

As an example, under the *old* rules there was a reasonable expectation that if you read a job posting and sent in a resume, you would receive a reply. You had every reason to believe the following, "They have a need. I have most of the qualifications. They will review my resume, either email me or call me and set up an interview or, at the very least, I will get a 'no thank you'."

---

[1] *See NEW Rule Number Five.*

The new reality? The new rules? Today you will be lucky if you get even a one percent response rate from your efforts, much less an interview—even if you are perfectly qualified! Why? The system is set up to find a reason to exclude you!

In *"Headhunter" Hiring Secrets*, I show you the *specific* things you need to do and not to do; the specific things to say and not to say in order to play effectively by the **new hiring rules**. For example, I show you, not how you can be *included* in the "pool' of job candidates, but rather, how you can minimize the chances of being *excluded* from that "pool." To some job seekers, there may appear to be a subtle distinction between these two perspectives, but believe me, **in 2010 and beyond the distinction is very real** and ultimately **of critical importance in your job/career search!**

THE FOUR STRATEGIC PHASES OF AN *EFFECTIVE* JOB SEARCH

After years of experience in the professional recruiting business, it is clear to me, and it will become clear to you, that there are **FOUR** major, quite distinct strategic phases involved in an *effective* job/career search:

- **Preliminary Planning & Preparation**

- **Developing a Marketing Plan**

- **Selling** (yourself to prospective employers)

- **Closing the Deal** (getting the job!)

"Headhunter" Hiring Secrets examines each of these four phases in detail, showing you how to capitalize on opportunities by learning, and then employing, the tactical "secrets" I share with you. I know from experience that, at least initially, some of these "secrets" will seem entirely foreign to you. That's entirely understandable because you'll quite likely still be thinking about a job search from *your* perspective, not from an employer's perspective. You'll still be playing off the old set of rules, not the new.

Conversely, some tactical "secrets" may seem intuitive to you, and you might even think, "That is no secret at all." Be that as it may, I still see the same mistakes being made over and over again daily to the detriment of hundreds of highly qualified, top-notch job seekers because they don't understand the NEW rules that hiring companies play by.

Over my more than seven years as a professional "headhunter," I have learned that the majority of people do not know how to conduct an *effective* job search. From observation, as well as from hundreds of conversations, what most people do is conduct their job search somewhat in the following manner: They put together a résumé, "hit the job boards," and fire off dozens of résumés, many to companies seeking to fill positions for which they are in no way qualified. They ask the *wrong* questions during an interview. They don't know how to properly answer the questions prospective employers ask them. Their résumés are full of easily avoidable errors, e.g., typos, grammatical errors, misspellings, etc. They approach hiring managers with a "what's in it for me" attitude, instead of a "what can I offer you and your company" attitude.

But you know what? All of this is perfectly understandable, in a way. Consider these facts:

- The typical person conducts a job search about **five** or **six** times in his or her working **life**! (Thus, the fact that they are essentially playing by the wrong set of rules when it comes to job hunting is therefore certainly understandable.)

- The typical company hiring manager *may* be involved in the hiring process **five** or **six** times in a **year**.

- As a professional "headhunter," I am involved in the hiring process **five** or **six** times a **day**!

In *"Headhunter" Hiring Secrets*, I share with you what I have learned from being involved in the hiring process on a *day-to-day* basis for over seven years. I share with you what I have learned from observing the hiring process both from the candidates' perspective *and* from the perspective of the hiring managers and the companies they represent.

I realize that what seems perfectly clear and logical to me may not seem that way to you at all. That's at least one reason why I decided to write this book—to share these "secrets" with you, so that you will be able to learn the NEW rules of the hiring game, and then apply the tactics and strategies that can help you *effectively* compete in today's significantly changed job market. If you will learn, and then diligently apply the tactics and strategies outlined in this book, you will be able to WIN in today's job market. You will be able to position yourself as a TOP candidate in the job market and get HIRED!

How well do these "secrets," this approach, work for a job seeker today? The candidates represented by The HTW Group, generally **have a 50-60% greater probability of landing the position versus candidates who have gone after the position on their own**. Why? Because we teach and coach our candidates on the NEW rules and how to play to WIN! Thus far, we have helped hundreds of candidates find stellar new careers over the past seven years, including during the recession. In the summer of 2009 a professional in the United Kingdom purchased the eBook version of *"Headhunter" Hiring Secrets* and sent us this unsolicited email, "I purchased your eBook, have implemented most of the ideas and I am here to tell you . . . they work!" A job seeker in Atlanta states, "Until I applied the techniques in 'Hiring Secrets,' I had not had even one single interview. After purchasing the book and using it, I have landed my dream job."

Now, with the print publication of *"Headhunter" Hiring Secrets*, we can help literally thousands and thousands of job seekers!

IF YOU ALREADY HAVE A JOB, SHOULD YOU STILL READ *'HEADHUNTER' HIRING SECRETS*?

If you are currently employed, you're probably thinking, *Well, I already have a job, so why would I benefit from reading* **"Headhunter" Hiring Secrets**? Good question, but also the *wrong* question. Let me tell you why.

Gone are the days when *any* job was considered a "safe" job, if there ever really was such a time or that kind of job. Today virtually everyone who is employed is at risk of suddenly—and unexpectedly!—joining the ranks of the unemployed. If you have been in your current position for a number of years, for example, you are at risk ("We need new 'blood'"). If you are relatively new in your job, you are equally at risk ("We need someone with more experience" or "We need to cut costs, so we're laying off those who have been with us the shortest amount of time"). If you are among the highly compensated (or even close to it), you definitely are at risk ("We need to cut costs"). In other words, in today's labor market there simply is no "safe" place to hide.

Is the current and future job picture bleak? It depends! It depends fully on which set of rules you play by.

One last thing: I don't want you to get the impression that *"Headhunter" Hiring Secrets* offers you some kind of "silver bullet," or any other kind of "guarantee" that you'll find a job. I can't guarantee such a thing and no one else can, either. What I can *guarantee* you, though, is this: If you will study and then **put into practice** the "secrets" that I have included in this book, you **will** significantly increase your chances of being among the **very top candidates** vying for jobs in any market. If anyone gets hired, chances are, it will be you! Job seekers who continue to play by the OLD set of rules, and who refuse to acknowledge and effectively adapt to the NEW set of rules, will not be in the same league as you. They won't even be close.

PHASE ONE
PRELIMINARY PLANNING & PREPARATION

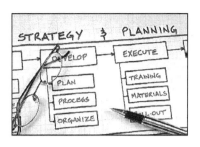

Most people conduct a job/career search somewhat in the following manner: They . . .

- Update or create a résumé.
- "Surf" the job boards.
- Send out résumés to postings that are "interesting" and *seem* "relevant."
- Call a few recruiters.
- Call a few networking contacts.
- Get frustrated when they don't hear back from a hiring manager or company, even though their credentials, at least in their opinion, seem a *perfect* match for the position.
- Begin to send out even *more* résumés, for even *more* postings, many of which, this time around, really aren't even relevant to their credentials.
- Finally get an interview with someone.
- Think they actually did well on the interview, but never hear another word from the hiring manager/company.
- Become more and more frustrated and the cycle continues—all to no avail!

My advice at this juncture is—STOP! Get ORGANIZED! Make a PLAN!

Without an *effective* job search plan, you are destined to play by the *wrong* set of rules.

In the following section, I'll show you how to prepare for the unique challenges you'll be facing in today's job market. I'll also show you how to come up with a good, solid, *workable* plan that will allow you the best chance of becoming a TOP candidate for jobs in *any* economic climate, in *any* job market.

THE 'DAILY MISOGI': PREPARE FIRST, TAKE ACTION! SECOND

If you are anticipating being laid off, or have actually lost your job, you are quite likely to have a very strong temptation to take ACTION! This is very understandable and a very human reaction under the circumstances. You want to pick up the phone and call a recruiter, contact people in your social and professional networks. You want to hit the job boards and start sending out résumés by the dozens, if not by the hundreds! You've got to get *something* going, and you've got to do it NOW!

STOP! It is critical that you take the time to collect your thoughts, to get adequately prepared *and* to formulate your plan. Rushing around helter-skelter without first preparing your mind and your spirit *and* your plan is unlikely to be very productive for you.

So, before I get into the "secrets" in *"Headhunter" Hiring Secrets*, let me share with you how you can—and must!—prepare your *mind* and *spirit* to effectively meet the challenges that lie ahead for you in your job search—before taking even the first step.

THE DAILY MISOGI

The Daily Misogi . . . no, it's not some kind of Japanese soup. Rather, it's an ancient Japanese *cleansing* ritual involving preparation of the *mind* and *spirit* for each new day. It's a ritual that can serve you well in preparing for your daily job search activities.

The majority of us start each day with at least some general plan regarding the *activities* that we would like (or have) to undertake. But most of us don't fully prepare our *minds* and *spirits* for the day.

Oh, some of us may start our day with prayer, reading a holy book, or even by going to a religious service. But how many of us really ever stop to think *deeply* and *quietly* about the issues of the day ahead and make a *definite* plan of activities?

MISOGI AS PRACTICED BY THE SAMURAI

My professional mentor and coach, Pat Scopelliti, taught me that ancient Samurai warriors, who were practitioners of Misogi, would get up before dawn every day, sit cross-

22

legged and sharpen their swords, often for a couple of hours. Did their swords really need to be sharpened for two hours? Of course not! While it may have appeared to the casual observer that the warriors were merely sharpening their *swords*, actually, they were really "sharpening" their *minds*.

The reality of each new day for a Samurai was that, potentially at least, he lived in a "kill or be killed" world. He would therefore visualize the day ahead, and analyze the results of previous battles. He would visualize victory. He would do "success/failure" analysis. What must he do to replicate past successes? What had he learned from past failures?

APPLYING MISOGI TO YOUR JOB HUNT

Preparing for the "job hunt" each day requires this same kind of intense, *daily* preparation of the *mind* and *spirit*. And once you find your next position (or even if you are currently employed), you would do well to continue such daily preparation.

Before the start of each new day's activities, you should quietly and deeply reflect upon and then set "drop dead" targets and/or goals, i.e., those things that you positively, absolutely must accomplish, as a minimum, for the day. Equally importantly, you should also quietly and deeply reflect upon the targets and/or goals you set for the *previous* day.

Ask yourself, "What successes did I achieve?" "How do I replicate those again?"

"What failures occurred?" "How do I learn from those failures?"

There are two types of failure: Honorable and dishonorable.

Honorable failure means that you didn't achieve your objective(s) for that day. However, you analyzed the failure(s), discerned lessons, applied them and simply collapsed on "the battlefield," exhausted, having failed, but still knowing that you didn't "surrender."

Dishonorable failure means one of two things. Either you didn't learn from your failures or you simply surrendered (quit) before completing the task(s) ("drop dead" minimums) that you had set.

HOW I PRACTICE MISOGI

Here is how I practice Misogi. When I get up in the morning it is still dark. The coffee has automatically brewed. I savor the aroma. I stumble downstairs and pour a large cup, groggily make my way back upstairs and turn on the shower as hot as I can stand it. I get in the shower, sit down with my legs crossed, let the hot water flow on my neck and back, and I slowly sip the coffee. (Taking care not to let water from the shower get into my cup, of course!) I am still groggy and sleepy. I let my mind wander. I think of the *known* issues of the day ahead. I think of the successes and failures of the past day.

After sitting in the shower for about twenty minutes, suddenly the synapses in my brain start firing rapidly, "dots" are instantly "connected." Ideas surface that I hadn't previously thought of. Solutions to persistent problems seemingly occur out of nowhere. My mind and my spirit are on full steam ahead by the time I exit the shower.

None of these things would likely have happened had I merely jumped out of bed, hopped in for a quick shower, dressed, grabbed a cup of coffee and made a mad dash to get out the door and head for my office. For what? So I could quickly fire up my computer and check my email, taking the day largely as it unfolded? Or, another way of putting it: I would be letting the day seize *me* rather than my seizing the day!

This isn't magic, of course, or any kind of strange "voodoo," but it has proven to work remarkably well, time and time again for me, and it can also work for you, although it wasn't until just the last couple of years that I learned that the practice (now a habit!) actually had a name—Misogi. (Some "purists" may debate me on this and say that I am not actually doing a Misogi. But again, the point is not *what* we call it. The point is that we do something each day to prepare our *mind* and *spirit* for the day ahead!)

Remember: Misogi—A Whole New Way of Preparing for the Day

Again, Misogi is different from praying, reading a holy book or a "how-to" or motivational book. This is a practice of *intensely* focusing on the day ahead and the *specific* tasks that must be accomplished, in light of both the successes and failures of the previous day, in order to develop creative solutions.

So, whether you do what I do or get coffee and just go sit in a swing or rocking chair on the porch, find a way to spend about twenty minutes waking up slowly, keeping your eyes closed and truly, thoroughly contemplating the day ahead. Consider some *"hard"* questions/issues such as these:

- What interviews do I have today?
- If I don't have any interviews, what must I do to start getting them?
- How do I best follow up on the ones I have had?
- How do I identify new companies and hiring managers to contact?

- What can I do today that is unique versus the other "job hunters" out there, so that I will be perceived as adding value to a potential employer?

This is how I have uncovered the secrets for hiring: I would ask myself questions such as, "Why didn't the candidate we represented get the job?" Or, "Why was the offer so low?" "What happened to enable the offer to be so high?"—higher, actually, than any of us imagined? By letting the brain ponder such things in solitude and quietness, solutions and answers come together that you probably would never think about otherwise.

The power of the human spirit, coupled with the human brain, is boundless. Overlay that with knowledge and you are ready to begin. So let's begin!

JOB HUNTING IS LIKE
HIGH SCHOOL
FOOTBALL 'TRYOUTS

Over the years, the job hunt has been compared to a variety of sports-oriented "crucibles," i.e., "tests." A marathon. A 100-yard dash. A "free-for-all." And while such sports analogies certainly have seemed apt at one time or the other, the best analogy, at least in my opinion, is high school football "try outs." Even though I fully understand that 95% of the U.S. population will never have tried out for football, there really is no other comparison as applicable or appropriate to the hiring process. Read on and see why.

Each fall, at virtually any high school in the nation, upward of 200 young men, in the case of the larger schools, show up to try out for the football team. All of the hopefuls know that, on average, only about one-third of them will actually make the team. Still, they show up, hoping they will be among the chosen few. The odds facing a job candidate, of course, are even worse! Only *one* candidate is going to be successful for any given job opportunity and the number of applicants generally far exceeds 200!

In order to quickly "separate the wheat from the chaff," most football coaches hold the dreaded "two-a-day" practice sessions, usually one two-hour session in the morning and another two-hour session in the afternoon. (These afternoon sessions can be particularly grueling in states like Texas or Oklahoma, where high school football is practically a religion, and afternoon temperatures are still flirting with the mid- to high-90s at this time of the day!) This extremely challenging regimen goes on for about two weeks in the typical high school football program.

At each practice session, the candidates run, run, run, oftentimes until many literally fall to the ground, exhausted and, at least for the time being, defeated. The goal, of course, is to push these young men to their absolute physical and psychological limits. Some of the hopefuls don't have to wait to

Like high school football coaches during fall 'try outs,' employers are not looking for people they can *include* on the team, they are looking for people they can *exclude* from the team!

be "cut," they merely take themselves out of contention because they either can't—or won't—make the sacrifices necessary to become part of the team.

To the casual observer, it appears that the football coaches are merely trying to determine which of, say, 50 to 70 young men they will actually select for the final team roster. In fact, nothing could be farther from the truth. What the coaches are actually trying to determine during this two-week period is which of the other 130 to 150 young aspirants they can *eliminate* from further consideration.

What does this have to do with job hunting? In a word: EVERYTHING! Because that's precisely how many, if not most, employers view any given pool of job candidates. They are not looking for whom to include, they are looking for those whom they can exclude! Harsh? Unfeeling? Not "fair"? Yes, yes, and yes, but that's still the way it works, and you need to understand this right from the start of your job search. Failure to understand this key concept puts you behind the rest of "the pack" before the try outs have even begun.

Consider these facts about the job picture in mid 2009. In comparison to the market of just a year or two ago, there are just *one-half* the number of jobs available. However, there are now *twice* the number of candidates seeking those jobs! That means it's *four times* harder to "win" one of those jobs in today's market.

So, just as is the case with the "football tryouts" analogy, you had better show up ready to "play"—not to "lose," ready to make the necessary sacrifices, or you stand virtually no chance of ever making "the team." You'll be among the first to be "cut (excluded)." Conversely, of course, if you do show up well-prepared, your chances for success are significantly improved! Remember, the objective in both football tryouts *and* job hunting is to make sure you don't get eliminated.

Now, if you haven't already done it, go get "suited up" for *your* "try out"!

BILE, BLOOD & PHLEGM

G ot your attention, didn't I? Good.

The ancient Greek Philosopher Hippocrates, a pioneer thinker in what later became the medical sciences, thought human behavior could be classified into basic types, with each personality being caused by an excess of a particular bodily fluid. For example, an *irritable* person had an excess of *yellow* bile, according to Hippocrates. A person who was *depressed* had an excess of *black* bile. If a person was *optimistic*, then he or she had an excess of *blood*. A *calm* person had an excess of *phlegm*, and so on.

Brilliant thinker that he was, we now know Hippocrates didn't exactly have it right when it comes to "classifying" the various causes for one's personality or emotional makeup. The point was—and is—that from time immemorial, we human beings have always felt the need to know something of ourselves (and others). We have always yearned to know the factors that contribute to, and ultimately shape, who we (and others) are.

Throughout this, the first phase of your job search, you will be developing an ongoing, dynamic assessment of the skills, talents, abilities, contributions and recognition that you will later use to market yourself to prospective employers. You will use this information, for example, to prepare your *final* résumé (I assume you already have a résumé, but in Phase Two, **Developing Your Marketing Plan,** I'll show you how to develop one that will make you stand "head and shoulders" above most of your competitors!) and cover letters, as well as the other "collateral" marketing materials you MUST use in your job search, e.g., your "smile file," networking business cards, emails, direct mail—virtually every single type and piece of communication used during the marketing phase.

You very definitely will also be using the information emanating from this assessment in telephone interviews and the all-important face-to-face interviews.

Ultimately, you should be able to come up with about **sixty attributes** for the "product" you will be marketing—you. These attributes will, of course, be unique to you! And attributes lead to accomplishments and achievements that SELL! Remember, numbers (#'s), percentages (%'s) and dollars ($'s) saved (or made) sell. What do they sell? You!

Maybe your "product" attributes will look something like this: Are you . . . Relaxed? Sociable? Assertive? Sensitive? Quiet? Fragile? Enthusiastic? Competitive? Driven? Creative? Patient? Persuasive? Courageous? One who thrives on pressure? Resilient? Do you know which traits actually describe *your* personality? I strongly recommend that, if you don't, you get a personality assessment. A thorough understanding of exactly *who* and *what* you are can help you emphasize those traits most sought after by prospective employers, while at the same time, downplay those traits that might get you excluded from further consideration.

Next, you must assess how these "product attributes" actually contributed to the success of the companies for which you have worked. Examples:

- **Fifteen years** of **progressive responsibility** in **key roles** in (your field of specialty).
- Among the **top 10%** of all salespeople for the past **eight years.**
- Led a team that produced a **new product** that **increased** the company's **net profit by 5%** in the first full year of production.
- Was a **keynote speaker** at the company's 2008 "Sales Roundtable."
- Received THREE "letters of commendation" for **Outstanding Sales Achievement** in 2008.
- Attained the **Professional Engineer (PE)** designation in 2008.

A FREE website that offers an excellent personality assessment, and can provide insight into this critical area, is available through North Carolina State University. Here is the link:

http://www.soicc.state.nc.us/soicc/planning/c1a.htm

Emotional Intelligence: Another critical area for you to explore as you analyze your abilities and attributes is the area of emotional intelligence. **Brent Darnell**, a leader in this field, states, "All things being equal, the people who excel in the workplace and beyond are the ones with higher levels of emotional intelligence. Not that technical ability is unimportant. In fact, it is extremely important. But technical ability and experience can only take you so far."

So what is emotional intelligence (EI)?

"Emotional intelligence is the ability to identify, assess and manage one's own emotions and those of others," states Brent. "This ability is like any other—it is naturally found in varying degrees from person to person.

However, emotional intelligence can be learned and improved through specialized programs."

For a snapshot assessment of *your* Emotional Intelligence, go to this website:

www.brentdarnell.com

In the upper left of the website, click on **"Download Center"** and register with the site. Once registered, go to **"Other Resources"** on the bottom left of the page and click on "**EI Mini Test**."

This **"EI Mini Test"** will provide you with a snapshot of your strengths and weaknesses in regard to EI. Self-awareness of these areas will not only help you develop your marketing plan, it will also help you in interviews. Plus, it can give you some ideas on areas of improvement that will help you in your overall career progression and development.

Career Progression: Your **ability t**o demonstrate career progression is extremely important in the eyes and minds of many hiring managers. This is demonstrated through promotions, title changes and/or increased duties and responsibilities. Think back over your career and be sure to include these as bullet points in your résumé, as well as conversation points during your interviews.

Examples include:

- Promoted to District Sales Manager of $20 million district with 12 team members.

— OR —

- New preventative maintenance procedures led to a $200,000 decrease in unexpected downtime in 2006. Consequently, **became maintenance team leader over two plant production units.**

"Winning Under Fire": This is the title of a book by **Dale Collie** and, as stated by Bob Danzig, former CEO of Hearst Newspapers, "A must read for every leader." Just as you will learn in Phase Three that every job seeker is a salesperson, it is equally true that every job seeker is a leader. A leader influences others toward achieving a goal. As a job seeker, you will indeed be influencing others toward achieving a goal—hiring you! Thus, you need to exhibit the qualities and characteristics of a leader in every phase of your job search.

Whether you are employed or unemployed, looking for a new position is stressful. If you let this affect you negatively, it will dramatically reduce your ability to play by the new rules of the hiring game and will derail your job search. In *Winning Under Fire,* Dale draws upon his experience as both a combat leader and a sales manager in two Fortune 500 companies and illustrates how to combine military know-how and business savvy in order to be able to:

- Stay resilient under all conditions.
- Prepare a game plan to get you through every battle.
- Channel stress into positive energy in order to achieve your goals.
- Channel fear into focus.
- Identify and control stress at the first sign of it.

"There is little glory for a company in bringing a 'me too' product to the market just to watch it share shelf space with the competition," Dale says.

As a job seeker now (or in the future) *are you a "me-too" product* or will you position yourself as the TOP candidate and GET HIRED?

If you read, learn, study and apply the principles in this book, it will be the latter!

KEEPING *ACCURATE, CURRENT* RECORDS OF JOB SEARCH ACTIVITIES, CONTACTS

The best time to get organized in any undertaking, particularly one as important as a job search, is *before* you actually need to *be* organized. During your job search, materials and information, as well as myriad details, can quickly accumulate and soon overwhelm you, if you are not organized. Such disorganization and failure to pay attention to detail can—and often does—easily derail your candidacy, as you'll see below. So get organized NOW, just as you are beginning your job search.

One system that works well for most candidates is to keep (religiously!) a **notebook** or a **journal** (I recommend a three-ring binder that can hold 8 ½" x 11" lined paper) in order to **stay up-to-date and ultimately organized** during your entire job search. This is the type of information you should include in it:

- A list of companies/positions that you have applied to on the job boards.
- The *specific* names and Web addresses (URLs) of the job boards to which you've posted your résumé. Also make sure you can "retrieve" your résumés, if necessary, i.e., write down your UserId and password(s) for these sites. Far too many people forget where they have posted their résumés, so old résumés, résumés with mistakes, etc., remain in cyberspace, possibly to come back and haunt them.
- A list of companies/individuals you have contacted directly or through referrals.
- A list, by name and company affiliation, of recruiters with whom you have connected.
- The notes/comments from any interview (telephone *and* face-to-face) you have had.
- Your daily thoughts (Misogi moments) regarding your career search.

If you are playing *not to lose*—and you had better be in that mindset in any job market!—it is imperative that you be able to recall, quickly and easily, ALL of the details involving your job search. You may think you'll be able to do this without keeping a diary or a notebook, but in my experience, you would be wrong. None of us can remember everything, and since a job search can quickly become physically and emotionally exhausting, the ability to recall *specific* details will be substantially diminished. And keep in mind, not being able to remember details can quickly cause you to be *eliminated* from further consideration!

In addition to your **three-ring binder**, I recommend that you also have a **three-hole punch** available, as well as **extra ink cartridges** (if you use an ink jet printer), plus a set of at least **seven tab dividers**. Here is what you should include on the tabs:

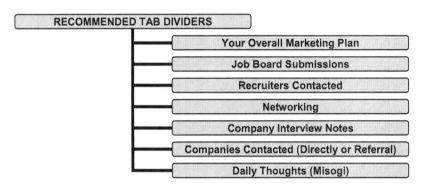

RECOMMENDED TAB DIVIDERS
- Your Overall Marketing Plan
- Job Board Submissions
- Recruiters Contacted
- Networking
- Company Interview Notes
- Companies Contacted (Directly or Referral)
- Daily Thoughts (Misogi)

Consider the following examples of what can happen to a job candidate who isn't organized, who doesn't take precise notes and keep a good record of his or her job hunting contacts and activities. (These are real examples from my work with both candidates and client companies, by the way.)

CAN YOU AT LEAST GET MY NAME RIGHT?

This example involves an email a candidate sent to a hiring manager after he (the candidate) had completed the initial phone interview with the hiring company. At the end of the call, the hiring manager had advised the candidate that they were moving forward and would like him to have a second phone interview later the same week. Understandably, the candidate was quite excited about his prospects at this point. He quickly fired off the following "Thank You" email to the hiring manager:

Dear Larry,

Thank you for the opportunity to speak with you yesterday on the telephone. The more I learn about XYZ Company, the more excited I become. Based upon our conversation, the three areas where I can add the most value are:

- **The First . . .**
- **The Second . . .**
- **The Third . . .**

33

Now, I know what you're probably thinking. Seems like a pretty good follow-up letter/email, right? Well, yes, at first glance. But there is actually one *major* problem with the email—the hiring manager's name was *not* Larry! To put it mildly, the response this candidate received back from the hiring manager was somewhat less than enthusiastic, as you can probably imagine. Here is the response:

First, my name is not Larry. It is Ron. Your information has been forwarded to HR and they will be getting back to you.

Ron was the person the candidate had actually phone interviewed with. Larry was the next person in line he was going to interview with. By not taking careful notes during the initial phone conversation, the candidate literally blew himself out of the water! One of the most carefully guarded possessions a person has is his or her name. Being addressed by the *wrong* name is particularly grating, especially to someone you're trying to impress.

The result of this *major faux pas* is quite predictable, of course. The candidate certainly didn't get a second telephone interview. Rather, soon thereafter he received an email from HR thanking him for his interest in the position and advising him, essentially, that he wasn't the "right fit" for the position.

Perhaps the biggest irony of all in this particular example is that the candidate was otherwise a *superb, highly qualified* candidate! He simply didn't pay attention to the necessary details and was quickly—and predictably—eliminated from further consideration

OK, You Got My Name Right, Now Can You SPELL it Correctly?!

This example is similar to the previous one. In this case, the candidate got the hiring manager's name correct . . . well . . . almost. She actually *misspelled* the hiring manager's name (by getting just one letter wrong)! And this error, which could easily have been avoided by the candidate paying closer attention to detail, occurred after the face-to-face interview! She practically had the job wrapped up at that point. As a matter of fact, the client company had already advised me that they were ready to make her an offer! As in the first case, this candidate was also magnificently qualified. She was, however, just as quickly eliminated from the running, as was the case with the candidate in the example above. Why? Because it was an engineering position and engineers must pay attention to details! Otherwise, a bridge may collapse!

Now, if you are at all typical, you're probably thinking, "I would never make a mistake like that!" I hope you're right, but . . . I see mistakes just like these all the time!

IF YOU DON'T EVEN KNOW WHERE YOU'VE APPLIED . . .

In this example, a candidate applied to us for a position that my recruiting firm had posted on one of the major job boards. He also was a well-qualified candidate. In our initial interviews with candidates, we routinely ask them if they have ever applied to the companies we are representing. In this case, he said he had not. So far, so good.

When we presented the candidate to the hiring company, we were advised that their records showed that he had already sent them a résumé through CareerBuilder.com. So what was the big deal, you might ask? "If he can't keep track of the fact that he has already applied with our company," said the hiring manager, "we certainly don't want him working for us."

Cruel? Petty? Perhaps, but that's the way it is in the job market. Employers, who are literally inundated with highly qualified candidates for virtually every job, can afford to be picky, and they are. Remember, employers are *not* looking for candidates to *include* on "the team," rather, they are looking for those candidates they can *exclude* from "the team"! And any reason is a good reason in their minds.

As you can readily see, had the candidates cited in the three examples above simply set up an effective, efficient method of keeping track of every single detail during their job search, the outcomes quite likely would have been far different, and certainly much more favorable, for them. Don't you make the same mistake!

GET A BUSINESS CARD FROM EVERYONE YOU CAN!

Virtually everyone you will come into contact with during your job search will have a business card. Ask *everyone* for a card, and then organize those cards, by including them in a Rolodex card file, taping them to correspondence you've sent (or received) from companies you have contacted, etc. The method you use to organize the cards is not half as important as the fact that you *do* organize them in some fashion for easy future reference!

KEEPING TRACK OF EVERYTHING ELECTRONICALLY

You don't have to "reinvent the wheel" (and waste valuable time!) when it comes to keeping your critical job search information organized by creating spreadsheets or some type of database. My recommendation is to investigate www.jibberjobber.com. This site offers a FREE, very user friendly way of easily keeping track of critical job search information . . . names . . . telephone numbers . . . email addresses, as well as other important information generated during your job search.

JOB BOARD 'SURFING'
IS NOT JOB HUNTING

What is the first thing most job seekers do when they start out looking for a new job? Jump online and go to the job boards, see what's available and start sending out dozens of résumés!

This is the time for *planning*, not for immediate ACTION! Actually, I strongly recommend that you do NOT distribute your résumé at all at this time, including—"especially" is probably a better word—to the job boards. (I'll discuss the appropriate time to distribute your résumé, as well as how to effectively use the job boards in Phase Two, the **Marketing** phase.)

It's also very important to keep in mind that the various job boards, Monster, CareerBuilder, et al., should only be considered as just one part—a very *small* part, as a matter of fact—of your total job search plan. Why? Because the typical "hit" rate on the job boards is only **one to two percent**. That is, for every 100 positions you might apply for on a job board, you can expect to receive some type of response (good, bad or indifferent) from only one or two hiring companies. That means you've got better odds winning at the Blackjack tables in Vegas!

Number of Résumés Sent to Companies Advertising on "Job Boards"	Expected Number of Responses (good, bad, indifferent)	"Hit" Rate
100	1 to 2	1% to 2%

Want more bad news about relying solely, or nearly solely, on the job boards? Only about one-half of all jobs are posted on the boards. And, statistics show that **only ten to twelve percent of all jobs advertised are filled with applicants from the boards!** This means that **only five to six percent of ALL jobs** (advertised *and* unadvertised) **are filled with applicants from the boards!**

Still, large numbers of candidates continue to make it a major point to visit the job boards each and every day, sending out sometimes hundreds of résumés. Most think they are spending their job hunting time productively, but in fact, they are doing nothing of the kind. They are wasting time that could be better and more productively spent in far more important job hunting activities.

THE *ONLY* TWO REASONS COMPANIES HIRE YOU: YOU CAN *MAKE* 'EM MONEY OR *SAVE* 'EM MONEY

Forget all about altruism . . . companies hire people solely for the two principal reasons cited in the headline above: You can either *make* the company money, or you can *save* the company money. If you can do one or the other, or preferably, *both*, your chances of being ultimately successful in your job search are significantly improved. However, just *saying* you can do either of these things (or both) isn't going to "cut it." You must be able to *prove* your ability to do them.

Very early in the planning stages of your job search, you need to sit down and give some serious thought to what accomplishments (with current or previous employers) you can cite regarding these two key factors. Example: "I was a team leader on a project to reduce overall costs of the company's Management Information Systems. Our team ended up reducing overall costs by nearly 25 percent." Or, "As one of the top salespeople in my company, I was instrumental in increasing total gross income for the chemical division by an average of 10% for each of the last five years."

You get the idea. The important thing to remember here is that you must cite *specific, concrete* facts and figures to bolster any claims of how you can make the company money, or save them money.

GATHER UP ALL YOUR AWARDS, PROFESSIONAL CERTIFICATIONS, TRANSCRIPTS, REFERENCE LETTERS AND LETTERS OF RECOGNITION AND/OR PROMOTION

Most of us have been admonished from childhood never to "brag" about ourselves and our accomplishments. While that may be good advice in social circles, it's the wrong rule to play by in the hiring game. Potential employers know virtually *nothing* about you. As a matter of fact, the only thing they can *ever* know about you is what you (or others) tell them about yourself. So don't even consider holding back *anything* that might give you a competitive edge over other candidates for the same positions.

Scour your personal and professional files and come up with any letters of recommendation you may have received during your career, awards, especially glowing performance reviews, etc. If you've been mentioned favorably in any company (or industry) publications, try to get copies of the articles (if you don't already have them). Assemble your letters of reference and any documents demonstrating that you have been promoted and/or given increased responsibilities.

In the event you don't have letters of recommendation, or if the ones you have are outdated, don't hesitate to ask influential colleagues, as well as other persons in positions of authority, to write some for you Simply call these people up and ask them for their help. A very good approach is to tell them that you know their time is very valuable, and that you would be glad to put some thoughts down on paper for them to consider for inclusion in the letters, if they indeed concur with those conclusions. Handled properly, such letters oftentimes produce remarkable results for the job candidate. Let me give you a recent example.

A SUCCESS STORY

In January 2009, I was working with a chemist who used our coaching and "headhunting hiring secrets" to become so well prepared that he had *two* solid job offers within just three weeks of beginning his search! After our coaching conversations, he went to his boss and his boss's boss and asked for letters of recommendation—in the right way. (The company was in financial difficulty, so they were willing to write letters, otherwise, obviously, he would have had to approach a previous company.) He asked if they would please use specific information that would demonstrate specific, quantifiable achievements. The first letter, the one from the boss, is shown on the next page. (Notice the *specifics* in this letter. Too many letters contain just broad generalities.)

January 2, 2009

To Whom It May Concern:

Jim Smith worked on our product development team at XYZ Chemical for five years as a formulations manager. During that period, we met personally every week to review projects, to work on cost reductions and product performance enhancements. Jim was a pleasant fellow to work with and was meticulous in his approach for formulation dilemmas.

Over his tenure at our company, his documented formulation efforts and plant integration expertise saved the company hundreds of thousands of dollars.

Examples include:

- Development of cationic cleaning systems
- Development of green secondary solvent surfactant systems
- Development of surface dewatering systems for automobile cleaning
- Reformulation of "safe" mineral acid cleaning systems and products
- Structure-activity relationship development - for narrow-range alcohol ethoxylate formulations in hard surface cleaners
- Formulation of Imidazoline-based surfactants into hard surface cleaning applications
- Other examples too numerous to mention

Jim can work independently, works as well in the plant as in the laboratory, and is excellent with customers and in product demonstration situations. Jim is a professional product formulations chemist and has good experience in many industrial and consumer product markets.

Jim is not a synthetic organic chemist; however, the talents he brings are the ones that translate molecular chemistry into products. He is very straightforward in explaining his work and his position on projects.

Had I the need for a product formulation chemist for developing industrial or consumer cleaning products, I would rehire him without reservation.

Sincerely,

Sam Beaumont

Sam Beaumont
Senior Vice President – Chemical Group

Here is the letter from the boss's boss. Notice the mention of *specific* dollar amounts and how our coached candidate had a direct (and *favorable)* impact on the company's bottom line.

1-24-2009

To: Whom It May Concern

Reference: Letter of Recommendation for Mr. Jim Smith

Mr. Smith reported indirectly to me in my position of Vice President for a period of approximately five years in his capacity as Formulations Manager for XYZ Chemical. Over that time I observed first hand his skill level as a chemist, his work ethic and personal integrity. The caliber of his work was excellent and his personal work style required limited direct management as he was keenly aware of his goals and objectives.

In the course of his work Jim had several key accomplishments. Some examples are:

- **Technical Innovation**. Led technical development on a number of surfactant projects by taking market requirements and converting them into performance chemical products. His work with cationic surface cleaners resulted in the launch of two products that resulted in **first year start up sales of approximately $250,000.**

- **Margin Improvement of Existing Products**. Jim did a critical analysis of raw materials where both pricing and supply were critical issues in 2008. This allowed several key products to be supplied with no market interruption and additionally the company was able to **post savings in the $150,000 range.**

- **Process Improvement**. He was able to creatively use newly available raw materials that were very economical to streamline formulations by creating offsets to existing products; this had a major impact on product costing with no deficiency in product performance. This process occurred over all product lines in the company with **upside for the company in the $300,000 range.**

Mr. Smith is the type of person that would be an asset to any company that would provide him the opportunity to showcase his skills. I can highly recommend Jim and am available for follow up by phone at 123-456-7890.

Sincerely,

Mike Roberts

Michael Roberts
Vice President - Surfactants

Further implementing our coaching and "headhunter hiring secrets," our candidate didn't stop with the two fine letters of recommendation. He also put together a very professional, "knock-'em-dead" presentation to *graphically* illustrate the results of key projects he was integrally involved in. (Remember, a picture is indeed sometimes worth a thousand words!)

Below is just a brief sample of what was featured in his rather extensive and quite impressive graphic presentation concerning his personal and professional involvement in a key product development project.

New Carpet Cleaner/Repellent

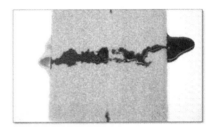

One-half of the carpet (left side) was cleaned with Resolve and the other half with a New Carpet Cleaner with Stain Repellent. Then grape juice was poured on. Compare the results of the two sides.

Notice how the grape juice runs off the half cleaned with our new carpet cleaner with stain repellent (right side), while the left side, cleaned with Resolve, immediately begins to soak up the grape juice.

Mr. Smith is just one of the many job seekers we have coached. His following our advice paid off quite handsomely. Can you be as well prepared as Mr. Smith? You better believe it! And you certainly *should* be, too, because, today, this is the type of job seeker you're going to be up against if he or she has been coached by our firm or has truly taken to heart the "secrets" in this book.

To ensure your file is complete, be sure to get copies of any professional certifications, e.g., Professional Engineer (PE) designation, Chartered Financial Consultant (ChFC), etc. And, if you graduated from high school or college in the last ten years, get a copy of your grade transcripts. If you are applying for a position that requires driving a motor vehicle, be sure to obtain a motor vehicle (MVR) report, too.

WHERE ARE YOU?!

This may be one of those secrets for which you ask yourself, "Why is this in the book?" Isn't this obvious? I have asked myself that dozens of times because it does seem rather obvious that you should make sure that you can *easily* be found by companies to which you have applied and by recruiters. But I am constantly amazed by how *difficult* some candidates make it for hiring managers and recruiters to be able to reach them!

 Email

Most job candidates today have an email address. Interestingly enough, one major problem is that many don't check their email on a frequent enough basis, nor do they respond in a timely fashion to incoming emails. Additionally, many forget to check their junk/spam folder for messages that were improperly processed by their email program. This can prove deadly during a job search. Get in the habit of checking your email at least **three times a day**—morning, afternoon and in the evening. Don't become addicted to it, just check it.

You should also make sure that your email address reflects professionalism. How would a prospective employer likely view the person who has this email address: golfintheafternoon@myisp.com? Or this one: fungalatnight@myisp.com or feistybitch@xyz.com? And then this one: lazydad@myisp.com! (All four of these are REAL email addresses of job seekers who corresponded with us. Needless to say, we did not contact any of them regarding any job opportunities!) Make sure you choose an email address that is far more suitable. The standard professional format is to use your firstname.lastname@myisp.com, e.g., john.smith@myisp.com.

Never use your email address at your current employer (if you still are employed) as your email contact during your job search. This practice could easily result in you having to *significantly* speed up your job search, if your current employer were to discover this practice (and many, if not most, employers today *do* monitor both email *and* Internet use among their employees!).

One additional comment regarding email use: Treat each and every email you send with the same care and attention to detail that you would if you were sending a regular "snail mail" letter. That is, make sure you use proper grammar, correct spelling, appropriate salutations (use "Dear Ms. Smith" instead of "Dear Sally," for example), etc. And, while email communications aren't generally held to the same formal standards as the traditional business letter, that doesn't mean it's OK for emails to be "sloppy," or "chatty," either.

 **Telephone**

Another critical consideration during your job search is to make sure that you have a *dedicated* "career search" phone number. Does that mean you must get another land line installed in your home during your job search? Of course not. Just dedicate an existing line or cell phone for this purpose.

The first thing to do is to make sure your voice mail or answering machine "greeting" is appropriate and professional. "Hey, you know what to do at the 'beep'" is *not* the kind of greeting you want the caller to hear while on your job search. Having your three-year-old record the message probably isn't a very good idea, either. Cute perhaps, but NOT a good idea when searching for a job. And make sure the dogs aren't barking in the background, or that the garbage truck is not out front when you record the greeting. (Yes, each of these examples is real!)

Also, actually record the greeting yourself. Don't let the voice mail/answering system use the computerized, built-in greeting message. When I call and hear the "robot" say, "No one is available to take your call. Please leave your message . . . beep. . . ." I don't know if I dialed the right number or not, nor do I even know if you check your messages. Once, out of interest, I kept a record of the number of voice mail messages I left on systems that had the "computerized" greetings. Less than 20% of the time did I get a call back versus an 85% call back rate from people who had an actual greeting. So, today, if I get a computerized greeting, I simply move on, and that's what hiring managers from companies do as well.

An acceptable greeting could go something like this:

"You have reached the voice mail of Jim Smith. I am not able to answer the phone right now, but your call is important to me. Please leave your name, number and a brief message and I will get back to you as soon as possible. Thank you!"

One other thing regarding your voice mail greeting: Make sure you put some *positive feeling* and *enthusiasm* in your voice when recording the greeting. If your voice sounds monotone and totally lacking in enthusiasm, then chances are, any hiring manager will conclude that *you* probably don't have much feeling and enthusiasm as a person! On the other hand, don't go overboard at the other extreme, either, by sounding "fake" or too "cheery."

Finally, ask some friends to call you and critique your greeting.

All of this should go without saying, but I learned a long time ago never to take *anything* for granted when you are in a job search. And remember, *every* opportunity a company can use to exclude you as a candidate will be taken. Check your voice mails frequently, and return calls *promptly*. Oh, you might be thinking, that's just common sense. Common sense or not, I have dealt with candidates whom it took me several days (and numerous phone messages) to contact. When finally I did reach them, and asked if they had received my messages, their answers, typically, went something like this: "I have been busy and haven't had time to check my voice mail"!

Needless to say, in most cases, any potential these candidates may have had for job opportunities largely evaporated because they couldn't "get around" to checking their phone messages.

One more consideration: Only put *one* phone number and *one* email address on your résumé. Two reasons:

- Don't make the hiring manager try to guess which email or voice mail you will check first.

- And as you will learn later, the larger companies use résumé inhaling software and generally only one phone number and one email address get inhaled into the database. You want them to be the ones you check frequently.

NEVER, NEVER QUIT A JOB
UNTIL YOU HAVE ANOTHER ONE!

This may sound like an absolute "no-brainer" to most people, but never, never, never quit a job you now have before getting another! Yet people do this all the time, and it can have devastating effects on a candidate, particularly if he or she is currently in the process of becoming a "finalist" for a new position. Whereas the candidate may have once had some degree of "leverage" with the prospective, new employer, as long as he or she had a job, once he or she quits that job, he or she will have virtually none! But what if the prospective employer doesn't *know* I quit my job? you may be asking yourself. Trust me, they will find out.

In today's economy, of course, downsizing and lay-offs occur. Fact. End of story. If you were downsized, do not bemoan the fact to a hiring manager. Do *not* be negative! Suck it up, remain positive and demonstrate that you are ready to move forward.

That said, the truth remains that employers still prefer to hire employed people.

If you feel your position is in any way "at risk," i.e., you get wind that something may be coming down, start looking. NOW! (Remember what the former CEO of Intel, Andy Grove, advised: "Only the paranoid survive!")

A candidate whose company was recently purchased by another firm knew that the position she had in her present company would not exist in the newly formed company, so she approached her boss with her (genuine!) concerns about her ability to survive in the new company. Her boss told her, "Do you really think I would let anything happen to you?" My candidate's response was, "Boss, I appreciate what you are saying, but the reality is, once the merger is finalized, you might not have a whole lot of say in the matter."

Note, in this example, the candidate did *not* suggest in any way whatsoever to the current boss that she was "going to start looking." (Never a good idea!) She merely presented herself as being "diligent." Following that conversation, she has since updated her résumé and is *actively* seeking other career opportunities. She wants to be able to choose her own fate, not have it chosen for her. You should take this same approach, if you ever begin to feel "tremors" in your current position.

Phase Two
Developing Your Marketing Plan

Product
Pricing

Promotion
Placement

How do you go about *effectively* marketing yourself? Simple. The same way you would market *any* product or service!

Marketing campaigns are generally based on a **Plan** that has four subsets: **Product, Pricing, Promotion** and **Placement** (the so-called "Four P's" of marketing). Here is how the "Four P's" apply to your job search:

- **Product** – It's YOU, of course.

- **Pricing** – How much you will cost the company (as compared to the value that you will bring to them).

- **Promotion** – Disseminating information about the **product** to the **target audience**. (Promotion and the concepts in Phase Three, **Selling,** are what communicate your value to a prospective employer.)

- **Placement** – How you **place** yourself in front of your **target audience**, also known as "channels to market."

But your marketing plan should do more than just *consider* the Four P's. You must study them! It's important that you *understand* the product (You). You need to research and understand your pricing (your cost versus your value). You need to develop your promotional literature. And finally, you need to identify and implement appropriate channels to market, i.e., placement—getting yourself in front of the right prospects (hiring managers).

In the previous section, **Preliminary Planning & Preparation**, you were building the foundation from which you will launch your campaign. The marketing phase that follows fills in many gaps and holes that most job seekers are unaware of and **exposes many of the rules of the hiring game that companies play by.**

DON'T BE A BTNA CANDIDATE!

How many people in your personal and professional life have you met who can be classified as "BTNA" people? That stands for **"Big Talk, No Action,"** by the way. Job candidates can talk until they are literally "blue in the face" about what they are *going* to do to market themselves to the job market, but until they actually *take* some definite ACTION!, they can only be classified as BTNA candidates! Many of your competitor job seekers will fall into this category.

Taking action, of course, requires a plan. A *personal* marketing plan. Here is how French novelist Victor Hugo put it:

> **"Where no plan is laid, where the disposal of time is surrendered merely to the chance of incident, chaos will soon reign."**

Imagine beginning a trip without first having a "map" to guide you from your point of origin to your planned destination. Wouldn't be a very good idea, would it? The same, of course, holds true when it comes to your job search. If you just set out willy-nilly, with nothing more than the vague goal of "getting a job," you'll certainly find it difficult to position yourself as a top candidate for *any* position that might become available. Without a plan, you have a greater probability of being excluded early.

By the time you have completed the bulk of your preliminary planning and preparation discussed in Phase One, you should have more than enough information to put together your *personal* marketing plan described here in Phase Two. If you don't, then you need to revisit this important preliminary phase of the job search!

In the simplest terms, a marketing plan is nothing more than a type of "map" to keep you on the right track when it comes to marketing yourself during the job search. Virtually every company that intends to stay in business has a marketing plan. Sometimes that plan is extremely complex and somewhat lengthy, particularly in huge companies marketing numerous and diverse products and/or services. Other times, particularly in the smaller companies—and in the case of your *personal* marketing plan—it can be relatively simple and brief, as long as all the important "stops" along the road to positioning yourself as a top candidate are included and clearly marked.

STEP ONE – WRITING THE 'MISSION STATEMENT'

Regardless of the complexity or simplicity of your personal marketing plan, it should contain the basic elements of a good plan. For example, most marketing plans begin with the so-called "mission statement." Yours should also. Here is how you might construct your mission statement:

"To leverage my skills and fifteen years of experience and progressively increasing responsibilities to my own advantage, as well as to the advantage of any future employer, in order to obtain a new job as a senior advertising copywriter in the retail products industry, within the next six months."

The power of the above mission statement is that it is both simple and complete. That is what you need. It will give you direction as you develop the rest of your plan. Please note, though, that this is your *personal* mission statement for guiding your action. It does *not* go on your résumé!

STEP TWO – PUT THE PLAN IN WRITING

Next, you will want to reduce to writing both the *strategies* and *tactics* you will employ, in order to accomplish your mission. Following is an example of just one strategy and several tactics you might employ to implement the strategy. Your strategies, as well as the specific tactics you will employ to implement your personal marketing plan, will, of course, be unique to you.

STRATEGY	Make meaningful contact with the Top 100 retail product companies in the U.S.
TACTICS	• Through Internet research and other appropriate sources, identify the Top 100 retail product companies, as well as the names and email addresses of the top advertising executives in each company. • Construct personally addressed emails and send to the top advertising executives. • Prepare very professional portfolio containing award-winning advertisements for which I was principal copywriter.

STEP THREE – DEVELOP AND IMPLEMENT THE PLAN

Creating a mission statement and reducing your marketing plan to writing alone are not enough. Developing and implementing your plan by focusing on the "Four P's" of marketing—Product, Pricing, Promotion and Placement—will separate you from your competitors. Additionally, a well-constructed, properly developed and implemented plan gives you the focus you need to leverage your time during your job search, a very important consideration.

Too many job seekers—too many people, actually—are "Big Talk, No Action." Make sure your talk, your ideas and your dreams are converted to ACTION! That will greatly improve your odds of being placed in the job/career of your dreams—and put you head and shoulders above much of the competition!

YOU ARE THE 'PRODUCT' BEING MARKETED

A product, any product, consists of two parts: 1.) the *contents* and 2.) the *packaging*. In the previous phase on **Preliminary Planning & Preparation**, you gathered the whole array of information about yourself that will most appeal to prospective employers. This information represents the contents. Now, it's time to "package" the contents and come up with the complete "product," you.

By now, you should be able to clearly and easily show an employer what you can "bring to the table," in the form of past accomplishments and demonstrated future potential. You should be able to present *concrete, specific* examples of *precisely* how hiring you (instead of another candidate) will benefit the company, i.e., you will either "*make* them more money" or "*save* them more money," or both. This certainly will make you stand out from other candidates! What's more, you also have the numbers, percentages and dollar amounts reflected in your résumé, letters of recommendation, etc., to prove it.

Always keep in mind that this type of information will not necessarily get you the position you seek, but it can help keep you from being quickly *excluded* in the great elimination process so characteristic of, and so constant in, any job market. When a hiring manager sees *specific, measurable, concrete* accomplishments and other information on your résumé, LinkedIn profile, in letters of recommendation, etc., he or she is far more likely to put you into the "maybe" pile. But a cautionary note is in order here: The "maybe" pile is *not* the "inclusion" pile. It is simply the pile of those *not* excluded—yet.

'PACKAGING' YOURSELF FOR SUCCESS

As I am sure you are quite aware, consumer product companies spend hundreds of millions of dollars to come up with just the right "packaging" for their products. There is a very good reason for that, of course. No matter how wonderful the contents may be, if the packaging isn't attractive and inviting to the consumer, the product likely will sit on store shelves for quite some time. Make no mistake about it, this same "packaging" principle applies to job candidates, including you!

A candidate could have an absolutely glowing résumé, great phone skills (demonstrated during the initial phone contacts), excellent references and letters of recommendation, but in 80% of the interviews if one isn't dressed

Nervous 'ticks,' such as nail-biting, hair-twirling, etc., during an interview can cause you to be quickly eliminated from further consideration.

conservatively and appropriately, he or she will be eliminated regardless of how casual our society has become. (Note: Conservative dress does *not* mean "old-fashioned," however.)

HIRING MANAGERS ARE A 'PICKY' BUNCH

Hiring managers are a very "picky" bunch of folks. Why? *Because they simply can be, that's why.* While you may consider some of the reasons hiring managers automatically *eliminate* candidates from consideration as being "unfair," "unreasonable" or "unrealistic," that still isn't going to change the situation. If you want to compete successfully in today's job market, get over it, suck it up, and get prepared to present yourself, i.e., "package" yourself, in such a fashion that you will stand head and shoulders above many of the other candidates against whom you will be competing for the same positions.

Be sure to brush *and* gargle before an interview! Bad breath is one of the most common reasons hiring managers eliminate job candidates during the face-to-face interview.

Just for starters, one of the top reasons hiring managers **eliminate candidates** right from the start is **bad breath!** (The solution to this, obviously, is to make sure you brush thoroughly *and* use mouthwash as soon as possible *before* meeting with the hiring manager. If you smoke, refrain from smoking until after you have left the hiring company's offices! Also, check out Colgate®'s new "Wisp®" waterless toothbrush.)

Here are some other things about personal "packaging" that puts off some hiring managers:

- Candidates who wear **aftershave or perfume**, particularly of the *overwhelming* variety. Why? Some hiring managers have allergies.

52

Or, you may be wearing a particular fragrance that the hiring manager associates with someone he or she strongly dislikes or at least prefers not to be around. (Petty? Yes. Nonetheless true? Yes again.)

- **"Exotic" hair styles** (both men and women)

- Women—or men!—who wear **"over the edge" earrings**. **Best advice:** Women, if you wear earrings, make sure they are of the *conservative* variety. (Men, if you do in fact wear them, leave them at home. Don't wear them to the interview.)

- **Any garment that is an outrageous** or **"loud" color**. Stick to the soft pastels, if you feel you absolutely must wear colored garments. (**True story:** I once had a candidate, who otherwise was very well qualified, eliminated from further consideration because he chose to **wear a bright orange shirt** to his face-to-face interview! The reason for his elimination? The hiring manager said she was concerned about what customers might think of the candidate, if he visited the customers' facilities dressed in such a fashion.)

If this is your idea of 'appropriate' footwear for a job interview, you had better be seeking a job in the rodeo! (Or, be interviewing in Texas!)

- **"Scuffed," unshined or inappropriate footwear.** (If this is the way you present yourself in the all-important first face-to-face interview with the hiring manager, he or she automatically will wonder if you will take the same approach with customers and colleagues.)

- **Clothing that is "spotted" with food or drink spills.** The fact that the plane you took to the interview site "hit an air pocket" won't satisfy many hiring managers. (**Best advice:** Avoid drinking coffee or colas on the way to the interview site, and take along an "emergency" change of clothes, so that you can dash into the nearest restroom to change, if you have time.)

Best advice: Dress like the person who can promote you!

- **Trousers or pants** that are **not the correct length**, i.e., too long or "high water."

- **Belts (and neckties) that are not the correct length**, i.e., either too short or too long.

- **Large purses** (I am going to assume that you men won't have to worry about this!).

- **Nails that are not clean and well groomed,** on both women and men.

- **Excessive** or **"gaudy" jewelry** (men and women).

- **Pens** that look "cheap."

The only thing that *might* be able to salvage this young woman's interview image would be a long-sleeved, high-necked blouse—and ditching the gaudy earrings!

- **Tattoos** (Not a taboo, but if you have them, cover them up for the interview, if you can.)

SOME OTHER 'PRODUCT' DEVELOPMENT CONSIDERATIONS

The final consideration in developing the "product" (you) is to know not only the types of *companies* you want to target, but the types of *positions* as well.

In-depth information is provided in the **"Placement"** section that will show you how to research companies and find the names of hiring managers. But, in considering who you are and what you want to do, there are some additional important "secrets" you need to consider.

A down economy is NOT the best time to 'reinvent' yourself. Companies are looking for 'current, relevant' experience!

For starters, a down economy is not the best time to "reinvent" yourself. One of the "secrets" is that job seekers who can have an immediate impact are the ones who have a higher degree of probability of remaining in the game as the culling process moves along. Having "current and relevant" experience that enables you to make a company money or save a company money will keep you in the game. More on all of this as we move along.

In every company, and in every role, people are ranked, if not formally, certainly in the minds of hiring managers. This, as you will soon see, is the secret to the "hidden job market." There may not be an official opening, but a hiring manager is unhappy with someone and suddenly you are available and, well, they might just make room for you and you're HIRED!

Regardless of your status within your current or previous company the following holds true:

"Everyone can be an 'A' player, today, in the right job, in the right industry, in the right league." – Brad Smart, *Topgrading*

To learn more about this, study Brad's book. The point is, go after and accept jobs in which you can be a solid contributor and make the company money or save the company money. Going after positions in which you cannot make an immediate impactful contribution will mean you will be one of the first to be excluded.

BY KNOWING YOUR STRENGTHS, YOU WON'T SPEW 'VENOM'

A critical element of knowing your product (yourself) is to know your talents, skills and abilities, i.e., your "product attributes." From the work you did during the **Preliminary Preparation and Planning** phase, you should be well on your way not only to *knowing* these, but more important, also knowing which ones to emphasize in your subsequent marketing and selling activities.

Show your list of key attributes to family and friends and ask them if they think you've left out anything important and relevant. How do they see you? What about colleagues and co-workers, former bosses, suppliers and clients? What do they say about you? What would you consider yourself an expert in? What would *others* consider you to be an expert in?

By now, you should have developed a list of about 50 or 60 skills and attributes. These become the points that you mention in cover letters, "thank you" notes and in both telephone and face-to-face conversations and interviews.

Some people elect to take a professional psychological assessment such as the Myers-Briggs. Such assessments can be helpful in further identifying strengths that you can discuss in interviews, or weaknesses that you will now know about so you can work on them and not expose them.

ATTITUDE IS KEY—NEVER SPEW 'VENOM'

You have now determined what you did for previous companies (or your present company) to "make 'em or save 'em money." You have your letters of reference in hand, or under development, and you are developing other materials that will represent you well.

By now you should know that you have a lot to offer. Focus on that and don't spew 'venom'!

If you are employed, then looking for a new opportunity requires a steady, highly disciplined approach. If you don't like your job, don't complain, i.e., "spew venom." Don't spend the day "bad mouthing" the boss and/or complaining to co-workers. You are programming your brain negatively. Those thoughts will come out later in an interview and get you quickly and summarily *excluded* from further consideration.

Having a "positive mental attitude" is much more than a cliché. It is critical. It is part of what enables the brain to find solutions to problems. You don't like your boss . . . don't criticize. Think of it as a problem to be solved. You aren't going to change him. So how do you respond? How do you keep a smile on your face? What does your boss do that is good? Why did the company put him in the position that they did? And in that interview when you are asked, "Tell me about your current supervisor?" you won't fall into the trap of telling them how you really feel. If you speak badly of your current or a former boss, you have just eliminated yourself from consideration, guaranteed. This is a *key* rule in the hiring game and another one of the **top reasons** hiring managers eliminate candidates during an interview.

If you are out of work, then your full-time job is to find your next job. Get plenty of rest. Get up as if you are going to work. Dress. I know one person who gets up, dresses, hops on public transportation and takes it to his favorite Starbucks® each day. Maintaining a positive attitude will help you persevere. A positive attitude is a magnet. It separates you from the hundreds of others out there on the playing field, competing against *you*.

Speaking negatively of a former boss (spewing 'venom') is one of the TOP reasons a job seeker is eliminated quickly from further consideration!

LEARN TO TELL STORIES

One of the most effective methods of communicating information about yourself, your achievements, accomplishments, and, most importantly, the contributions you can make to a prospective employer, is by telling stories. By using stories and anecdotes in your answers to questions asked by hiring managers, they not only will *hear* your answers, they will be able to *see* the answers as well.

You certainly can expect to be asked questions about your accomplishments and achievements, both professionally and personally, with the heavier emphasis, of course, on the professional. Construct some stories you can tell about your *most* significant contributions. This will accomplish two important goals. First, it reminds you that you have a proven track record of success, thus enabling you to maintain a positive attitude. Second, it serves to constantly remind you that you can overcome obstacles and win.

As an added bonus, it can also prepare you for many of the behavioral-based questions you'll undoubtedly be asked during various interviews with prospective employers. Here is an example of the type of questions I'm referring to:

"Tell me about a time when you had to overcome tremendous odds to accomplish something."

Once you answer a question like this, be prepared for myriad "follow-up" questions, such as these:

"What did the odds consist of?"

"What resources did you make use of to overcome the odds?"

"Did you have to overcome conflict with anyone? If so, how did you deal with the team member who was creating conflict?"

"Give me an example of how you dealt with a team member not fully contributing to the project."

If you've adequately prepared yourself before you begin your job search in earnest, you should be able to easily deal with virtually any questions that can—and will be!—thrown at you, including questions such as these.

It's also very important to keep in mind that those who do NOT have accomplishments and achievements listed on their résumé, and backed up by letters of reference and recommendation, will have a much higher degree of probability of being eliminated earlier on in the job search process. Remember: Job hunting is a process of *elimination*—not of inclusion.

By the time you make it to a face-to-face interview, you certainly should have a thorough understanding of and appreciation for both your accomplishments and achievements, how they can be translated into contributions for your new company and how they can be communicated through stories. That enables you to position yourself in terms of the value you can bring to the employer. In interviews, do not focus on what you may have done for a current or previous employer. That is in your résumé. In an interview, focus on what your accomplishments and achievements can do for your *new* potential employer!

Here is an example of a behavioral-based interview question answered with a story:

"Think back over your career for just a moment. What would you consider to be your most significant career accomplishment?"

This is a real answer from a job seeker our office coached:

"Earlier in our conversation, we discussed the importance of taking market share from the competition. At the time, I had been in industrial sales about six months. I sold products that supported utility systems and wastewater systems. One of my target accounts was a chemical plant about an hour and fifteen minutes from where I lived. The competitor had had the business there for about 10 years and I was told that many a sales representative before me had called on the plant, but was unable to cultivate the account. I identified the utility manager who would have been one of the major decision-makers, and after numerous attempts, got him on the phone, introduced myself and asked for an appointment, which I was given.

"Pretty excited, I showed up early that day, had my literature, business cards, etc. A big, husky guy with a mustache, sunglasses and a hard hat walked into the lobby and asked, 'Is Jim Smith here?' I stood up, walked over to him, stuck out my hand and asked, 'You must be Richard?' He didn't bother to shake my hand. Instead, he took off his sunglasses, looked me square in the eye and said, 'There is one reason and one reason only why I agreed to see you today. I kicked your company out of this plant ten years ago and neither you nor anyone else from your company will ever set foot in this plant again as long as I am here, and I wanted to be able to tell you that to your face.' He then abruptly turned and walked out of the lobby.

"I sat down, caught my breath, tried to slow down my rapidly beating heart and said to myself, 'Just hide and watch.' This was in 1987, so we didn't yet have cell phones, lap tops, or easy access to information. So I picked up the company directory in the lobby and called the engineering department. I just started talking to people trying to identify who the wastewater engineer might be. (Sometimes wastewater and utilities are connected and sometimes they aren't.)

"I identified the wastewater engineer, called, introduced myself, told him I was in the lobby and he agreed to see me. In that conversation, he told me that they were building a new wastewater treatment plant and it would be finished in about a year. There could be an interest in having me quote on the treatment of it.

"I told him, 'Larry, a wastewater treatment plant is very finicky, as I know you know. In order to provide you an effective treatment proposal, I will need to know the system inside and out, the character of all of the waste streams, how my products interact with the differing streams, etc. May I suggest coming up each Friday at 7 a.m., gathering samples, running tests and developing data for you? I won't get in anyone's way and that way I can put together something for you that will truly be our best solution.

"He agreed. And so began a one-year journey of my leaving home every Friday at 5:45 a.m., arriving at the plant by 7 a.m., getting to know the operators, the treatment methodology, the waste streams, the impact that my different products would have on the waste streams and how my company and I could provide a cost-effective solution.

"It was six months before Richard discovered I was coming into the plant every week. By then, Richard couldn't stop me from coming in. I brought in upper level managers from my company to meet with upper level managers at this company. The quality movement (Deming, Juran, et al.) was in vogue at the time, so I structured my reports to mirror their language and what the plant was emphasizing.

"When it came time to write our proposal I had data, charts, graphs, pictures and a team in place. Yes, Richard ended up being one of ten decision-makers. He voted against us, but we had eight for us.

"We took $500 thousand of business from our competitor and ultimately took another $250 thousand from other sections of the plant. We ultimately had Richard surrounded. He was the lone holdout in the middle of the plant. I was a 'Top 10' sales representative in 1988. I could have turned tail and run after Richard's comment in the lobby that day, but he actually motivated me to figure out the ways to attack the problem and win the business.

"I hope that answers your question. Are there any points you would like for me to clarify further?"

When read out loud, this "story" is two minutes and 15 seconds long. Sometimes brevity is good and sometimes it isn't adequate for the task. In this particular case, the candidate was able to convey numerous important details that outlined determination, a competitive spirit, work ethic, commitment, perseverance, relationship building, resilience, creativity. . . . "Jim" was able to "package" his attributes, a significant accomplishment, and their associated contributions into one story. Because of the individual's "stories," this person was hired by this company.

By using stories you are "painting" imagery. Stories told correctly are 90 to 150 seconds in length, are vivid and illustrative and use action verbs, adjectives and adverbs. They also contain *numbers, percentages, dollar amounts* saved and earned—all of which serve to *quantify* the points you are making with the stories. But remember, what we're talking about here are *stories*, not novels! They also need to be stories that are *relevant* to the things that are important to the hiring manager. In the example above, the job seeker had inferred (correctly) that taking business away from the competition was critically important to this hiring manager.

But "Jim" is hardly the only professional who has a story or two to tell when the time is right, such as in a job interview. You have them, too. I know you do. You know you do. Develop them, tell them and use them to your advantage. Taking such an approach will indeed help you become one of the top candidates for any job you set your sights on and are fully qualified for— in today's job market or any other job market. That I *will* guarantee.

THE *TOUGHEST* INTERVIEW QUESTION: SALARY

In developing your marketing plan, you have now addressed the first "P" of the "Four P's" of marketing, i.e., the **product** (you). Now, let's address the second "P," **pricing**. How much you are "worth" in the job market is based upon how much *value* you can bring and how much the company is willing to pay for that value.

Many suppose, erroneously, that the *toughest* question they might be asked in an interview is one (or all) of the following:

"Tell me about yourself."

"What are your strengths and weaknesses?"

"Why would you want to work for us?"

Or, maybe, they think one of the perennially favorite "Gotcha!" questions is the toughest, such as this one:

"Tell me about your current boss."

The fact of the matter is, far and away, the *toughest* question you'll be asked by a hiring manager concerns *salary*. Here are common ways to be asked the salary question:

"What is your current salary?"

"What salary would it take to hire you?"

"What salary are you expecting?"

Answer the salary question the wrong way and you will be *excluded*. To learn why, read on.

Salary is hardly ever the only factor most of us consider when deciding whether or not to accept a job offer from a particular company. To be sure, salary is an *important* factor in the whole equation, but very rarely is it the *most* important factor. It's also probably the most misunderstood, and poorly negotiated element of a job offer, at least from the standpoint of many candidates.

Always keep this in mind: The salary offered is what the *company* thinks the position is worth—not what *you* think it's worth, or *ought* to be worth!

All of us want to be paid a fair and reasonable salary and receive competitive benefits. But rarely does the typical candidate have any legitimate idea about what any particular position is actually worth in the *current* job marketplace within a particular company. Rather, what they usually have is a strong *belief* regarding what they *think* it is worth. There can be—and quite often is!—a vast difference between these two extremes, particularly in a down economy.

In the simplest terms, salaries for virtually any position are driven the most by the old "supply and demand" phenomenon. When there is a shortage of qualified candidates for any particular position, then the salary being offered for the position tends to be driven upward, if the company genuinely wants and needs to fill the position. Conversely, when there is an abundance of fully qualified candidates for open positions, salaries are driven downward.

It's also important to realize (if you don't already) that the larger the hiring company, the more "set in stone" are the salary ranges for virtually any position within that company. So, no matter what you may have been earning at XYZ company, that doesn't mean you can necessarily expect to be offered either the *same* amount of salary, or better yet, an even *higher* salary at a new company. Let me give you an example of how this works.

Let's assume you are being considered for a **manager's position** in a large consumer packaged goods company. Say the company's salary range for this position is $80,000 to $98,000. It generally will be administered in quartiles, in order to provide flexibility within the salary range, on the basis of experience, skill level, etc.

Salary Range Quartiles	
First Quartile $80,000 to $84,500	**Second Quartile** $84,501 to $89,000
Third Quartile $89,001 to $93,500	**Fourth Quartile** $93,501 to $98,000

As a fully qualified, very experienced candidate, who may have been paid, say, $110,000 in your previous position, you probably would expect to be placed in the Fourth Quartile ($93,501 to $98,000 range). Actually, though, unless you virtually have no peers when it comes to job performance, knowledge and skills (an unlikely situation for most of us mere mortals), that expectation probably won't be realized. It won't matter what you earned in your previous position.

The company will look at it this way: Your former company had its way of administering salary and benefits and the new company has its way. The new company's way is essentially going to prevail in this situation. (There might be an opportunity to increase the *total* compensation package by negotiating a "signing" bonus, more vacation days, etc., but such things are becoming increasingly rare.) And, in a larger company, you seldom get a starting salary in the top quartile. Also, as a new hire, you will seldom be paid a salary higher than anyone else in that pay grade within the work group for which you are interviewing.

If, within this particular consumer products company, the highest paid person in the work group is paid, say, $90,000 a year, you can almost be guaranteed that you will not receive a starting salary greater than $90,000.

Ironically, the smaller the company is, the less "set in stone" salary administration tends to be. In other words, usually, though certainly not always, the smaller companies have more flexibility when it comes to salaries.

'HOW MUCH ARE YOU EARNING IN YOUR CURRENT POSITION?'

Be prepared for this question, but if at all possible, avoid answering it directly as long as possible. Why? Because it's tantamount to another player in a card game asking you, "What do you have in your hand?" Remember the whole hiring process is essentially a "game," a very serious game, of course, but a game nonetheless. And that's particularly true when it comes to issues involving compensation. If the company wants to hire you (and you must cross this first hurdle before salary will even become an issue with the hiring company), they are going to make every effort to get you for the lowest, though still fair (in the company's opinion, at least) salary possible.

A good way to respond to a question about your *current* salary (or your salary at your former company, if currently unemployed) is to say something like this:

> "Mr. Hiring Manager, I appreciate your interest in knowing what I am earning in my current position. I really do. More importantly, at this point in the process how do you see me

bringing value to you based upon our conversation thus far?"

The object here is to get the manager's attention redirected on other issues and off the salary issue, at least for the time being.

Again, keep in mind that salary negotiation is a *game*. If you're dealing with a seasoned hiring manager, he or she will know that as well, and perhaps respect you for holding your "cards" close to your chest. Perhaps not, too, and then you will have no choice—particularly in the latter stages of negotiation—but to specify your current (or last) salary amount, or risk alienating the manager, who may perceive that you're simply being contrary or evasive.

'WHAT SALARY WERE YOU EXPECTING TO RECEIVE IN THIS POSITION?'

At least this question is easier to field. A very good response to this question is the following:

"If I am your candidate of choice and, in turn, if this is the right opportunity for me, then I know the offer will be more than fair."

If you were actually to specify an amount of expected salary, you could easily end up "painting yourself into a corner." If the figure you were to cite is too high, the hiring manager will immediately eliminate you as a candidate because he or she knows they cannot meet your expectations. Cite a figure lower than what the hiring manager is in a position to offer you (assuming, of course, that you actually are *made* an offer!), and you just left "money on the table."

Under no circumstances should you respond to this question in any of the following ways:

"I just need a job; I'll take whatever the job pays."

"This position reports to you so you should know what the pay range is. You tell me what it pays." (I just finished reading a book that actually *recommended* this kind of flippant answer!)

"What's it pay?"

Any answers along these lines—and I have known too many job seekers who actually said things like this in job interviews!—will put you *immediately* out of the running.

Here is yet another way to look at and approach the question about current (or last) salary. You already know that virtually all companies, particularly the larger ones, place a dollar value on each position within the company. The company will hire you and pay you what *they* feel the position is "worth," if they truly need your abilities *and* you have sold them on the fact that you can make 'em money or save 'em money.

So, recognizing this, another way of answering the question, then, is to say something like this:

> "Mr. hiring manager, I am sure you have a salary range in mind for this position. I would imagine that the most important issue for you is finding the best person to do the job. If indeed I am that person, then I believe we will be able to find a 'win-win' salary within the boundaries of what you deem the position is worth. What additional questions can I answer for you to help you determine if I am your candidate of choice?"

If you are ultimately "pushed to the wall," simply say, politely and professionally,

> "I am currently making X dollars. But, Jim, the most important thing here for me is the opportunity. Again, I truly believe that, if I can bring value to you, and XYZ is the right company for me, salary certainly can be worked out."

SO, HOW MUCH *SHOULD* YOU EXPECT TO RECEIVE IN SALARY?

Obviously, if you are currently employed and at least making a *livable* salary, and are reasonably content in your current position, it is going to be far easier for you to effectively negotiate salary with a new employer than if you're unemployed. (This assumes, of course, that the new company will actually reach the salary negotiation stage with you!) Sure, it's not fair, but whoever said life was fair?!

Too many job seekers take this approach: "Well, I am making 'X' dollars per year now, and I won't be able to take another position unless I am offered *at least* ten percent more in salary." So, I will restate the rule here: Most companies, particularly the larger ones, really couldn't care less what your current (or former) salary is (was). If a new company actually gets to the salary negotiation stages with you, their salary administration and structure will almost always dictate salary, not your current (or previous) company's salary structure.

The best advice: Do your homework. Research current salary levels for your field of specialty, based upon locale, company size, industry, etc., with regard to any new company you may be considering.

Also, don't get entirely hung up on the *salary* amount. Include some of the more subtle components of many companies' benefit programs into the overall equation. For example, the company may offer substantially reduced premiums to employees on health insurance coverage, free life insurance, increased 401(k) matching, etc. These all add up and all too often I have seen job seekers not take the total package into consideration. (More on this in Phase Four, **Closing**.)

A very powerful tool for doing your salary research can be found in the "Tools" section of indeed.com:

www.indeed.com/salary

For example, let's research the position "SAP Programmer" in "Denver, CO."

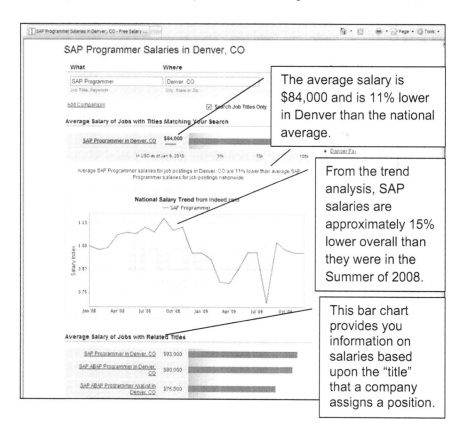

The average salary is $84,000 and is 11% lower in Denver than the national average.

From the trend analysis, SAP salaries are approximately 15% lower overall than they were in the Summer of 2008.

This bar chart provides you information on salaries based upon the "title" that a company assigns a position.

Armed with this information, you are able to make well-informed decisions regarding positions you are going after, you will be able to answer interview questions "properly" during the "Selling" phase (Phase Three) and negotiate effectively during the "Closing" phase (Phase Four). As an example, if you were making $95K as an SAP Programmer in Atlanta, GA, and you want to move to Denver (or must move to Denver), you can't necessarily expect to make $95K. Or, if you were making $95K in Denver in 2008 and were laid off, there is a very low probability you will be able to get hired again at $95K, since today's SAP salaries are 15% lower than they were then.

Also, if you are anticipating relocating, or find that it is *necessary* to relocate, this tool provides a city-by-city comparison. Below, for example, is the salary comparison for SAP Programmers in Denver, CO, and Atlanta, GA.

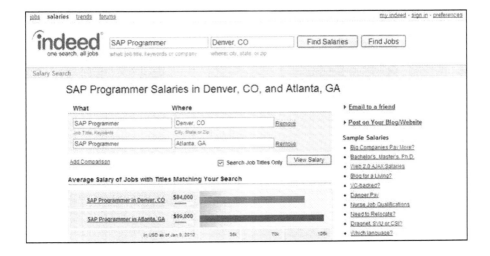

YOUR RÉSUMÉ IS
YOUR 'MARKETING BROCHURE'

Say you're planning a family vacation to Universal Studios®. In preparation for the trip, you go online and request a brochure. A few days later, you anxiously pick up your mail, expecting to get a Universal Studios® brochure. Instead, you receive a brochure on the Appalachian Trail! Far-fetched, you say? Not really because that's precisely what many job seekers do when it comes to their résumé, i.e., *their* marketing brochure! They craft a résumé essentially designed for one job (or one *type* of job) and then send it out for jobs that aren't even related to what's in their résumé!

Very rarely does a "one size fits all" approach work in any endeavor. That's particularly true when it comes to your résumé. Be prepared to tailor your résumé, perhaps many times, to fit the unique requirements for the position(s) you apply for—or be prepared for your résumé to spend a lot of time being hit with the DELETE key and excluded from further consideration.

Most products and services worth even considering normally have at least some type of marketing brochure that describes the various attributes and benefits of those products and services. Generally speaking, the higher the quality of the product or service, the higher the quality of the marketing brochure and other collateral materials. If you've been paying attention thus far, and heeding my advice and recommendations up to this point, you are ready to create *your* "marketing brochure," your résumé.

Quite literally, your résumé is your "ticket to the ballgame." And if *you* want to be perceived as a *high-quality* job candidate, you will ensure that your "marketing brochure" amply and very effectively illustrates that fact.

Very few prospective customers initially "study" any company's marketing brochure. At best, they may scan it for thirty seconds or so, and if it's particularly attractive and inviting, perhaps even as much as a minute. Only later, after a prospective customer has looked at a number of options, will they come back and begin to really dig into the company's brochure in any great depth. The same is true for your résumé. Simply because of the sheer volume of résumés received at hiring companies—not to even mention the poor quality of many of those received—on average, the "typical" résumé, if it gets read at all, receives about 45 *seconds* of attention from the screener or hiring manager. So, like any marketing brochure, you had better make sure there is something "eye-catching" about your résumé, or it won't get read at all.

FACT: The 'typical' résumé receives about *45 seconds* of the screener's or hiring manager's attention—if it's 'eye-catching' and 'inviting' enough to be read at all! And, over one-half of ALL résumés have some type of error that will *immediately* get the candidate *excluded*!

A RÉSUMÉ IS A *SUMMARY* OF EXPERIENCE, ACCOMPLISHMENTS, NOT YOUR LIFE HISTORY

Just as most companies' marketing brochures don't address every single characteristic or attribute of a particular product or service, neither should you make your résumé your life history. The literal definition of the word *"résumé,"* a French word, is *"to summarize."* Make sure that's what your résumé does—*summarizes*, with pertinent, compelling details, which of course introduces another important consideration for your résumé: The appropriate length.

As a general rule, your résumé should be no longer than two pages, one, if you are a recent graduate or relatively new to your career. Candidates for very senior positions, i.e., Chief Executive Officer, Chief Financial Officer, Executive Vice President, et al., can have a résumé of three to four pages, but only in the most unusual of circumstances (none of which, by the way, leaps immediately to mind) should *any* résumé exceed four pages. (Documentation of research, lists of projects, etc., normally are included in a separate document.)

WHAT WORKS WITH RÉSUMÉS, AND WHAT DOESN'T

I sincerely wish I could tell you that there is one, and only one, résumé format or approach to use, in order to successfully get you in front of a hiring manager. (And, by the way, that's the **principle purpose of a résumé**: To **get you an interview**! A poorly crafted one will quickly get you *excluded* from the pool of candidates; a well-crafted one *might* get you *included*.) Unfortunately, neither I nor anyone else can legitimately lay claim to such omniscience. I can, however, tell you that, based upon years of experience in the recruiting business and being involved with hundreds of *successful* candidates, I know what tends to work—*most* of the time, at least—with résumés. Equally important, I know what tends *not* to work with résumés. Let me share that information with you.

Avoid Multiple Submissions to the Same Company. You might think that, if you send your résumé to a company, particularly a large one, and you hear nothing back, it's all right to shoot off another one to them and another and another. Well, no, it's not! That's because some companies, especially the larger ones, normally use software designed to "inhale" incoming résumés. Chances are, if the company's system rejected your résumé the first time, it quite likely will reject it on subsequent submissions. However, if your résumé did indeed "survive" the software screening program, it normally would be sent to the hiring manager for further review. If he or she finds it compelling, be assured that you will soon receive a call or other contact. If you *don't* receive a call (or a contact) within a reasonable period of time, say, a couple of weeks or so, then it's OK to resubmit one more time. After that, move on to another prospective player. (In the "Define and Develop Your Channels to Market" section, I will give you tips on how to avoid this altogether.)

Carefully Evaluate Advice from "Résumé Experts." Ever since the job market soured, it seems résumé "professionals" have been literally coming out of the woodwork. Now, don't misunderstand me here. There are many reputable, highly professional individuals and companies that provide very good résumé services and advice. Still, there seems to be a nearly equal number who clearly do not know the proper way to create a résumé. The former group can provide very valuable services to job candidates; the latter can easily do *significant* harm to even the most highly qualified candidates, by recommending such things as printing your résumé on brightly colored paper stock, using oversized paper (greater than 8 ½" x 11"), putting a fancy border around your résumé, etc. Sure, some people will tell you that these techniques will get you noticed and, yes, sometimes you will be hired. But such situations are definitely the exception, not the rule. In fact, such techniques may just get you *excluded.*

So, if you decide to seek professional résumé assistance, make sure you're dealing with a true professional entity.[2]

> **"I want to see a job seeker stand out on their own because of what they can do for my company, not because they put their résumé on bright yellow paper with fancy borders,"** stated one hiring manager I have worked with.

---

[2]**Shelly Rosenberg** is a professional résumé writer with whom our recruiting firm has had excellent success. (www.shellyrosenberg.com)

Make Sure You Use a Standard Heading. This is the format for a standard heading:

Your Name
Address
Phone Number/Email Address

Why is this detail important? Because **if your résumé is "inhaled" or "parsed" into a company's candidate software program** (and most are today, regardless of the size of the company), the software is designed to capture the information in just this order.

Thus, if you use a *non*-standard heading such as this:

The Résumé of
John Jones
123 Main St., Anywhere
USA 12345
Phone Number/Email
Address

You will now be in the database with the first name of "The," the last name of "of" and your street address will be "John Jones." This makes it kind of difficult for the company to locate your résumé, don't you agree?

Use Only *One* Contact Phone Number and *One* Email Address. (This was addressed earlier and this is just a reminder.)

Use the Same Type Face, Type Size, and Formatting in Similar Sections in Your Résumé. For example, if you use **14-point, Times New Roman Bold Face** for section headings (examples shown below),

Education
Professional Experience & Training

make sure *all* your section headings use this same type size and face.

Likewise, if you choose **10-point, Times New Roman** for the body of your résumé (example: body copy), use this same face and size in *all* body copy in your résumé.

Failure to observe such basic principles of typography and formatting in your résumé not only is extremely distracting to the person scanning your résumé, it also makes you look extremely *unprofessional* and *disorganized*. The usual treatment of such résumés? You guessed it, the DELETE key!

Make Sure the Tone of Your Résumé Reflects CONFIDENCE and a Strong Bias Toward ACTION! and Measurable Results, and That the Writing Style is Clear, Concise and Very Much "To the Point." If all of this sounds like a pretty tall order, it is. But observing these principles when creating your résumé can pay very high dividends; by not observing them, you're again just one of the masses.

Consider these three ways to say the same thing:

"I was responsible for overseeing the second-shift production line."
"Responsible for overseeing the second-shift production line and increasing production."
"Managed and led a second-shift production team of 12 while increasing production 4%."

Which of the three statements *best* reflects *confidence* and a *bias toward ACTION!* and *measurable results?* If you said the third statement, you are getting the idea!

Long, rambling sentence structure must also be avoided. In other words, get right to the point, make it and move on. Consider the differences between the following two sentences. The first is a sentence in the résumé of one of our candidates before our coaching, the second after coaching:

Before
"During my tenure with this company, I had many opportunities to demonstrate both my leadership skills and my superior communication skills, by virtue of the fact that I was charged with interfacing with the customer base on nearly a daily basis, and had to make decisions 'on the spot' that could affect the company, either positively or negatively, depending upon the quality of the decisions I made in this capacity."

After
"Continually demonstrated team leadership and effective communication skills while interacting daily with customer base, resulting in an overall increase of 25% in the team's customer satisfaction scores."

I am sure you can see the *significant* differences between these two sentences!

Use ACTION! Verbs and Powerful Adjectives. American author Mark Twain perhaps said it best:

"The difference between the right word and the almost right word is the difference between lightning and the lightning bug."

Consider the following word choices:

Verbs		Adjectives	
Weak	Strong	Weak	Strong
Supervised	Led	Varied	Dynamic
Ran	Coordinated	Important	Effective

Avoid Using the Personal Pronoun "I." You've undoubtedly heard it before: "There is no 'I' in 'team.'" And that's precisely what many, if not most employers today are looking for, strong *team* members or leaders. There may be rare times when you simply can't avoid using "I," but keep such usage to an absolute minimum.

Use Bullet Points and Other Graphic Devices to Highlight Key Accomplishments, Experience and Career Progression. Used somewhat sparingly and *discriminately*, bullet points can bring considerable clarity and focus to a résumé. If you're using Word® as the word processing program to create your résumé, you are offered a wide variety and good selection of bullets. Here are some examples of the types of bullet points I recommend:

- This is one of the "basic" bullet points and you normally can't go wrong using it.

Want a little more "Pizzazz" in your bullet points? Try this one:

➢ This bullet point is perfectly acceptable for using in your résumé, too.

Check mark bullets are especially useful for highlighting key duties or responsibilities in your résumé:

✓ This bullet point can make your accomplishments really stand out, particularly when used in a table, if you feature one in your résumé.

Another very effective graphic device you can use to tightly focus attention on key accomplishment and experience featured in your résumé is very selective "highlighting" and bolding. Here is how you could use these techniques:

➢ Led sales team to record sales increase of 25% in 2008
➢ **Promoted** from Sales Rep to Area Sales Manager

A note of caution here, though. When using *any* graphic or design element in your résumé, remember this: "Less is More." Just as a little salt added to a meal can enhance the flavor and the taste experience, if you pour the whole *container* of salt on it . . . well, you get the idea, I'm sure.

Use a *Reverse Chronological* Approach in Your Résumé. Almost without exception, your résumé should be arranged in reverse chronological order, i.e., your most recent (or current) position (and company), followed by the previous one and so forth. This lets a screener or hiring manager quickly and easily skim your résumé. Although used rarely, the so-called *functional* arrangement in your résumé, i.e., where specific job experience/skills are placed in "buckets," sometimes even *without* dates, makes it far more difficult to review your résumé. About the only time you might want to consider using a *functional* approach to your résumé is when you have been out of the job market for some length of time, such as when raising your children, getting an advanced degree, going on a very long mission trip, an extended illness, etc.

Check and Re-Check Dates Used in Your Résumé and be Prepared to Explain any "Gaps." Make sure all dates in your résumé are accurate—and verifiable. "Gaps" on your résumé will immediately raise "red flags." Thus, include the gaps on your résumé and just briefly make a statement of fact. Examples: Caring for sick child, family time, degree completion, etc. Never lie on your résumé. If you become a serious candidate, all facts contained in your résumé will be checked by a prospective employer through companies that provide background screening services. You *will* be found out and you will be quickly *eliminated* from further consideration! Use the résumé cover letter for any additional explanation of the gaps. Never make comments on a résumé (or in a cover letter) such as "I was fired" when explaining gaps. Or worse, "I was downsized because my boss and I could never see eye to eye." (Yes, a real job-seeker's résumé!) Any statement along these lines *will be* "translated" into the hiring manager's mind as, "This person must be difficult to get along with. I probably will have problems with him/her also, therefore, I pass."

When Should You Use a Picture with Your Résumé? This is a simple one—**never, never, never**!

When Should You Include Personal Information on Your Résumé? This too is a simple one—**never, never, never**!

"Why?" you might ask, for both of these questions. Equal Employment Opportunity Commission. EEOC. EEO. If a Human Resources person sees your picture or learns of your personal situation (married or single, children or no children, "good health," etc.) then they could be faced with dealing with a discriminatory situation, so they take the "safe" route and *eliminate* you right up front.

Should You Include a Cover Letter with Your Résumé? This is another easy one to answer: Yes, definitely, without question! There is an important caveat here, though—make sure it is *not* a "generic" cover letter, as so many candidates use!

Have Someone Proofread Your Résumé. Every good writer needs a good editor, or at the very least, a good proofreader. Since nearly one-half of **ALL résumés contain at least one or more errors**, e.g., misspellings, improper word usage ("their" vs. "there"), grammatical errors, etc., why take a risk that your résumé will be among this group? Why risk having *your* résumé end up the same place that this group will end up, in the trash can? Ideally, you would seek the assistance of a *professional* résumé writer (or service) so that you can come up with the very best, most accurate, most appealing résumé possible.

Create Your Résumé in a Document Employers can Open. Since Microsoft® Word® is the industry standard word processing program, you can't go wrong using it to create your résumé. Be sure to also save a copy of your résumé in "Plain Text" format, so that you can easily "paste" it in job boards and company websites when the time is right, that is. (See the "Define and Develop Your Channels to Market" section).

Abbreviate *and* Spell Out Types of Degrees, Professional Designations. For example, if you have earned a Master of Business Administration degree, cite that accomplishment this way: **Master of Business Administration (MBA).** Additionally, use this same approach when citing professional designations, e.g., **Chartered Life Underwriter (CLU)**, **Professional Engineer (PE)**. This ensures that there are no misunderstandings *and* that the résumé screening software will correctly identify your credentials.

Use Keywords, but Never "White Font" or "Blackline" Them. Hiring managers, résumé screeners and computers are looking for key words in your résumé, so make sure they are there! Do not, however, "white font" or "blackline" the key words. "White fonting" is the practice of including key words at the bottom of your résumé, then selecting "white" as the font color, so the human eye can't see them but the computer can. "Blacklining" is using a font so small that, to the human eye, an entire series of words merely looks like a straight black line. Computers today are programmed to screen out résumés that use such practices.

Where do you find the *right* key words? In the job postings themselves. Use them, but don't go overboard. Make sure any key words you use are used in the appropriate context.

If the person(s) (or computer) "screening" your résumé is looking for some specific key words and your résumé doesn't contain them, at least include them in your cover letter. Let me give you an example.

Let's say the hiring manager is looking for a candidate with experience in SQF 2000. (Don't worry if you don't know what SQF 2000 means. It still works in this example.)

Now, not having SQF 2000 may ultimately be a deal breaker for the position, but right now the object is to get the résumé past the screener(s). So, in your cover letter, you might say something like this:

"Even though I don't have experience in SQF 2000, I do have four years' experience working in food safety. . . ."

That way, the key word "SQF 2000" will be picked up by the screener(s), and there will be a higher probability that your résumé will survive another round!

IN REFERENCE TO YOUR REFERENCES

When it comes to citing references on a résumé, most candidates use a statement such as this: "References available upon request." And that is OK, as long as you actually have made contact with people you would like to use as references, that they have agreed to be a reference, and that you have absolute confidence that they will help you and not hurt you. What's that? you say, references that *hurt* you? That is precisely what I mean. References, though sometimes taken rather lightly by job candidates, can either make or break a candidate's chances for a new position. More often than you might imagine, I've seen references *break* the candidate's chances—and the candidate wasn't even aware of the potential until it was too late!

Whom should you use as a "professional reference"? Only those professionals with whom you have a *personal* relationship and ones that you know, without any doubt whatsoever, will only say **stellar things about you**! If you don't have this level of comfort with a professional whom you are considering using as a reference, don't use them! Let me give you an example of how using the wrong references can cause irreparable harm to a candidate.

I called the reference for an engineer I was going to present to a company. After I introduced myself, and told him why I was calling, the person asked me, "He told you I was one of his references? Why on earth would he do that?" After a long pause of uncomfortable silence, I asked, "So, is this something you would like to pass on?" The potential reference said, "I can't believe he would ask me to be a reference for him. Yes, I will pass."

Wow!

Don't let this kind of thing happen to you!

Get Six References. Former bosses, colleagues, clients, suppliers, consultants—all of these professionals can serve as good references for you. Most likely, they will know your work ethic, the quality of your work, accomplishments, achievements, etc. Why do I suggest six references? So you don't "burn out" your references. For example, you might use three of your six references for prospective employers, and use the remaining three for recruiters working with you on different opportunities.

Ask for Permission. Many candidates simply *assume* that "so-and-so" would be "glad" to serve as a reference for them, so they don't even bother to ask the person. Not a good move at all. (We just saw how not properly "screening" references can backfire on a candidate!) Never use someone as a reference without first asking—and getting—their permission. After getting permission from your references:

> ➢ Send them a copy of your current résumé.
> ➢ Get their current phone number and email address.
> ➢ Advise them of the type of position(s) you're applying for.
> ➢ Advise them to emphasize certain areas of expertise, contributions you've made, etc.
> ➢ Gently "coach" them to be enthusiastic when they speak to a potential employer or recruiter.

Let your references know that you are willing to return the favor, if they ever need you to serve as a professional reference for them. (And, in today's job market, that could be sooner rather than later!)

Be Ready to *Produce* Your References. Even though it is perfectly acceptable to indicate on your résumé that references are available upon request, make sure you do in fact have them, including all the most recent contact information just mentioned above. They should be listed on a sheet of paper that you can hand to a hiring manager in an interview or email at the appropriate time. Keep in mind that developing references that are most applicable to the positions or companies you are applying for can help position you even more strongly as a TOP candidate.

HOW TO HANDLE THE ISSUE OF MULTIPLE POSITIONS IN A SHORT PERIOD OF TIME

As you will learn through *"Headhunter" Hiring Secrets,* the ideal profile of a candidate is someone who is . . .

* Currently employed.
* Has demonstrated stability in his/her career.
* Has a proven track record of accomplishments and achievements in which they have made a company money or saved them money.
* Has current, relevant experience.
* Is fairly priced in terms of salary and doesn't scare the hiring manager ("shadows on the wall") in the interview process.

That being said, most people do NOT have the perfect profile, especially in this environment of downsizing, rightsizing, companies going out of business, facilities closing and the like. So what does one do? Current relevant experience, accomplishments and achievements, solid references and being competitively priced are the keys, if your tenure with companies is on the thin side.

Plus, as you will study in **Phase Three**, this is both a numbers game and a skills game. You may have to just make more contacts with more companies and hiring managers.

It *is* a game. You are learning the *real* rules, so you know how best to play *not* to lose.

RÉSUMÉS, I GET RÉSUMÉS

We get dozens of résumés each and every day. Some are quite good, others "not so good." You can find many books and articles on how to write a résumé. Yet, even after reading such books and articles, most people's résumés still are so problematic that they cause them to be *eliminated* from further consideration.

Rather than my spending any time on how to write and résumé, I believe it would be far more instructive to illustrate how we "dissect" a résumé. On the next several pages we show a résumé from an extremely talented individual who is well thought of in the chemical industry. Though he has a stellar reputation, this particular version of his "marketing brochure," i.e., his résumé which he was sending out, was actually *increasing* his probability of *exclusion* rather than decreasing it, due to errors, irrelevant points, inconsistencies and confusing information. You will note that we have highlighted in gray the phrases/sentences that we felt were problematic and included our coaching points to the candidate as **bold face Italics,** underscored, parenthetical remarks next to those problem areas.

Then, following this "dissection" you will see the final version of the résumé that we used in actually marketing this individual to prospective companies and hiring managers. In the final version, for illustration, we highlight in gray the areas where our recommended changes were incorporated into the revised résumé.

You will be able to see the dramatic difference between the candidate's first résumé version and the final one used to market this individual. (And, yes, he was hired!) This is where a professional résumé writer can save you thousands of dollars. How? You get hired—sooner rather than later!

SALES MANAGEMENT EXECUTIVE

Bottom-line driven manager supported by Executive MBA and a successful 29-year career progression *(Don't hide the fact that you have a 29 year career...just don't put it in flashing neon lights right at the beginning of your resume)* with leading specialty chemicals manufacturing, distribution services organization. Diverse qualifications include process improvement, operations management, sales management, procurement, business development, and acquisition integration. Exceptional skills in all functions of general management, financial management, and strategic partnership development. Ability to convey vision, strategize action plans and implement solutions. An individual possessing a positive outlook with a good sense of humor, high values, solid family relationship, strong work ethic and unyielding integrity. Specific qualification includes:

➤ Strategic Business Planning	➤ P&L Management
➤ Sales Force Redesign	➤ Market Analysis / Research
➤ Productivity Improvement	➤ Sales Presentations / Strategy
➤ Reach US Position	➤ New Market Identification
➤ Solution Selling	➤ Budgeting / Cost Control
➤ Project Planning / Analysis	➤ Measurement Systems

Industry specific experience includes: Responsible Care, SAP, MRP, ISO-9000, and Process Safety Management.

EXPERIENCE PROFILE

Global Chemical Company   **1980 to present**

9 Billon *(Either put $ sign or the word dollar. Spell "Billon" correctly, i.e. "Billion")* Company with operating income from specialty manufacturing & distribution business (ascended quickly through ranks with increased responsibility & various management positions that position the company to capitalize on growth and new market development)

2002 – 2009

Director of Sales responsible for Central Region Distribution Business (distribution buys chemicals from manufactures and repackages to meet customer requirements / sales for my region was $750MM). I had nine district managers and 75 sellers reporting to me. *(Put the ")" after requirements, never use the word "my." Also, remove "I" and "me" . . . never use these.)* The region covered sales in Illinois, Missouri, Kansas, Minnesota, Wisconsin, Dakota's, Michigan, Ohio, Indiana, Kentucky, West Virginia, Western Pennsylvania, and Eastern Canada.

- Developed new sales strategy / process & market focus for chemical distribution that resulted in adding $40MM in gross margin.
- P&L responsibility that increased operating income from break even to $85MM.
- Created Vision for sales team that united the effort to achieve the desired revenue & operating income results.
- Increased annual revenue from $500MM to $750MM in 2002 -2009 *(Dash needs to be in the middle and spell out "MM")* through volume growth and price management.
- Lead *(should be "led")* change management for sales force that projected positive & energetic vision for the company.
- Improved working capital by working *(Even though working and working are used in two different ways, the fact that they are so close together is confusing when one glances at a resume for 45 seconds. Change the second "working" to "teaming")* with operations to take out cost and stream line *("Streamline" is one word.)* services that resulted in $65MM savings with out *("Without" is one word)* effecting *(The correct word is "affecting")* customer satisfaction rating.
- Worked with our suppliers and purchasing to increase our *(Take out the second "our")* margins and developed price book that resulted in 3% GM increase.
- Implemented SAP in 2007 with out *("Without" is one word)* negative customer impact during system switch over.
- Developed and implemented restructuring of the business resulting in a 15% reduction of sales force.

Problem areas - Areas/sentences highlighted in gray are phrases/sentences in the original résumé that we felt were problematic.

(Our Coaching Points) - The coaching points that we offered to the writer of the résumé.

2000 - 2002

Regional Supply / Purchasing Manager responsible for purchasing $400MM in chemicals negotiate & determine our purchase price for product purchased in North East. *(Way too long and too much detail)*

- Set pricing for NE Region seller price book.
- Negotiated & determined purchase price for products distributed in North East.
- Developed supply plan for NE Region (who we bought from and what % of our business they received). *(Delete)*
- Negotiate and find new suppliers & products for distributor sales and then introduce them to sales force to sell. Activity resulted in adding 5 new product families and over 25 new products to distributive market. *(Way too long and complicated. Also, need to be using some different words by now. We reworded this to read "Researched and developed new suppliers & products resulting in adding 5 new product families and over 25 new products")*
- Provide prices to be quoted on contract and bid business. *(Useless information. Delete.)*
- Work with operations and buyers to establish and implement supply chain.

1996 - 2000

Strategic Alliance Business Manager responsible for setting up corporate account program across North America East Coast.

- Established key account strategy resulting in increased revenue from $75MM to $350MM.
- Developed regional business model and hired 8 account managers to focus sales and relationships with active / potential corporate account customers that resulted in double digit volume growth at key global accounts.
- Developed key supplier relations to support our new corporate account initiative.
- Worked with operations and customer support to develop new supply chain offering to these strategic customers that resulted in increase customer base from 30 active customers to 175 active customers with improved customer satisfaction index.
- Developed sales strategy, business plans, and budget and had P&L responsibility. *(Way too wordy by the time we are getting to this point in the candidate's career.*

1992 - 1996

District Manager of Fine Ingredients Division.

This assignment *(How about the word "mission"? Let's use an ACTION verb.)* was to manage 7 regional sellers and establish Distribution in the fine chemical business into the market segments of personal care, food & beverage, and *(Remove the comma before the word "and")* pharma. *(In a professional document, spell this word out.) (Thus, reworded this to read, "Mission was to establish a strong presence in the fine chemicals business. Target markets were personal care, food & beverage and pharmaceutical.")*

- Established new district sales team to focus on Fine Ingredient Business that resulted in growing the sales from $5MM to $80MM. *(Combine this bullet point with the 5th one.)*
- Responsible for finding suppliers and brokers to support our introduction into this new market that resulted in establishing over 50 new suppliers. *(Reworded to, "Rapidly identified and established 50 new suppliers to support our aggressive entrance into this new market.")*
- Developed training tools and product literature for new sellers and division. *(Combine this bullet point and the last bullet point into one succinct idea.)*
- Worked with operations to set up new warehousing to meet FDA requirements and EH&S guidelines.
- Responsible for setting up annual & 5 year strategic plan for business performance.
- P&L responsibility for district.
- Responsible for setting up trade shows to promote our introduction into the fine chemical business. *(These 7 bullet points can be reduced to 4)*

Problem areas - Areas/sentences highlighted in gray are phrases/sentences in the original résumé that we felt were problematic.

(Our Coaching Points) - The coaching points that we offered to the writer of the résumé.

1989 - 1992

Sales Manager responsible for closing down the Dayton, Ohio plant and consolidate the business to our Cincinnati Plant and managing 4 sellers with $30MM annual sales.

- Dayton, Ohio Plant consolidation resulted in $20MM cost savings.
- Achieved double digit volume growth while consolidating business. *(Who cares what the names of the plants were, especially 20 years ago? How about, "Responsible for consolidating 2 manufacturing facilities resulting in $20MM in cost savings" followed by "Managed 4 account managers and achieved double-digit volume growth")*

1986 - 1989

Market Develop Manager for North America responsible for setting up suppliers and train our 230 chemical sellers to sell into the ingestible market. At the time we started with the Pfizer line of Citrates and we were able to get a full line of complement ingredients to eventually start a separate division within xxx Distribution. Through this role I was successful in positioning xxx to enter into and compete in the fine chemical market. The sales grew from zero to $150,000,000 during this time. *(Whoa. Way too wordy and complicated. See revised resume to see how we fixed this.)*

1982 - 1986

Corporate Account Manager responsible for marketing our refined products (hydrocarbons, methanol, maleic) through the Eastern half of USA & Canada to all major chemical companies. Overall territory size was $75MM.

- Responsible for developing new corporate relationships and to base load our maleic anhydride production (outside Xxx own captive requirements). Results were that I grew the customer base from 7 accounts to 20 accounts with sale revenue increase from $20MM to $45MM.
- Developed annual business plans resulting in growth from $20MM to $75MM. *(Huh? I'm confused. Which was it? $20MM to $45MM or $20MM to $75MM? Plus this whole thing again is way too long. At the end of the resume it has to be succinct. We converted this whole thing to one sharpened sword: "Throughout Eastern USA and Canada grew customer base from 7 accounts to 20 and increased sales from $20MM to $75MM")*

1980 - 1982

Sales Representative responsible for local sales territory in Southern Indiana with base business of $1,000,000 and after two years the territory grew to $2,000,000. *(Why did we suddenly go from using the MM and start putting all of the zeros?)*

Education & Professional Development

Bachelor of Business Administration with Degree in Marketing – University of Kentucky, Lexington, KY *(Year of graduation? As stated earlier, 1/3 of the people who did not put the date actually did not graduate. By now any hiring manager is going to know this person is over 50. If they are going to discriminate, they are going to discriminate so go ahead and put it here. Remember, this candidate started off his résumé by stating he had a 29-year career so don't cause yourself to be eliminated by skipping the date here.)*

Indiana University Kelly Executive Finance Program
North Western *(One word)* University Kellogg Business Executive MBA Program

Problem areas - Areas/sentences highlighted in gray are phrases/sentences in the original résumé that we felt were problematic.

(Our Coaching Points) - The coaching points that we offered to the writer of the résumé.

This is a very typical résumé hiring managers and recruiters *routinely* receive from highly skilled, very talented candidates! Unfortunately, unlike this candidate, most never get a second chance to make a good first impression.

Next, this candidate's revised résumé, incorporating our coaching points and providing him with a résumé that has IMPACT! (Gray areas are where our recommended changes were incorporated.)

Richard Jones

123 Main Street	Phone: 123-456-7890
Anywhere, USA 12345	Email: rjones@myisp.com

Sales Management Executive

Bottom-line driven manager supported by Executive MBA and successful career progression with leading specialty chemicals manufacturing, distribution services organization. Diverse qualifications include process improvement, operations management, sales management, procurement, business development, and acquisition integration. Exceptional skills in all functions of general management, financial management, and strategic partnership development. Ability to convey vision, strategize action plans and implement solutions. An individual possessing a positive outlook with a good sense of humor, high values, solid family relationship, strong work ethic and unyielding integrity. Specific qualifications include:

☑	Strategic Business Planning	☑	New Market Identification
☑	Sales Force Redesign	☑	Budgeting/Cost Control
☑	Productivity Improvement	☑	Measurement Systems
☑	Reach U.S. Position	☑	Continuous Improvement
☑	Solution Selling	☑	Change Management
☑	Project Planning/Analysis	☑	Staffing/Training
☑	P&L Management	☑	Regulatory Compliance
☑	Market Analysis/Research	☑	Business Plan Implementation
☑	Sales Presentation/Strategy	☑	Mergers/Acquisitions

Industry specific experience includes: Responsible Care, SAP, MRP, ISO-9000, and Process Safety Management.

Experience Profile

Global Chemical Company   *1980 to Present*

A $9 Billion company with operating income from specialty manufacturing & distribution. (Ascended quickly through ranks with increased responsibility & various management assignments that position the company to capitalize on growth and new market development.)

2002 – 2009

Director of Sales - Responsible for $750 million Central Region Distribution Business (Distribution buys chemicals from manufactures and repackages to meet customer requirements). Region covered sales in Illinois, Missouri, Kansas, Minnesota, Wisconsin, Dakota's, Michigan, Ohio, Indiana, Kentucky, West Virginia, Western Pennsylvania, and Eastern Canada.

- Developed new sales strategy/process & market focus for chemical distribution that resulted in adding $40 million in gross margin.
- P&L responsibility that increased operating income from break even to $85 million.
- Created Vision for sales team that united the effort to achieve the desired revenue & operating income results.

Page 1 of 3 Pages

We did even more "tightening" and "smoothing out" of the copy on page two:

- Increased annual revenue from $500 million to $750 million in 2002 - 2009.
- Led change management for sales force that projected positive & energetic vision for the company.
- Improved working capital by teaming with operations to reduce costs and streamline services, resulting in a cost-savings of $65 million and significantly improving customer satisfaction ratings.
- Worked with suppliers and purchasing department to increase margins and developed price book that resulted in 3% gross margin increase.
- Implemented SAP software solution in 2007 without negative customer impact during system switch over.
- Developed and implemented restructuring of the business resulting in a 15% reduction of sales force.

2000 – 2002

Regional Supply/Purchasing Manager - Responsible for purchasing & price negotiations for $400 million in chemicals.

- Set pricing for Northeast Region seller price book.
- Negotiated & determined purchase price for products distributed in Northeast.
- Researched and developed new suppliers & products, resulting in adding five new product families and over 25 new products.
- Worked with operations and buyers to establish and implement supply chain.

1996 – 2000

Strategic Alliance Business Manager — Developed sales strategy, business plans and budget and had P&L responsibility. Responsible for setting up corporate account program across North America East Coast.

- Established key account strategy increasing revenue from $75 million to $350 million.
- Developed regional business model. Hired 8 account managers to focus sales/relationships with active/potential corporate accounts that resulted in double digit volume growth at key global accounts.
- Developed key supplier relations to support our new corporate account initiative.
- Worked with operations, suppliers and customer support. Developed new supply chain offering increased customer base from 30 active customers to 175 active customers with improved customer satisfaction index.
- Developed sales strategy, business plans, and budget and had P&L responsibility.

1992 - 1996

District Manager, Fine Ingredients Division — Mission was to establish a strong presence in the fine chemical business. Target markets were personal care, food & beverage and pharmaceutical.

- Developed and implemented five-year strategic business plan and established new district sales team, ultimately growing sales from $5 million to $80 million.
- Rapidly identified and established 50 new suppliers to support the company's aggressive entrance into this new market.
- Developed all new training tools, product literature and implemented trade shows.
- Teamed with operations to set up new warehousing to meet Federal Drug Administration (FDA) requirements and Environmental Health & Safety (EH&S) guidelines.

Page 2 of 3 Pages

And here is the last page of this candidate's résumé. You'll note that the year the candidate graduated from college has been added. Hiring managers and recruiters are always on the lookout for candidates who do not include the year they (supposedly) earned their college degree because nearly one-third of those who omit this information actually never graduated!

1989 - 1992

Sales Manager

- Responsible for consolidating 2 manufacturing facilities resulting in $20 million cost savings.
- Managed four Account Managers and achieved double-digit volume growth.

1986 - 1989

Market Development Manager, North America

- Started with Pfizer line of Citrates, aggressively increased the product line and trained 230 chemical sales representatives. Grew sales from $0 to $150 million in the ingestible market.

1982 - 1986

Corporate Account Manager, Refined Products

- Throughout Eastern USA and Canada grew customer base from 7 accounts to 20 and increased sales from $20 million to $75 million.

1980 – 1982

Sales Representative, Indiana

- Grew business from $1 million to $2 million during this recessionary period.

Education & Professional Development

Bachelor of Business Administration with Degree in Marketing – University of Kentucky, Lexington, KY 1980

Indiana University Kelly Executive Finance Program

Northwestern University Kellogg Business Executive Master of Business Administration program

Page 3 of 3 Pages

WRITE A 'LAZY' COVER LETTER, GET EXCLUDED! GUARANTEED!

Is a résumé cover letter really that important? Yes it is, provided it is *customized* for the position or for the hiring manager. Generic, "lazy" cover letters will get you *excluded*. It actually is better *not* to include a cover letter than to include one that is generic, ambiguous and otherwise what I call "lazy." Let me first show you an example of the "typical" cover letter that I am referring to, and then we will examine how you *should* write a cover letter.

This cover letter is *very* characteristic of scores of cover letters that I (and again, hiring managers!) get each and every business day of the year! The person who wrote this cover letter would have been better off not sending one at all.

The person who sent me this cover letter, along with his résumé, was responding to a posting my firm had on one of the job boards. The position was for someone with either a chemical or mechanical engineering background who had some refinery experience and some sales/business development experience in industrial sales. The position itself would involve selling process chemicals to refineries.

I "dissected" this "lazy" cover letter in the "call-outs" featured below:

January 31, 2009

Dear HR Manager;

> My name was in my email address on the posting. So, the correct salutation should have been "Dear Mr. Freeman" or "Dear Skip." Plus, I am NOT an "HR Manager."

My name is Jim Smith and I am 38 years old mechanical engineer. (Single) (sic)

I live in Houston / Texas.
Phone: **713-123-4567** (Houston / Texas)

My field is **HVAC** (Heating, Ventilating Air Conditioning).

> Because of EEOC considerations, NEVER include age & marital status.

[Also I have Fire Fighting, Plumbing, Automatic Control, Instrumentation & Control Project Experience]. I have international offshore&onshore (sic) (Oil Platform,Terminal (sic) Buildings), industrial plants (Power Plant, Chemical Plant etc.), commercial buildings (Hotel, Stadium, Shopping Mall etc.) construction experience include calculation, design, procurement, cost control, planning, installation, testing & balancing, commissioning and start up activities.

You can find the my résumé and references at the attachment. (sic)
I would be grateful if you would tell me a convenient time and place when I may talk with your further about my qualifications as the **hard working estimator you want**.

Thank you.
Jim Smith

> Candidate should suggest time & place for follow up conversation.

87

Additionally, there are other "deficiencies" in cover letter, such as the poor formatting, lack of organization, etc.

Of course the most glaring deficiency of all is that *this individual has none of the prerequisite experience*. My guess was—and is—that this candidate found a job posting for an estimator's position, created a cover letter for that position, sent it out, and then continued clicking away, sending out more and more of the same irrelevant, lazy "cover letters" and résumés to all of the positions he found in Houston, thinking he was "job hunting" and being productive. All he really was doing was becoming more and more disappointed when he wouldn't hear back from anyone. That's why I call it a "lazy" cover letter. This candidate, like so many other candidates, was simply too *lazy* to *customize* his cover letter.

Now, let me be fair here. He might not be lazy at all. He simply may not know the rules of the hiring game. But in this game, the recipients of his cover letter will view it as "lazy" and exclude him because he did nothing to set himself apart and show me—or anyone else, for that matter—why he should be considered. He gave me many, many reasons to hit the DELETE key!

But just in case you think the previous example is an isolated one, I want to share just one more with you. I get dozens of these types of cover letters every single business day! (And so do *hiring managers*, incidentally.)

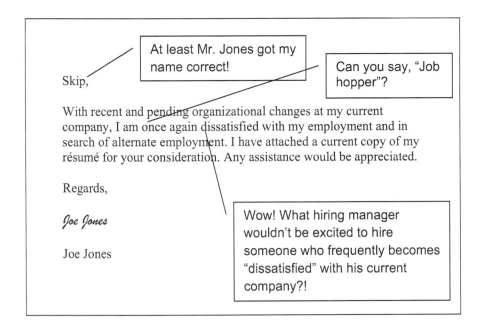

How to Create a *Cover Letter* with IMPACT!

You've gone to considerable lengths to create a résumé with IMPACT!, so now let's create a *cover letter* that also has IMPACT! Let's examine precisely how to accomplish that.

First and foremost, if at all possible, come up with the *specific* name, title and business address of the person you want to see your résumé. (Methods for identifying the right people are covered in the **Placement** section.)

Once you have determined the name and the title of the person to whom you will send your cover letter and résumé, make sure you use the correct salutation. Let's say, for example, that you were able to come up with the name of the person actually hiring for the position you seek, James R. Smith. In that case, here is the *correct* (read: *safest*!) way to phrase your salutation:

Dear Mr. Smith:

Do *not* automatically assume a degree of familiarity you simply don't enjoy with Mr. Smith by addressing your cover letter to:

Dear James, (or even worse!) **Dear Jim,** (Maybe Mr. Smith despises the nickname "Jim"!)

Failing to take this simple little rule of business etiquette into consideration can quickly get your cover letter and résumé excluded. That's how sensitive some people can be about how they are addressed by strangers.

Notice also, in the *correct* salutation above, a *colon* is the proper punctuation to use—*not* a semi-colon and *not* a comma. (For the record, colons are used in *formal* salutations; commas are used in *informal* salutations; and semi-colons are not used at all in salutations.)

In virtually ALL cases, *avoid* using such "lazy" salutations as these:

Dear Sir/Madame ("Madam" often implies something far different!)

To Whom It May Concern

Dear Human Resources Professional

Dear Recruiter (if you are indeed applying to a recruiter for assistance)

Dear HR Manager

By far, the most important sentence in your cover letter is the *opening* sentence. This is where you need to quickly and effectively "grab" the attention of the reader. Don't beat around the bush, don't apologize for contacting them. Get right to the point and don't waste the recipient's valuable time.

Below is an example of a cover letter to a recruiter (me!) that tends to get read.

April 20, 2009

Mr. Skip Freeman
President
The HTW Group
190 Camden Hill Rd. Su
Lawrenceville, GA 3004

Dear Mr. Freeman:

Notice that this person took the time to find out, precisely, to whom to send this cover letter and his résumé.

He also used the correct salutation.

He gets right to the point in the opening paragraph.

In the course of your search assignments you may have a requirement for an accomplished IT leader with extensive experience meeting global business needs and requirements. Additional aspects of my background, which may be of interest include:

• Expertise in leading an initiative to convert the IT function into a project-based organization.

• Experience in developing strategic plans that provide vision, direction and operational synergies.

• Broad technical and managerial skills and perspective, allowing me to partner effectively with business executives to identify high-impact, cost-effective solutions.

A résumé highlighting my experience and accomplishments is attached. If it appears that my qualifications meet the needs of one of your clients, I would be pleased to discuss my background with you. I will call you Thursday, April 23, at 3:00 PM ET to follow up.

Thank you for your consideration.

Bullet points let me see instantly what he has to offer.

Excellent closing paragraph.

P.S. If 3:00 PM ET is not convenient for you, please advise a time that is.

Using a "P.S." is one of the keys in a good cover letter. It usually makes a reader stop and actually read the "P.S." However, a "P.S." that deals with ACTION is usually the most effective.

SOME ADDITIONAL COVER LETTER CONSIDERATIONS

Never, never attempt to fashion a **"one size fits all"** cover letter. There is no way you will be able to effectively accomplish this, and you will fool no one, particularly a hiring manager.

Length

Your cover letter should be no longer than 250 to 300 words.

Typographic Considerations

Use bullets to illustrate key points in your cover letter. Use Italics and bold face type to emphasize certain words and concepts featured in your cover letter.

Identify the Position You're Applying for

This relates to trying to use a "one size fits" all approach in your cover letter. Make sure you always identify the specific position you are applying for.

P.S. (Use One!)

Numerous studies have shown that using a P.S. in a cover letter results in greater readership.

Opening Statements

Use a creative, "value" opening statement, i.e., *your* value to a prospective employer.

Attitude/Tone

Never, never convey any degree of desperateness. Offer no apologies for writing. Show confidence!

Envelope

Using a computer printer (not handwritten), address the envelope to the individual and put CONFIDENTIAL on the outside.

Paper

If the cover letter is mailed, use only high-quality *résumé grade* paper, which can be purchased at an office supply store. Do not use brightly colored stationery. As a general rule, use only 8 ½" x 11" paper. There is somewhat of an argument for using paper that is *slightly* larger, say, just ½" larger, but certainly no larger than that. The reasoning goes, if your résumé clearly "stands out" from the rest, merely because it is slightly larger in size, it may get noticed and then reviewed. Maybe.

Send No Gifts!

Some candidates attempt to get the attention of a hiring manager by sending a "gift" (pizza, lunch, flowers, coffee mug, etc.) along with their cover letter and résumé.

Some candidates actually send *gifts* with their résumés, trying to 'impress' the hiring manager. If you do this, you *will* make an impression, but probably not the one you intended!

Sending gifts may work every now and then, but the comments from most hiring managers are negative regarding this tactic, **especially in the larger companies where there are strict policies on "gifts," no matter what.**

DIFFERENTIATE YOURSELF
WITH NETWORKING BUSINESS CARDS

If you're currently employed, chances are very good that you have a business card, and, if you are at all typical, you make sure that your business card gets as widely distributed as possible. That's particularly true if your position entails interacting on a regular basis with customers. Why? Because you want to make sure people know *who* you are and *what* you do, correct?

These same criteria apply during your job search—whether or not you're still employed. (Under NO circumstances should you use your business card from your present employer, if you are still employed, to network for a new position. That could really "backfire" on you!) Make sure you have what is referred to as a **networking** business card, and disseminate it as widely as possible—to as many people as possible—during your job search, so that they will remember *who* you are and *what* you do.

A networking business card can be really simple in design, and is quite affordable. Here is an example of a perfectly acceptable, basic networking business card:

James R. Johnson
123-456-7890
Sales Professional
jrjohnson@myisp.com

Some job seekers take the networking business card one step further and use it as a "mini-résumé," by featuring special job qualifications, skills and talents on the *reverse* side. Here is an example of how you could do that:

✓ I can increase your sales by *at least* ten percent—regardless of the products or services you sell!

✓ I have continually been in the "Top 10%" of any sales force I've been a member of and have the numbers to PROVE it!

✓ If you're looking for a "Top Tier" Sales PRO, you and I need to talk—soon!

93

Note that, unlike my recommendation to avoid the use of the personal pronoun "I" on your résumé, such usage on a networking business card is perfectly acceptable, and even strongly recommended.

There are many local printers, as well as quite a number of online printers, that can print some high-quality networking business cards for you at a very affordable price. Using Microsoft® Word®, and business card templates offered by companies such as Avery®, you can also easily and quickly print your own networking business cards. (Remain conservative in your design!) I also strongly recommend that you check out these two online printers for your networking business card needs:

www.vistaprint.com (FREE)

www.novaoffset.com (Features dual- and tri-fold cards that are quite attractive and versatile.)

NO 'THANK YOU' FROM YOU
MEANS 'NO, THANK YOU'
FROM THE HIRING COMPANY

Two simple words that can mean so very much to most people—Thank You. Yet the reality is that few people actually take the time to make the effort to send a "Thank You" note, letter or email following a face-to-face job interview. In almost every case, *not* observing this simple, basic courtesy,

Sending a *hand-written* 'Thank You' note card (preferable) or email after a face-to-face job interview is simple *and* powerful. Still, many job seekers don't do it!

more often than not means, at least figuratively speaking, a "No, thanks" from the prospective employer.

Why do so many candidates fail to exercise the simple, common courtesy of sending "Thank You" notes? A common "excuse" (and that's what it is, an *excuse*, not a "reason") I have heard from candidates is that they believed they had no further chance at the position they were seeking, so they didn't feel it necessary to go to the "trouble" of sending a "Thank You" note. Another one is, "I don't want them to think I want the position that badly. Besides, if they are interested, they should contact me."

One of the "rules" of the hiring game that *hasn't* changed: Companies *expect* "Thank You" notes or emails! You are right, if a company has already indeed excluded you after the face-to-face interview, sending a "Thank You" note in fact won't change the decision. However, what if—despite what you may *perceive* to be the case—you are, in fact, "still in the mix"? What if the company is still trying to decide which one of, say, two or three candidates, they ultimately will select? And *you're* one of those candidates. The common courtesy of sending a "Thank You" note just might tip the scales in your favor! In other words, the two who did not send the "Thank You" note are the ones who were excluded, not you. Or, what if several months down the road, there is *another* position that comes open in the company for which you might be qualified. Which of the candidates for the current position is the company likely to remember? Recently, one of the job seekers we were coaching was in the final two. Our candidate followed our advice and sent the

"Thank You" note (after we had reviewed it and helped her ensure it was powerfully worded and contained no spelling or grammatical errors). The other candidate did *not* send a "Thank You." That proved to be the deciding factor! The hiring manager told me, "We're offering your candidate the position. They sent a well-worded 'Thank You' follow-up. The other candidate did not; they are out of the running."

TIME IS OF THE ESSENCE

Timing is everything when it comes to sending "Thank You" notes, letters or emails. The quicker you send it the better. A late "Thank You" really is no better than not sending one at all. You might even "overnight" it!

WHAT TO SAY, HOW TO SAY IT

If you send a note keep your message brief, while still including some very specific information. Don't make the note so brief and general that it is largely meaningless. Here is an example of a "lazy" "Thank You":

Dear Larry (make sure that actually is name, too!),

I just wanted to tell you how very much I appreciated visiting with you yesterday. Hope to hear from you soon!

Best Regards,

James Johnson

Here is a significantly better approach to use in the "Thank You" note:

Dear Larry,

It was a genuine pleasure to meet with you, Dan Stevens and Steve McLaughlin yesterday to discuss the tremendous opportunities offered by the chemical engineering position in your company.

I sincerely appreciate the time each of you took to present and thoroughly discuss the position with me.

It is obvious that the position offers exceptional career growth potential, as well as a genuine opportunity for the successful candidate to make a substantial contribution to the overall success of ABC Chemical.

Best Regards,

James Johnson

In this example, you have kept your note relatively brief, while still including enough specific detail regarding the interview, so that the hiring manager should more easily be able to connect a face, name and professional experience with the position he or she is trying to fill.

GOOD IDEA TO FOLLOW UP 'THANK YOU' LETTER/NOTE CARD WITH EMAIL

A powerful, dual approach is to send two "Thank You" communications. One is the letter or note that is sent overnight or mailed and the other is an associated email. One of the two can be framed similar to the "Thank You" on the previous page, while the other is a more specific "Thank You" where you "resell" yourself and your unique qualifications and career accomplishments. Additionally, you must address any concerns that a hiring manager may have expressed in their interview with you. This dual approach can definitely set you apart from *most* of your competition!

Featured below is an example of how candidate James Johnson might construct an *effective*, very *specific* follow-up email. Again, it is always a good idea to put yourself in the place of the hiring manager. What impression would *you* have of Mr. Johnson, if you were the hiring manager for this position, and you received not only a very nice "Thank You" note, but also this carefully crafted follow-up email?

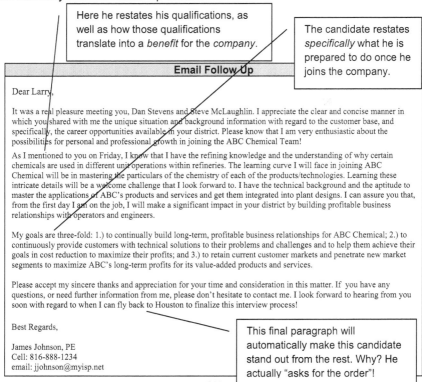

Here he restates his qualifications, as well as how those qualifications translate into a *benefit* for the *company*.

The candidate restates *specifically* what he is prepared to do once he joins the company.

Email Follow-Up

Dear Larry,

It was a real pleasure meeting you, Dan Stevens and Steve McLaughlin. I appreciate the clear and concise manner in which you shared with me the unique situation and background information with regard to the customer base, and specifically, the career opportunities available in your district. Please know that I am very enthusiastic about the possibilities for personal and professional growth in joining the ABC Chemical Team!

As I mentioned to you on Friday, I know that I have the refining knowledge and the understanding of why certain chemicals are used in different unit operations within refineries. The learning curve I will face in joining ABC Chemical will be in mastering the particulars of the chemistry of each of the products/technologies. Learning these intricate details will be a welcome challenge that I look forward to. I have the technical background and the aptitude to master the applications of ABC's products and services and get them integrated into plant designs. I can assure you that, from the first day I am on the job, I will make a significant impact in your district by building profitable business relationships with operators and engineers.

My goals are three-fold: 1.) to continually build long-term, profitable business relationships for ABC Chemical; 2.) to continuously provide customers with technical solutions to their problems and challenges and to help them achieve their goals in cost reduction to maximize their profits; and 3.) to retain current customer markets and penetrate new market segments to maximize ABC's long-term profits for its value-added products and services.

Please accept my sincere thanks and appreciation for your time and consideration in this matter. If you have any questions, or need further information from me, please don't hesitate to contact me. I look forward to hearing from you soon with regard to when I can fly back to Houston to finalize this interview process!

Best Regards,

James Johnson, PE
Cell: 816-888-1234
email: jjohnson@myisp.net

This final paragraph will automatically make this candidate stand out from the rest. Why? He actually "asks for the order"!

TO MAKE A REAL IMPACT,
CREATE AN 'IMPACT PLAN'!

You probably have been able by now to infer that there is a dominant theme running throughout each of the "secrets" featured in *"Headhunter" Hiring Secrets*. It's a relatively simple and straightforward one, too. Successful candidates in today's job market, or in *any* job market, for that matter, tend to have one principal attribute in common: They are men and women who are *always* willing and able to take that "extra step," and walk that "extra mile," throughout the entire job search process.

Candidates who want to make an even greater impact, an even more positive impression on prospective employers, should consider doing what many candidates I coach do. They put together a **90-Day Impact Plan** (using Microsoft® PowerPoint®) showing their prospective employers *precisely* how they would perform the duties involved in the positions each candidate seeks. Of course it takes extra time (though not as much as you perhaps might imagine), and extra effort also is required. Still, the extra time and effort pay off handsomely. Below are examples of two impact plans put together by our candidates—each was offered the position sought!

Here is a portion of the impressive presentation created by a candidate seeking a **Business Development position**.

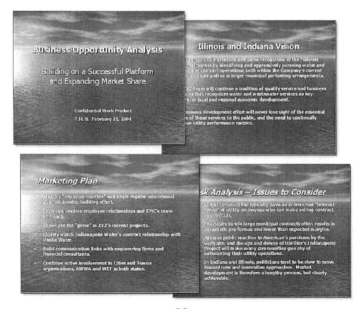

And here is just a portion of the presentation created by the other candidate, for a **Sales Manager** position.

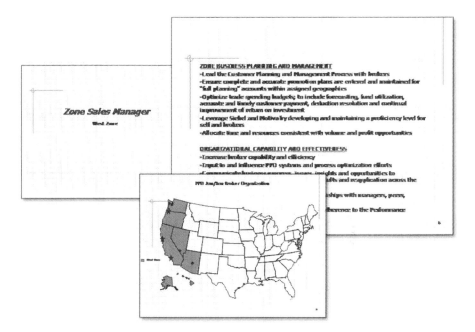

These plans are generally put together **after the first face-to-face interview, in order to progress the process toward the second face-to-face interview**.

DEVELOP A 'TOUCH' PLAN

An essential component of virtually any marketing strategy is the so-called "touch" plan, which involves keeping in touch with customers and prospects regularly, in order to build and maintain a good, solid, ongoing relationship. The rule of thumb is that it takes *seven* "touches" before you're able to "break through the clutter" that surrounds most people today, before the prospect actually begins "hearing" you.

What I said earlier about not responding to the same posting more than twice, however, still holds true. The "touch" plan is for when you are **actively engaged** in the placement process (next section) and are reaching out to real decision-makers.

I strongly advise you to use this same approach in prospecting for new job opportunities. But keep in mind, there is a very thin line between being persistent and simply being obnoxious. Being persistent is seven or more touches over time. Being obnoxious is trying to do it all in one week.

Since it can take a number of months to find the right opportunity in any job market, we circle back to your notebook (**Preliminary Planning & Preparation**). As pointed out in that section, it is absolutely vital that you keep an accurate, ongoing record of the people and companies you've connected with during the course of your job search.

Understandably, many job seekers wonder why they never heard back from a company or hiring manager they so painstakingly pursued, using perhaps a number of key contact methods. Unfortunately, the reason can be quite simple, though also somewhat bruising to one's ego: You may not have been on the hiring manager's "top 100 things to do" on that day! Or, perhaps your information was discarded without any further action. Maybe the hiring manager did indeed review your résumé and other application information, even liked what he or she saw, but put it aside for "later review," and the "later review" basket now is six inches high, with your information on the bottom of the pile (or email inbox)!

The point is, there could be any number of reasons why you have heard absolutely nothing from any given hiring manager. Obsessing about it won't do anything to change the situation. Periodically "re-touching" with the hiring manager, however, can go a long way toward preventing such an occurrence in the first place. My recommendation is to "re-touch" about three weeks after the initial contact and every three to four weeks thereafter.

What should you include in these "re-touching" contacts? Maybe an article about the competition in the appropriate industry. If you write a blog of some sort, and it's related to the business or industry the company is part of, send that. Show the hiring manager that you are an *expert* in your field and that you stay constantly engaged in that field. Become "The Rag Man"!

THE 'RAG MAN'

Who in the world is the "Rag Man"? you might ask. Let me briefly explain the role he played.

Back in the 1800s, in the Wild West, pioneers got a good deal of their news from a person everyone referred to simply as the "Rag Man."

Because it was so painful for the family when a person died, it was the "Rag Man's" job to come and clean out all the deceased's personal effects—clothing, jewelry, whatever—and take them away. The "Rag Man" traveled from town to town, village to village, either in a horse-drawn cart or merely using a push-cart. At each stop along the way, upon his arrival he would shout, for everyone to hear, "Rags for sale, rags for sale. Come and get your rags!" People of course flocked to greet the "Rag Man" at every stop. It wasn't that they were particularly all that interested in the "rags" he had for sale, although some people did indeed purchase them. More to the point, the people gathered around to hear the latest "news"—the "stories"—that the "Rag Man" had learned from other stops along his way.

As you expand your network, you should consider becoming a modern-day "Rag Man," the person to whom others turn to learn what's going on, in the industry, at various companies you've had contact with, etc. I suppose the modern term for such a person would more likely be something like "center of influence." Whatever you choose to call it, if you can occupy this vital role and serve as a reliable source of useful information to others, it can benefit you greatly because soon you will be perceived as, if not *the* expert, at least *an* expert. That can pay dividends for you.

If you choose to become a modern day "Rag Man," however, make it a point to always take "the high ground," to always put a *positive* spin on all information you convey to others. Or, as previously said, "don't spew venom." Anything you ever say about another person should build them up, and if you build others up more than yourself, you will build up your own image.

Other activities you could conduct as a modern day "Rag Man" might include such things as setting up and conducting professional seminars. Or forming a LinkedIn group oriented toward your profession or industry. If you have the talent, write and submit professional articles to industry publications or online forums. (These communication outlets, while most don't offer compensation, are continually looking for fresh, informative material from people perceived as "experts" in a particular field.)

Obviously, the opportunities to be perceived as an "expert" who is totally *engaged* in your profession are limited only by your imagination and willingness to explore them. One thing is certain, though, a hiring manager will quite likely view you as somewhat more than just the "average" candidate if you do become engaged in such activities. He or she will view you as someone who thinks strategically about his or her profession, about the relevant industry, someone who is *action-oriented*, not just another candidate "looking for a job."

CREATE A 'SMILE' FILE
(AKA, YOUR 'BRAG' BOOK)

In Phase One, you gathered all of your letters of recommendation and reference, awards, certifications, etc. Now it's time to assemble all of these things, along with a copy of your current résumé, into what is known as a "smile" file, also known in sales circles as a "brag book." It's merely a brief compilation of the achievements and awards, as well as other professional acclamations, for you to share with a hiring manager and any other people who may be in attendance at an interview.

Select a portfolio-type presentation book with a *professional* look. Insert the various documents you want to share into plastic sleeves, preferably those designed to fit into a three-ring binder portfolio.

Obviously, you will want to wait until the appropriate moment to share your "smile" file with prospective employers. That is, don't shove it into the hiring manager's face the moment you meet! Sometime early in the interview, you can expect the old, "Tell me a little bit about yourself" question. After responding with the type of answer mentioned later in the **Selling** section, you might want to introduce your "smile" file—if it seems an appropriate time to do that.

Having a "smile" file to present at the appropriate time can do several things for you. It can show that you obviously have had some noteworthy achievements and accomplishments during your professional career. It also shows that you have a good sense of organization. And, depending upon what's contained in the file, it shows that you definitely have the potential to accomplish some noteworthy things for your prospective employer.

Smile! ☺

DEFINE & DEVELOP YOUR 'CHANNELS TO MARKET'

The final element of the marketing plan, the Fourth "P" (**placement**), refers to the way the "product" gets "placed" into the market, aka, "channels to market." In this case, of course, the "product" is you, and your market consists of the *targeted* companies and hiring managers you want to reach with your marketing efforts.

This is actually your **first action step** in which you begin to get your information in front of potential hiring managers. There is an old saying, "Marketing fills the funnel. Sales executes at the narrow end." Here we begin to fill the funnel.

THE SIX PRIMARY CHANNELS TO MARKET' OR 'PLACEMENT' METHODS

For the purposes of your job search, you will be using **six primary "channels to market" or "placement" methods** (shown in the table below):

Channels to Market	Methodology/Activities
The Job Boards (Monster, CareerBuilder, Yahoo, HotJobs, niche boards, et al.)	• Posting your résumé • Properly applying to positions online ✓ Identifying an internal sponsor first through networking. ✓ Identifying a potential hiring manager. ✓ And, if these two approaches fail, modifying your résumé and cover letter to capture the key words and requirements of the position and applying online.
Recruiters	• Determining if it makes sense for you to work with a recruiter, and if so, how?
Networking	• Learning and applying the methods to properly and effectively network.
Direct Mail	• Learning how to craft direct mail communications to hiring managers/companies.
Phone Calls	• Learning and applying approaches and scripts that will get you results.
Job Fairs	• Learning how to work them and putting such events into proper perspective.

Before discussing how you should effectively place yourself in front of the hiring managers, it is necessary to identify the companies you wish to target and the names of people within those companies. *Sending résumé "blasts"* to a wide spectrum of companies across an equally wide range of industries, for example, **does not work**. It might make you *feel* as if you are accomplishing something, but you seldom are. Applying for positions in industries or companies for which you have no experience or qualifications makes you appear desperate and nothing is going to happen anyway. It is therefore necessary to considerably narrow your focus. You're not interested in—or at least you *shouldn't* be interested in—applying to *all* employers, for just *any* positions. You're interested in—or, again, you *should* be interested in— applying only to those positions for which you are qualified by your skill set, experience and education and training, in your particular field of specialty!

Though this sounds logical, and it might be to you, many of your competitors (i.e., other job seekers) do not do this. Thus, if you follow the guidance laid out, you will have a greater probability of not being excluded. To illustrate, we ask job seekers who contact us what industries, and positions within those industries, they are particularly interested in. All too often we receive responses like this: "I don't really care. I'll take any job I'm qualified for." As far as a hiring manager is concerned, if the job seeker doesn't know what she seeks from a job, or what she might be able to contribute to a hiring company, the hiring manager certainly isn't going to take the time to "coax" such information out of her!

Failure to properly identify the appropriate companies and industries that should comprise the 'target market' for you in your job search will communicate to a hiring manager that you are unfocused and ill prepared.

Let's recap:

- **Phase One: Preliminary Planning and Preparation**
  - You gathered collateral materials (letters of reference, awards, etc.).
  - You determined skills, talent and abilities.

- **Phase Two: Marketing**
  - You assessed the **product** (you).
  - You determined the value you bring to the marketplace in terms of how you can "make 'em or save 'em money" (which helps determine your **pricing**).

o   And you have developed and crafted your **promotional materials** (résumé, networking business cards, etc.).

Thus, by now, you should truly have a good idea of what it is you are good at, what you want to do and the types of companies you can do it for! The rest of *"Headhunter" Hiring Secrets* is basically helping you to learn how to get in front of the right people (**placement**), demonstrate your value (Phase Three - **Selling**) and **close** "the deal" (Phase Four).

The secrets in this book will enable you to position yourself as a top candidate in *any* job market. But, again, let me caution you, in a down economy, it will take much longer to find a new job if you try to reinvent yourself. For example, you hear that "green" is the future and it is. In the 2009 stimulus package, significant blocks of money are focused on energy (as well as healthcare and infrastructure).

Let me give you the reality of the situation, though. If you are currently, say, a mortgage broker and you want to get into a "green energy" field such as "wind," no matter how good a mortgage broker you are (or were) you will *not* be qualified to sell the electricity generated from the wind farm to the power company—unless you have prior experience in extremely complicated negotiations involving liabilities, liquidated damages, and other "what if" scenarios. For example,

"What if the wind farm doesn't produce enough electricity (due to wind speeds and the weather)?"

"What if the grid can't take the power? Or, conversely, what if the grid needs more power than the wind can even produce?"

Some people will say, "I can learn that." And, given time, perhaps they can. In a down economy, companies hire people who can do the job NOW—not a year from now, not three months from now, but NOW! In a down economy, companies generally do not hire people they have to develop. The two ways to reinvent yourself are either to go back to school or to make a significant career shift. The probability of making a significant career shift without the schooling or the prerequisite requirements is greatly reduced in a *down* economy! Such career shifts are best done in a rising economy. So, if you wish to reinvent yourself, either go back to school or wait for a rising economy.

I have had job seekers literally get angry with me for telling them this. So, let me provide a couple more examples of what I'm talking about. Here is what a solar power company recently had to say about this matter: "We admire anyone who is interested in 'green technology,' but what we need are engineers who already have experience when it comes to solar panels." And here is what a medical device company adds to this matter: "Sure, healthcare is growing. However, calling on doctors and hospitals can only be done if you have some experience doing that. A business degreed person with experience selling sports equipment will not be effective when it comes to calling on a hospital buying group. Can they learn it over time? Most likely, yes. However, we don't have time for 'on the job training.' We need someone who has done it, not someone who 'wants to do it'."

By now, you should truly have a good idea of what it is you are good at, what you want to do and the types of companies you can do it for!

That is the reality of trying to "reinvent yourself" in a "down" economy. It is therefore critical that you know the reality of what you can do and the types of companies you can do it for. **You cannot be, and you are not going to be, all things to all people,** so don't waste your time and energy trying to be! Let your competitors do that so that they are the ones excluded, not you.

AVOID RÉSUMÉ 'BLASTS'

Though résumé blasts were briefly mentioned previously, this is important. Often, if a job seeker is at all typical, one of his first inclinations, in addition to "hitting" the job boards, probably is to "blast" his résumé out to the marketplace. After all, this would appear to be the most efficient, easiest way to simultaneously contact large numbers of hiring managers and companies, as well as professional recruiters. **Let me strongly advise you against using this approach.**

One of the principal reasons I suggest not using résumé blasts is because this approach emphasizes "quantity" over "quality." It's not only taking the "one size fits all" approach, but is equivalent to everyone in high school trying out for the football team, not just those who have a chance of making it. Translation: Most "blasted" résumés get hit with the DELETE key. In the recruiting business we use a term to describe this approach—"spray and pray."

METHODS THAT DO WORK (AND AN EFFECTIVE
MARKETING PLAN USES THEM ALL!)

THE JOB BOARDS

 **Using the Job Boards.** Earlier we pointed out that the "hit rate" for the job boards is just 1-2%, or as we indicated in that section, **"job board 'surfing' is NOT job hunting!"** It is just *one* tool out of many in your complete marketing plan. When it comes to using the job boards, the problem is, far too many job seekers tend to make it a primary (if not *the* primary) component of their marketing plan.

Using job boards is a component of a complete marketing plan . . . a *small* component. Too many people make it their primary component.

That said, the job boards still can serve as an effective component in your entire marketing plan when used appropriately, as we will discuss. The two ways you should use the "boards":

- **Posting your résumé**
- **Applying to positions online—properly**

POSTING YOUR RÉSUMÉ

Once you have crafted your résumé according to the guidelines earlier outlined, posting it on the boards is a tool—if confidentiality isn't an issue. If confidentiality is important, though, then you do *not* want to do this. (Human Resources departments will often search the boards to see if current employees have résumés posted.)

The three primary, "generic" job boards that are the most well known, as well as the most widely used, are **Monster, CareerBuilder** and **Yahoo HotJobs**. If you post to these three boards, you will have exposure to over 80% of the recruiters, hiring managers and Human Resources professionals who use boards to find prospective job seekers. But this isn't all! Remember, you need to *focus* your job search, so at this point I would recommend that you also locate three "niche" job boards that relate to *your* industry or specialty.

How do you find the best niche or specialty employment websites? At www.weddles.com you can order a book that contains, in their opinion, the 350 best employment websites. Of course, you can do your own research, or you may already know the websites that are considered the best for your particular field of specialty.

In any case, you do not need to focus on any more than **six** job boards. After that, you should be spending your time on the other facets of placement that we will be discussing.

PROPERLY NAMING YOUR ONLINE RÉSUMÉ

When you get ready to upload your résumé to a job board (let's take www.monster.com as an example), you will encounter the following:

> **Résumé Name:** [_____]
> (Employers will see this title. Note: Some formatting may not appear in your Monster résumé.)

When hiring managers and recruiters do a search on the boards, key words are used. For illustration, as I am writing this, I have just put into Monster.com the Boolean key word phrase: "medical device" and engineering.

What is returned is the name of the résumé followed by the information shown in the table below:

Résumé Name: Senior QE Medical Device			
Candidate's Name: Jim Smith,. US Authorized			
Most Recent Job Title: Quality Engineer			
Most Recent Job Description: N/A			
Most Recent Employer	Self Employed Consultant	**Highest Degree**	Bachelor's
Desired Status	Full Time	**Desired Job Type**	Employee
Target Job Title	Validation Engineer	**Relocate**	No

It is from this information that the recruiter or hiring manager decides **whether to open the résumé or not!**

Let's take a further look at the results of this particular search. The complete details of the search criteria that I used in www.monster.com are:

- **Key words** (Boolean): "medical device" and engineering
- **Geography**: All of the U.S.
- **Degree**: Bachelor's Degree or higher
- **Experience Level**: Experienced, Non-Manager
- **Time frame**: Posted within the last 30 days

A total of 499 résumés were returned using these criteria. Am I going to look at all 499 résumés? Of course not! I have to quickly begin to cull through the résumés to develop a call list of possible candidates to contact. **In other words, first I look for whom I will** *exclude.*

How do I decide? The first item I look at is the résumé name. This is where **YOU** must use key words that will help me decide if I want to open your résumé.

Here are the names of the first 13 résumés of the 499 returned in this search:

- **Senior QE Medical Device**
- **Validation Engineer**
- Professional
- Resume April 2009
- **Manufacturing Engineer 3 Yrs Medical Device, BS Materials Eng***
- **Medical Device Development Engineer**
- QE CV Q2 09
- Resume
- **Biomedical Project Engineer**
- Highly motivated individual looking for a job
- Expereincd Proejct Engineer **(sic)**
- Tenacious Hard Working Results Driven Individual
- **Mechanical Engineer, Medical Device Design and Manufacturing***

It takes time (and costs money) to open and review a résumé, therefore, I will only open the résumés of the job seekers who give me a **"résumé name" that relates to the job and skill set**. The **résumé names that are in bold face type** are the six of the 13 shown above that I will take the time to open and review.

I have put an **asterisk (*)** after the two résumés shown above that are *most* clearly named and are good illustrations of how you should "name" yours. Notice the process here. It is one of exclusion. "Resume April 2009" might be the best candidate of them all, but whoever posted that résumé did not give me any compelling reason to open their résumé. I passed on them.

And the résumé name "Expereincd Proejct Engineer" (sic) . . . well, I think you get the picture there. I (and most others) will never open up that résumé, for obvious reasons!

And what about the boards that charge you a fee to upgrade your résumé so that you will come up first in a search? **DON'T WASTE YOUR MONEY**. The cheapest (and best) approach is to use the right descriptive key words, both in the "name" of your résumé and within the body of your résumé.

Look at it another way, if 300 people ahead of you each paid $150 to upgrade their résumé, you still aren't going to appear until the sixth page of a recruiter's or hiring manager's search. And if you pay $150 to get your résumé to appear ahead of others and still use an inept description, it won't be opened.

Additionally, there is an easy way to get your résumé posted on the Internet so that you can be found if someone uses AIRs (Advanced Internet Research) techniques on Google. It is: www.slideshare.net.

What does this do for you? Google's search engine optimization technology purposefully looks for PowerPoint® presentations on the Web and returns them at the top of a search. Thus, you can create a version of your résumé in PowerPoint®, save it to your computer, log onto www.slideshare.net and upload your PowerPoint® résumé. Use your "key" keyword in the title and additional keywords in the summary section and you will potentially be one of the first "hits" in a Google search, if a hiring manager or recruiter is looking for someone with your background and credentials.

There are additional strategies for being found on the Internet. Remember, however, that computers do not hire people. People hire people. It is easy to lull yourself into a false sense of security, feeling that, if you sit behind the computer all day and post your résumé and apply to positions online, you are doing something. Again, this is just one part of a full marketing campaign, so **do not fool yourself.**

APPLYING TO POSITIONS ONLINE (THE 'UNHIDDEN' OR 'ADVERTISED' JOB MARKET)

In this section we will be studying three things:

- **Identifying an internal person (sponsor) first through networking.**
- **Identifying a potential hiring manager.**
- **If these two approaches fail, applying directly through the Internet.**

Posted positions on the Internet (or in any other medium, such as the newspaper classifieds, radio, etc.) are referred to as the "advertised" positions. These are the positions that have the highest degree of visibility, as well as the ones to which hundreds (if not thousands) of people will respond!

I am going to show you a way to increase your probability of success in this "channel to market." First, how do you effectively and efficiently find the open positions and not spend hours on the Internet?

Use these Job Aggregators:

- www.indeed.com
- www.simplyhired.com
- www.hound.com

Jobs from Monster, CareerBuilder, Yahoo HotJobs, company websites, recruiter websites and many, many "niche" sites are all accumulated by and featured in these sites.

These three aggregators, properly used, will enable you to find 80% of all of the posted, advertised jobs.

Let's examine the utility and usefulness of **www.indeed.com** in more detail and see how this tool can accelerate your job/career search by providing you with a wealth of powerful information. From the home page of www.indeed.com you can launch a simple search using the "where" and "what" cells provided or you can click on the "Advanced Job Search" link.

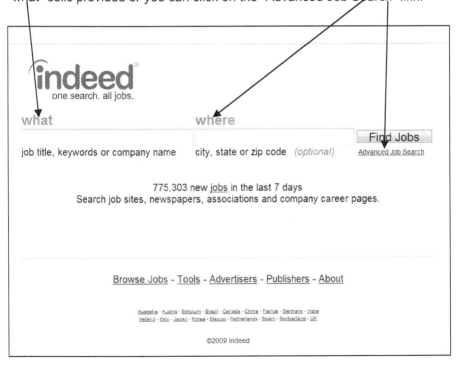

For an example of the simple search, let's put into the "what" cell the following Boolean phrase:

accountant OR accounting OR finance

And enter **Birmingham, AL** in the "where" cell.

Shown are the current openings within a 25-mile radius of Birmingham that have either "accountant" or "accounting" or "finance" in either the job title or in the position description. Let's examine some of the available information in detail.

The menu items on the left side (Refinements) enable you to further refine your information in regard to salary estimate, title, company, location, job type and whether or not the position was posted by a company (employer) or recruiter.

You can expand or contract your search from the exact location up to 100 miles out. This search is for a radius of 25 miles.

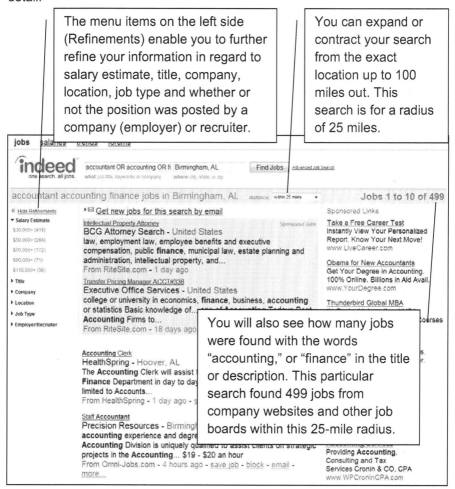

You will also see how many jobs were found with the words "accounting," or "finance" in the title or description. This particular search found 499 jobs from company websites and other job boards within this 25-mile radius.

As mentioned, jobs with "accountant" or "accounting" or "finance," either in the title or position description, will be returned by the search (the very first item). However, jobs that don't strictly meet these criteria may also be returned. Note, for example, that a job for an "intellectual property attorney" is also shown in this search. This is where the power of the **Advanced Job Search** function comes into play, as shown below.

On the "Advanced Job Search" page, enter words that you *don't* want to come up, find jobs from a particular company, use exact phrases and even refine your search to the age of the job posted ranging from "anytime" to "your last visit."

indeed
one search. all jobs.

Advanced Job Search

Find Jobs

With **all** of these words	
With the **exact phrase**	
With **at least one** of these words	accountant accounting finance
With **none** of these words	
With these words in the **title**	
From this **company**	
Show jobs of type	All job types ▾
Show jobs from	All web sites ▾
	☐ Exclude staffing agencies
Salary estimate	per year
	$50,000 or $40K-$90K

Where and When

Location	within 25 miles of ▾ Birmingham, AL (city, state, or zip)
Age - Jobs published	anytime ▾
Display	10 ▾ results per page, sorted by relevance ▾ [Find Jobs]

A powerful time-saving tool is the **Save Alert** function found at the bottom of the job search page. You can save the search and have email alerts sent to your inbox each day as shown below.

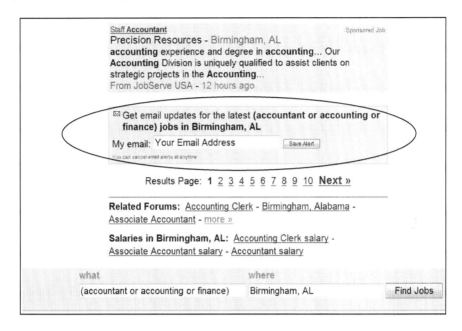

If you wish to see jobs by state or by category, click on the **"Browse Jobs"** link at the bottom of this page in the website:

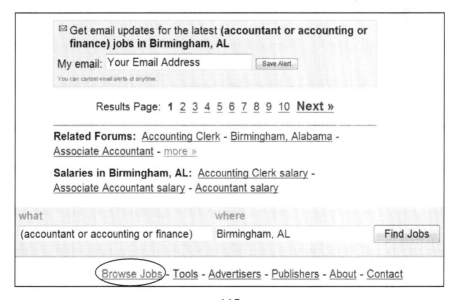

Shown below is the screen you will be taken to if you click the "Browse Jobs" link to explore jobs by state or by category.

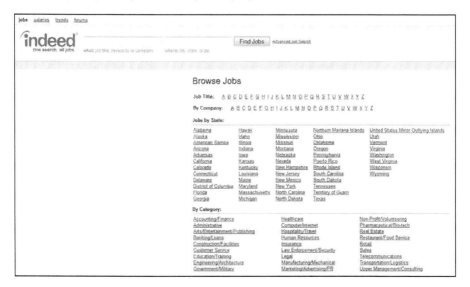

Job Trends, Job Market Competition and Industry Trends can all be accessed and studied from Indeed's **"Tools"** link at the bottom of their website. Shown below is the trend for "sales engineer." (Note trend improvement since July 2009.)

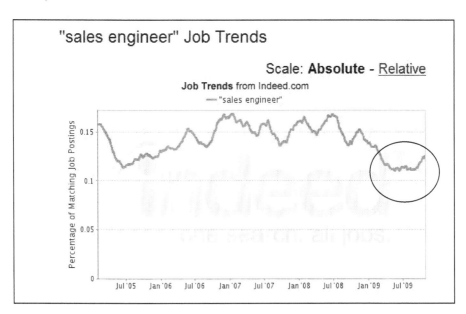

Shown next are the industry trends for our original search for accounting, accountant and finance jobs.

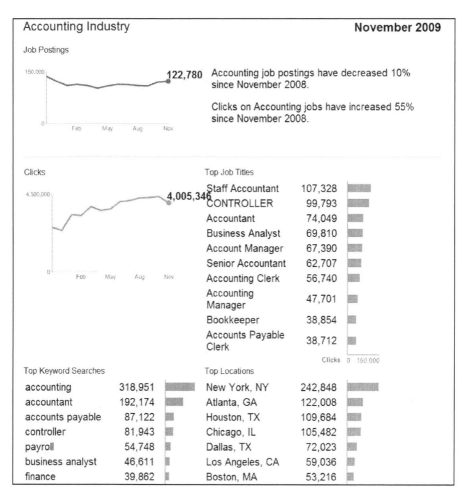

Proper use of www.indeed.com and the other job aggregators prevents you from wasting time and enables you to turn it into *productive* time, i.e., spending your time identifying hiring managers and contacting them as we will be showing you how to do. By the way, Craig's List is *not* indexed by the aggregators. Many local positions are posted on Craig's List so it can be a valuable resource for you, although high-level jobs are seldom found there.

Networking (discussed next) is a more powerful approach for finding your next opportunity than is using the Internet alone or applying online for positions. But, if you *combine* knowledge of the open position (gleaned from the Internet) with a **networking contact** who will represent, i.e., sponsor you, then you will have a distinct advantage over people who "just network" or "just apply online." (Details on how to have this conversation are in the **Networking** section.)

Before rushing into applying for the position online, use networking skills to see if you can identify an internal person who will *sponsor* you for the position.

Larger companies frequently offer a "referral bonus" to employees who recommend someone who subsequently gets hired. Such bonuses can range from $1,000 to $3,000. So, if you see an opening with a major company that you are a fit for, i.e., you truly have the credentials that are required, use your networking skills (which we will coach you on two sections from now) to identify someone who works in that company, get them to review your résumé and credentials and, if they feel you would be a good fit, ask them if they would be willing to sponsor you and submit your information internally. And "What is in it for them?" of course, is the "finder's fee."

Note, however, that this technique will NOT work if you have already applied for the position, plus it will alienate your networking contact—possibly forever. This is one of the reasons why you must keep accurate records and not just apply online indiscriminately to every position you come across. If you have already sent your résumé to the company, you will be "inhaled" into their automated computer databases. If an internal person now chooses to sponsor you, Human Resources will tell them, "We already have the résumé because they applied online," and that person will not get the referral bonus.

Only as a last resort should you apply directly online. If you do, make sure you use a *customized* cover letter *and* résumé, powered by the key words and requirements from the posting.

Even if a company does not offer a referral bonus, it is better to find someone through networking who will represent you internally versus going it alone.

The next best method (after looking for an internal sponsor) for applying to an advertised position is to use your "investigative reporter" skills. Determine who the potential hiring manager might be for the position, write a letter and use the "channel to market" of direct mail, followed up by a phone call (discussed in the following sections).

When you have someone sponsor you internally, or you send your information to a potential hiring manager, be sure to customize your cover letter and résumé, **using the keywords and requirements from the posting**.

Only as a last resort—after you have exhausted your efforts through networking and research and have come up empty handed—should you apply directly online through the job board or company website. Here is where many people fall into the trap of now just emailing their "generic" cover letter and "generic" résumé. It is still critical to *customize* each and every cover letter *and* résumé for the position being applied for. A lot of work? Yes! Not doing it, however, will ensure you are *excluded* and then it was all wasted time and effort, anyway.

EMAILING YOUR RÉSUMÉ

Why a special section on e*mailing* your résumé? you might ask. After all, this is a no-brainer, isn't it? Well, not exactly, and not if you want to make sure your résumé is received—and categorized—properly.

Take the simple task of *naming* your résumé, for example, when used as a Word® document attachment. Here are two examples of how I recommend doing that:

Jim Smith Resume – 01.11.10.doc

-OR-

Jim Smith Resume.doc

Be sure to keep updating the date portion of the first résumé name used in the first example above, i.e., "01.11.10." Sending out your résumé dated 04.15.09 in January 2010 makes it appear that you're having significant difficulty getting hired. That would be a "red flag" for most hiring managers.

You might suppose that, when it comes to naming your résumé, a name is a name is a name, right? Actually, no! It's vitally important that you select a name for your résumé that will allow a hiring manager (or recruiter) to easily access it for future reference. Name your résumé in some haphazard fashion and you could easily get "lost in the shuffle"!

Let me explain how that could happen, as well as how you can take steps to avoid it.

Here are some names of résumés we have received just this year:

résumé.doc*
resume2.doc
mysalesresume.doc
résumé-engineering.doc
mechanicalengineering.doc
salesspecialist.doc
mydadsresume.doc**
13x48hgg.doc***
mypostedresume.doc****

*Top name for résumés, which puts *your* résumé in a stack of thousands and thousands!

**Sort of makes you wonder why good old dad couldn't write his own résumé, doesn't it?

***I especially liked this highly descriptive one.

****This tells any recruiter or hiring manager that the job seeker is "all over the place," using a shot gun approach versus a targeted "here is what I can do for you" approach.

Résumés named in such a fashion help no one, particularly YOU. Let's say, for example, that a hiring manager receives your email, opens your résumé as a Word® document named "resume.doc," and then prints a copy for review within the next several days. Then, suppose the hiring manager likes at least some of what he or she sees on the printed version of your résumé and would like to email a copy of it to another person within the company. If you did not use an email address that is associated with your name, a relevant subject line or a "Word Doc" name that is relevant, you will never be found again.

Let me give you a real example:

Email address of person sending me the résumé: ac5@myisp.com
Subject: Posted position
Attachment: resume.doc

FACT: I have dozens and dozens of emails in my inbox. This person's name is "Tom." How am I going to easily find him again in my inbox? The email name ac5@myisp.com doesn't help me find Tom. The subject line, "Posted position," doesn't help because I have a dozen posted positions, so I don't know which one to look under, and finally, resume.doc doesn't help me find "Tom." Tom is now excluded because he made himself "non-findable" and I move on. (Remember the section "Where ARE you?")

Here are some more pointers about the **subject line** you use in your résumé email:

Avoid using typographic symbols, such as dashes (—) in the email subject line, because spam filters sometimes kick out such conventions. For example, avoid constructions such as this in the subject line:

Posting — Sales Engineer — Chicago — Joan Jones

Absolutely DO NOT use any of the following type of subject lines:

Posted Position
My resume
Seeking Employment
I Saw You Were Hiring
Your Monster Posting
Resume Attached for your Review

So what type of subject line could you use? Here is what I suggest:

Joan Jones Resume for Sales Engineer Chicago

It provides the required information so no one is guessing, and it most likely will not get picked up by a spam filter. It will also be easy to find again and is not too long.

As is the case with any communication you initiate in conjunction with your job search, when it comes to email, always put yourself in the mind, heart and soul, as well as the shoes, of course, of the intended recipient. It will make it harder for a recipient to exclude you if you clearly communicate to them that you know *precisely* what you hope to accomplish, and even more importantly, how you can benefit them.

You've undoubtedly listened many times to that **popular radio station, WIIFM**. You know, that station virtually *everybody* listens to, regularly, particularly hiring managers and the companies they represent. The "call letters" represent "What's In It For Me?" Stay tuned!

RECRUITERS

TYPES OF 'HEADHUNTERS' & HOW THEY EARN THEIR INCOME

A sizable number of good, reliable recruiting firms generally contract with businesses to locate and recruit candidates for the positions they need to fill. The fee charged by the recruiting firm normally is 25% to 33% of the successful candidate's first-year salary (paid by the client company, not the candidate). These recruiting firms actively seek out *fully qualified* candidates to present to companies that are hiring.

Retained Search Firms. This type of recruiting firm normally charges client companies a fee that is in the range of 33% of the total first-year compensation of the successful candidate, to include salary, signing bonuses, commissions, etc. (Again, this fee is paid by the hiring company, not the successful candidate.) A retained firm is generally paid the full 33% fee by the company, even if that recruiting firm's candidate is not the successful candidate.

Retained search firms normally deal only with *executive*-level candidates, so unless you are currently employed at that level, or have been in the recent past, don't expect them to come knocking on *your* door anytime soon.

Contingency Search Firms. Our firm, The HTW Group, is this type of search firm. There are some criteria that must be met in order to work with a contingency firm and, if you meet these criteria, you should consider contacting these types of recruiting firms as another component of your marketing plan. It is important to note that ninety-five percent of the time a contingency firm is working to fill an opening for a company where that company has been unable to fill it through other means. When a contingency firm gets a "job order" from the client, they look for **stellar talent** that would be a good fit. In other words, the candidate is right for the company and the company is right for the candidate.

Five percent of the time, however, we will work with you to help you find a new position. In other words, only 5% of the time is the recruiter *proactively* seeking to find you a position and "take you to market." Ninety-five percent of the time, the recruiter is looking for the right slate of candidates for presenting on an open position, and it may or may not include you. We will review the criteria a recruiting firm looks for in terms of that 5% they will proactively work with, in a moment.

If you contact a recruiter, be forewarned: Most recruiters will *not* **work with you** on a position if . . .

- You have already applied to that position online.
- You had your credentials submitted to the company through another recruiter.
- You submitted your credentials to the company directly yourself.

That's why it is so vitally important, as cited in the **Preliminary Planning & Preparation** section, to keep your notebook current regarding *where* and with *whom* you apply.

Let me give you an example of how the work originates and flows through the typical contingency search firm.

A company communicates to the contingency search firm that they need help filling a position (or positions). Normally, this occurs because the contingency firm, through *proactive* telephone prospecting among hiring companies, uncovered the need. Very rarely is it the hiring companies doing the initiating. (More on how YOU can also successfully do *proactive* telephone prospecting for yourself in the next Phase, **Selling**.)

The hiring company not only provides a job description and a salary range to the recruiting firm, they also will discuss the "must haves" of the position and the "nice to haves." Once the recruiter has a thorough understanding of *precisely* the type of candidate the hiring company is seeking—and normally such a thorough understanding can be obtained *only* by talking directly with the hiring manager, not the Human Resources department—he or she then initiates a search of the recruiting firm's internal candidate database, in an attempt to identify possible candidates to present to the hiring company. The recruiter also constantly monitors candidate résumés that come into the office on virtually a daily basis, looking for possible candidates. But most high-quality candidates are identified through *proactive* telephone prospecting!

And where do I find you? From referrals, networking and in www.zoominfo.com, www.linkedin.com or www.facebook.com. Occasionally, we might find your résumé posted on one of the job boards, but we actually like to find candidates from Google searches over candidates posting their résumé on a job board. (Recall how to use www.slideshare.net.)

Contingency firms will not—and cannot!—present just *any* candidate to a hiring company. That is, they can't and won't, if they want to maintain the credibility, reliability and the trust they have built up over the years. Only candidates who are fully qualified and have an impeccable work record with solid credentials will normally even be considered by a contingency search firm. If, for example, you are a "job hopper," don't have "**current, relevant experience**," or otherwise have any type of "stain" on your record, most contingency firms will avert their eyes! So be forewarned. That again is why **working with a recruiting firm is just one step of a complete marketing plan**. And just because one recruiter won't work with you doesn't mean another one won't. Each recruiter has his or her own criteria, based upon the needs of that client for that position. So don't be offended, just move on if a recruiter tells you that you aren't a right fit.

And what does "current relevant experience" mean? It means that the job seeker is currently doing the job or has most recently done the job. A company will not pay us 25% to 33% of a person's first-year's salary if that person cannot "hit the ground running." If they have to significantly train them, if the candidate is a "work in progress," they will not hire that person from a recruiter. **Let's be clear here**. That is NOT to say they won't hire that person. It is to say they won't hire that person from a recruiter. So, if you are a recent college graduate, have been out of the workforce for some time or haven't done the job within the last two to three years, there is probably very little a recruiter can do for you. You will have to use the other means described to land your new position.

MAJORITY OF 'HEADHUNTERS' WORK A MARKET 'NICHE'

A large majority of recruiters work a clearly identified market "niche." We "headhunters" have an acronym for this approach—DIG, which stands for "Discipline, Industry and Geography." My niche, for example, is sales and engineering (discipline), chemicals or petrochemicals (industry), and North America (geography). Many times, because my search firm is located in the Metro Atlanta, GA, area, I have candidates contact me because they want to relocate to Atlanta and hope that I can "find them a job." As you can see, it seldom works that way and most times, if they aren't fully qualified candidates for positions in my market niche, I simply can't help them at all. This usually is the case for other search firms as well. If a candidate doesn't fit into the firm's niche, the candidate seldom can be helped.

IF YOU DECIDE TO WORK WITH A 'HEADHUNTER' . . .

If you do end up working with a "headhunter," here are some critical key points to keep in mind:

- Always be 100% honest with the recruiter and keep him or her fully informed about everything you do in conjunction with your job search.

- Call the recruiter back within four hours of him/her calling you, i.e., if they leave you a voice mail message.

- Ask the recruiter questions about the opportunity so that you know all about it and are sure that you can *do* the job and *want* to do the job.

- Call the recruiter back within two hours of *any* interview.

- Be prepared to make a decision within 24 hours after any final interview.

- Good recruiters will *never* present you to a company without your permission, i.e., reveal your identity. If they do, you need to move on immediately!

FIRMS THAT CHARGE CANDIDATE FEES ARE NOT RECRUITING FIRMS

There are some firms that do charge the candidate fees and some of them are excellent. They will help you write your résumé, coach you, help you prepare for an interview, provide advice regarding offer negotiations, etc. The legitimate ones that charge fees are coaching firms and outplacement firms. And it can be in your best interest to consider such a firm. The legitimate ones will NOT guarantee you a job nor will they guarantee you an interview. No one can do that. If any company does offer such guarantees, be extremely leery. Do your due diligence and make sure that you know what the company can and cannot do for you.

TIMES WHEN A RECRUITING FIRM WILL *PROACTIVELY* MARKET YOU—THE MPC CONCEPT

Remember my mentioning that 5% of the time a contingency recruiter will work for you and actively market you? How do you know when that is? We call a candidate who meets the majority of the criteria in the following table a Most Placeable Candidate, or simply, an MPC. In this case, the focus of our efforts is concentrated on *proactively* presenting the candidate to a wide range of targeted companies and hiring managers.

The chart on the next page shows the characteristics of an MPC.

Who is a Most Placeable Candidate? Someone Who . . .

Has exceptional work performance as noted by quantifiable accomplishments and achievements.
Is not a "job hopper."
Has current, relevant experience.
Has a strong desire to make a career move AND a valid motivation for making that career move.
Is just beginning their search and is thus unknown in the job hunting market.
Is *not* working with other recruiters.
Agrees to work with one recruiter *exclusively* for an agreed period of time.
Is predictable and consistent in their dealings with the recruiter.
Is mentally sharp and has an affable demeanor.
Is affordable, i.e., desired salary in line with skills, marketplace demand.
Is willing to take résumé off any job boards where they may have been posted.
Is fairly flexible in terms of geography.
Will interview with client companies that express a desire to interview them.

If you meet the *majority* of these criteria, then a niche contingency recruiter *may* consider you an MPC. That can mean they will "take you to market" to several hundred companies, helping you gain exposure and the opportunity to explore any appropriate career opportunities that may exist for you at those companies. No guarantees, of course, but not a bad position to be in, either, whether we are talking about today's job market, or any other job market.

If you do not meet the majority of the above criteria a recruiter may still work with you and present you on appropriate opportunities. They just won't proactively market you, and remember that is 95% of the time. Thus, that is why I am making this book available to you—so that you will know what to do on your own and can develop a full plan for yourself and not have to rely on anyone else.

Recruiters are motivated to place you, if they can. That's how they make their money!

Remember, recruiters are motivated to place you if they can. After all, that is how we recruiters make our money! You should also keep in mind that a *legitimate* recruiter will *not* charge you money to market you. The role you must play in this arrangement is simply to cooperate. Let the recruiter have three weeks to market you exclusively and provide you updates. If you don't receive progress reports, feel free to work with other recruiters. But, if the recruiter is marketing you, give them the chance. It is hard work to research companies, make the calls, follow up and sell the hiring managers on the idea of speaking with you. When a recruiter markets you, it is as if they are your agent. Don't abuse that relationship. If you play one recruiter against another, then word gets out, you won't have anyone who will want to represent you.

If you would like to find a recruiter, I recommend that you study these two sites:

www.mrinetwork.com — **MRI** (Management Recruiters International) is a global network of approximately 800 recruiting firms and 4,000 recruiters. You can do a Boolean keyword search to find a recruiter within your area of interest, i.e., "niche.")

www.recruiterredbook.com — Ability to obtain online access to 13,000+ recruiters for $60 from Kennedy Information Network.

NETWORKING

Networking . . . we hear this term used all of the time. Certainly, most of us are familiar with the concept, yet many people continue to be "afraid" to network because they feel it involves asking friends, family members and acquaintances for "a job."

In fact, the **key to successful networking is, actually, *not* to ask for a job!** As I have helped job seekers over the years understand this fact, they usually have breathed a big sigh of relief and then have been able to effectively approach networking from a totally new perspective.

So, exactly, what is networking? It is about gathering information and exchanging ideas with people who have the same (or similar) interests as you. But the *real* power of networking is the *reciprocal* aspect of it, i.e., being able to give back, infusing your approach with the expressly implied understanding of "If you help me, I will gladly return the favor whenever I get the chance."

HOW TO MAKE A NETWORKING CALL TO FAMILY, FRIENDS

Let's say you haven't spoken to your cousin Sue in three years, so you give her a call.

"Sue, this is your long lost cousin Jim," you might say. After engaging in some chit-chat conversation (the "warm-up") you continue:

"Sue, I have recently been laid off. I have a solid track record in chemical industry sales. Whom do you know, or whom do you know who might know of someone in the chemical industry who could provide me with some insight as I progress in my career search?"

Obviously, if you haven't been laid off, simply modify the approach:

"Sue, I have a solid track record of performance in chemical sales. I have been reevaluating my career and would like to explore my options. Whom do you know or whom do you know who might know of someone in the chemical industry who could provide me with some insight as I progress in my career search?"

(Of course, this concept applies to engineering, HVAC installation and repair, home building, remodeling, accounting, etc.)

Sue says she doesn't know anyone.

"Sue, I understand, and no problem. If within your networking groups, church, Sunday School, college alumni association (i.e., offer some suggestions) you run into anyone who might have some connections in the chemical industry, I sure would appreciate the opportunity to network with them. By the way, if I can ever network for you, please let me know."

As the conversation now winds down, ask,

"Sue, may I email you my updated contact information?" After getting her email address and providing your own, close by asking, "Is there anything I can do for you now?"

That's it! That is a simple networking call to a family member whom you haven't seen in three years. A lot of people are afraid to make this call. They are afraid Sue won't help them out. But now you see it is *not* about *asking for a job*. It is about "whom do you know," and offering *reciprocity*. Look at it this way, if you never *make* the call, you can be absolutely assured that Sue will not help you out!

Key phrase: 'Whom do you know?'

Do *not* ask, "Do you know. . .?" Most people "don't know" anyone, or at least don't *think* they know anyone who might be able to help you in your job search. "Whom do you know or whom do you know who might know of someone in . . . ," takes them "off the hook" and they, more often than not, will actually give your request some serious thought and get back with you.

You have to approach each networking contact with an open mind. There is a human being on the other end with their own dreams, goals, desires and fears. Why should they help you? They don't have any reason to, in most cases. You have to give them a reason, such as being a source of information that can help them (reciprocity).

Approach networking with the overall perspective of building lifelong relationships. It is as much about the other person as it is about you, so be sure to ask good questions about others and have good conversations, follow up and do what you say you are going to do (which is why you keep your notebook or Outlook® calendar or Blackberry® calendar, etc.).

NETWORKING WITH THE ANSWERS
TO THE 'WHOM DO YOU KNOW?' QUESTION

Through attending luncheons, alumni events and association events, as well as by getting names from the "Whom do you know?" question, you now have the opportunity to reach out to people who are closer to the "stranger" side of the list than the "friend" side of the list. Just remember that a stranger is simply someone you haven't yet met or had an opportunity to develop into a friend.

This is when you use what is called your "90-second elevator speech." The four components of that "speech" are:

- Who you are.
- What you do.
- How you can solve someone's problem(s) or make a contribution that will make 'em or save 'em money?
- And what the listener/recipient should do next.

Back to your cousin Sue. Let's say she gave you "Jim's" name, so you call him up. Your conversation might go something like this:

(Who you are) "Jim, my name is Todd Smith. You and I have not spoken before, but I was referred to you by Sue Jones. Do you have a moment?"

(If they say no, then ask when they could schedule five minutes. If they say yes, then continue . . .)

(What you do)

"Jim, what I do is help companies significantly improve their fixed asset accounting by identifying business, system and operational

129

issues that affect the fixed assets and provide recommendations for improvements."

(How you can solve someone's problems)

"Recently, as an example, I reviewed the work flow on a pharmaceutical manufacturing line that enabled us to modify our existing depreciation schedule, adding over $40,000 to our bottom line for the year. I have a BS Degree in Accounting, a CPA and an MBA."

(What the listener should do next)

"Jim, I am looking for an opportunity with a progressive manufacturing company that is interested in improving their bottom line in this economy. Whom do you know who might have contacts within the manufacturing sector?"

— OR —

"Jim, are there any companies within the manufacturing sector that you are particularly impressed with right now?"

— OR —

"Jim, what trends do you see in accounting that might affect fixed assets?"

As you can see, ask a question in order to get the other person talking, have a conversation and see where it leads. If it doesn't come back to accounting, near the end of the conversation you circle back and ask,

"Jim, by the way, I am sure you are well networked. Whom do you know in the manufacturing sector that I could further network with?"

And be sure to use "power words" to describe what you do:

- If you are in sales, then a company may want to "turbo charge sales in turbulent times."
- If you are a chemical process engineer, a company may want to "distill their processes down to the most efficient possible."
- As an accountant, a company may want to "account for every penny to wring out waste."

Notice, again, what you are *not* asking during these telephone networking calls:

- You are *not* asking about their company and whether or not there is a job opening. Don't put them on the spot.
- You are *not* asking for a job. You are looking for information that will lead you to opportunities.

Now this is very important: Conclude *any* networking conversation with,

"Jim, what can I do for you?"

AN APPROACH THAT DOES NOT WORK IN NETWORKING

Chances are, the following "networking" call is probably the type you're used to thinking of when the subject of "networking" comes up:

"My name is Todd Smith. I am an accountant and I do fixed asset accounting. I grew up in Rochester, NY, as one of three kids. Went to Syracuse University and got my degree in accounting and later an MBA. I recently worked for XYZ Company and got laid off and am looking for a fixed asset accounting job."

This approach does *not* work! There is *no* value proposition in this rendition. So you are an accountant, so what? So are many others. You don't demonstrate how you can deliver value to anyone, and you conclude by asking for a job. This approach seldom leads to success.

Another key about networking is that *no one*—and I mean *no one!*—wants to hear your "sob story." If you come across as "poor, poor, pitiful me," guess what? You will remain "poor, poor, pitiful me."

MAKE SURE YOU CAN BE FOUND!

Part of any successful job search, of course, is being able to be found! It's particularly important when it comes to networking. We have discussed the appropriate naming of your résumé for job boards and on the Internet. There are some other extremely effective, additional methods that you need to consider. Featured below are some of these methods:

ZoomInfo (www.zoominfo.com)

This database is hugely popular on the recruiting side of the business, but still relatively unknown on the job seeker side.

Check it out by searching for yourself on ZoomInfo, and if you aren't there, you can—and should!—add yourself. If you are there, update your information so that people will learn about you and you can easily be found.

Thousands of recruiters and companies use ZoomInfo everyday to find potential candidates for the mission critical positions they are recruiting for, so make sure they can find you, too!

LinkedIn (www.linkedin.com)

Over 55 million people are now on LinkedIn, but I have conversations everyday with people who are not there. LinkedIn is a networking tool that helps you connect with others and, at the same time, discover "inside" connections within many companies.

HOW TO QUICKLY GET 'UP AND RUNNING' ON LINKEDIN

There are basically **four** steps to quickly getting "up and running" and effectively using LinkedIn:

> ➤ Develop a complete profile that does *not* conflict with your résumé.
> ➤ Begin to connect (grow your network).
> ➤ Ask for recommendations (a good target is three).
> ➤ Join appropriate groups.

Now, let's explore some of these steps and components of LinkedIn in a little more depth, so that you can effectively use it to be found and, in turn, do critical research for finding companies and names.

DEVELOPING YOUR LINKEDIN PROFILE

Everything that's in your résumé does *not* have to be in your LinkedIn profile, but make sure that the information contained in the profile and your résumé are in sync! In other words, don't say that you were with a company *four* years in your LinkedIn profile if your résumé shows you were with the company only *three* years!

How about a picture to include with your LinkedIn profile? While you should *never* put a picture on your résumé, it is perfectly acceptable to consider putting a professional, flattering picture of yourself on LinkedIn.

Be sure you use enough *keywords* in your LinkedIn profile to enable people to find you when they do a search.

Shown below is my LinkedIn profile. Note that at the top of your profile is a small section where you can tell people what you are doing now. Use this section. It is effective.

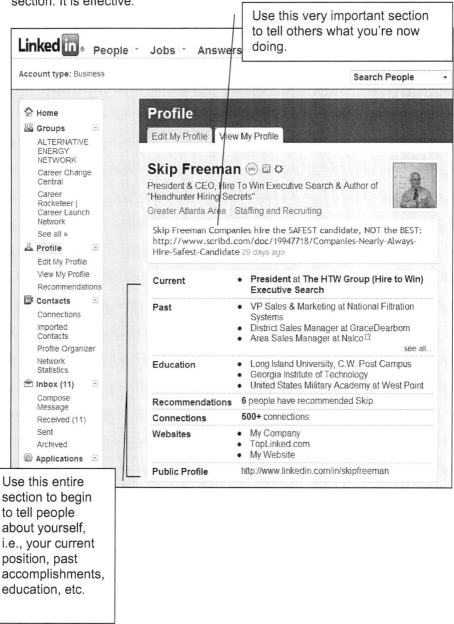

Use this very important section to tell others what you're now doing.

Use this entire section to begin to tell people about yourself, i.e., your current position, past accomplishments, education, etc.

BEGIN TO CONNECT (GROW YOUR NETWORK)

In addition to people being able to find you, the parallel strength of LinkedIn is that you can find colleagues, friends, relatives, classmates and many others you may know—*or want to know.*

LinkedIn works on the concept known as "degrees of separation." You know someone (your first-degree connection) who, in turn, knows other people (your second-degree connections) and they obviously know people who are considered your third-degree connections. As of this writing, I have over 9,000 first-degree connections and nearly 1.2 million second degree connections. I am connected to nearly 17 million people through three degrees of separation.

People tend to use one of two approaches to LinkedIn. The first approach is to connect *only* with the people you know and who know you, or only with people who are in your industry, specialty, niche, etc. There is a lot of validity to this approach and it does result in a very tight, high-quality network. The second approach emphasizes that "quality" comes from "quantity," i.e., you don't know whom you don't know. So by growing your network and connecting with as many people as you possibly can you will be able to connect with many stellar people whom you can help and who, in turn, can help you.

People respond extremely favorably to the email or phone call that begins with, 'I found you on LinkedIn.'

If you choose to grow your network by rapidly expanding your connections, it is easy to do. You can find "open networkers" by visiting www.toplinked.com, as well as others. Also, if you become a paid member of LinkedIn, you can join the OpenLink Network on LinkedIn. You identify yourself as an open networker and you can search for and find other open networkers with whom to connect. (But you do not need to become a paid member of LinkedIn to take advantage of the majority of its benefits.)

The power of reaching out to open networkers is that, theoretically, they should always accept your invitation. Sometimes, non-open networkers have a tendency to click the "decline invitation" button if they don't know you. If your invitations are excessively declined, you are temporarily blocked from inviting additional people to join your network until you send a message to

LinkedIn telling them that you "won't do it again."

If you use Microsoft® Outlook® (and have a version newer than 2003), then you can use the **LinkedIn Outlook Toolbar** to enable you to easily add connections. (Versions of Outlook® 2003 and earlier have a tendency to "lock up" if this toolbar is added.)

(Below is an illustration of how the Microsoft® Outlook® toolbar is featured on LinkedIn.)

If you use Microsoft® Outlook® as your email program, LinkedIn features an Outlook® toolbar, which enables you to easily and quickly add connections to your network.

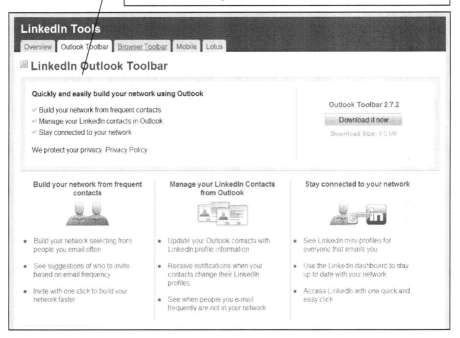

ASK FOR RECOMMENDATIONS

The more complete your profile is, the higher up you will appear in someone's search. Having at least one recommendation is necessary to begin to gain maximum exposure. Additional recommendations enhance your credibility. Three to ten recommendations is a solid range. (More than ten can begin to appear "fake." "Is this person for real?" someone may ask.)

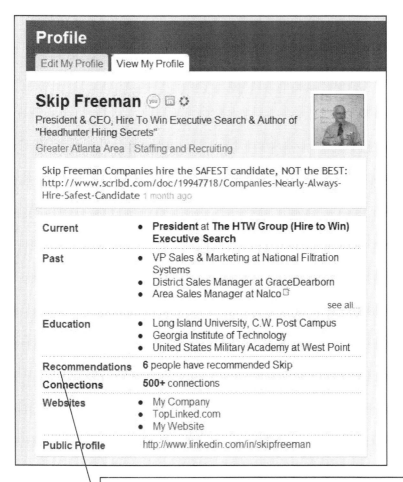

You must have *at least* ONE "recommendation" to begin gaining maximum exposure in your network. Some people go overboard. THREE is a good, solid number to start with.

JOIN GROUPS

One of the most powerful functionalities of LinkedIn is "Groups." You can join up to 50 groups.[3] The main reason it is so powerful is that you can search and find people within the groups you are a member of even if they are not part of your three degrees of separation network. Hence, **groups add a lot of power to your LinkedIn networking capability**.

Click on this tab in LinkedIn to search out groups you may want to join to enhance your networking connections and activities.

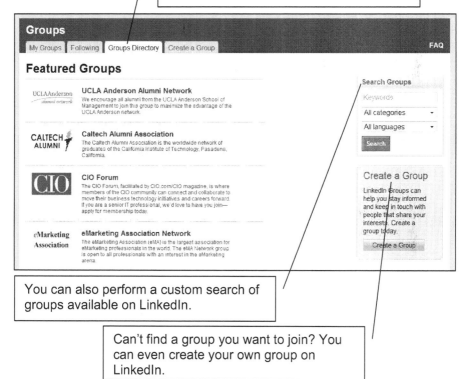

You can also perform a custom search of groups available on LinkedIn.

Can't find a group you want to join? You can even create your own group on LinkedIn.

---

[3]*You can easily leave a group that you are not actively involved in and join another group. To stay up to date and empowered regarding the NEW rules of the hiring game, join our LinkedIn group, **Job Hunting Power**.*

FINDING COMPANIES/FINDING NAMES

In your career/job search, before you can connect with the right people, you have to find the right, *relevant* companies, so let's continue our study of LinkedIn by seeing how you can locate companies using this tool.

First, click on the "Companies" tab in LinkedIn.

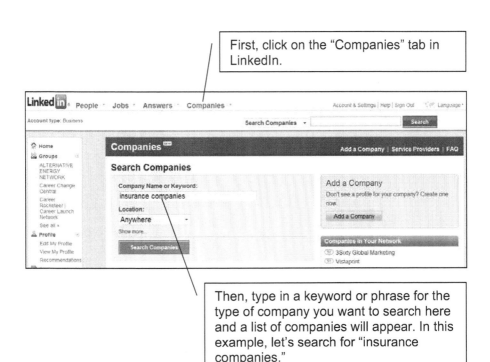

Then, type in a keyword or phrase for the type of company you want to search here and a list of companies will appear. In this example, let's search for "insurance companies."

Go to the "Companies" tab, type in a keyword and a list of companies in LinkedIn will appear. Click on one of those companies and people within your network who are currently (or were previously) with that company will be shown.

If you want to narrow your search to a specific geography, you can. For example, enter a ZIP code into the "Lookup" box under "Postal Code." (You can go to www.usps.com and easily obtain zip codes.)

There are a number of ways you can narrow your company search, simply by completing information in this section of the "Search Results" screen, e.g., by ZIP code, company size, only companies featuring jobs on LinkedIn, etc.

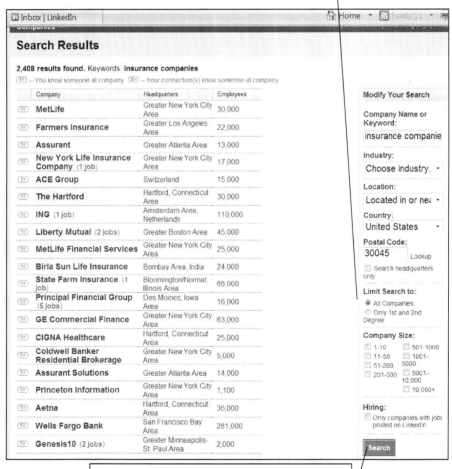

Once you're satisfied with how you have narrowed your search, simply click on the "Search" button.

Here is the list of insurance companies that came up when a search of the Metro Atlanta, GA, area was conducted. Let's click on the first company listed, Assurant.

You'll find a wealth of information on the company profile page: company information, people in your network who work there, former employees, new hires, promotions, common job titles, median age of employees, etc.

You will also find information such as gender percentages, top schools employees attended/graduated from, stock information, affiliate companies, and much, much more!

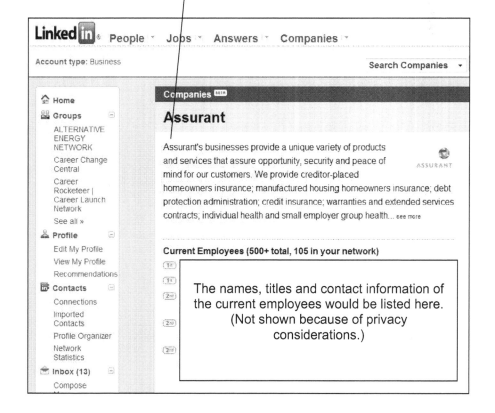

Linked in®   People   Jobs   Answers   Companies

Account type: Business   Search Companies ▾

Companies BETA

Assurant

Assurant's businesses provide a unique variety of products and services that assure opportunity, security and peace of mind for our customers. We provide creditor-placed homeowners insurance; manufactured housing homeowners insurance; debt protection administration; credit insurance; warranties and extended services contracts; individual health and small employer group health... see more

Current Employees (500+ total, 105 in your network)

The names, titles and contact information of the current employees would be listed here. (Not shown because of privacy considerations.)

Sidebar:

- Home
- Groups
  - ALTERNATIVE ENERGY NETWORK
  - Career Change Central
  - Career Rocketeer | Career Launch Network
  - See all »
- Profile
  - Edit My Profile
  - View My Profile
  - Recommendations
- Contacts
  - Connections
  - Imported Contacts
  - Profile Organizer
  - Network Statistics
- Inbox (13)
  - Compose

FINDING PEOPLE ON LINKEDIN

Now, let's leave the company page we were on in LinkedIn and explore how to use the site to find people.

To leave a company screen and redirect your search to people, click on the drop-down menu and select "Search People."

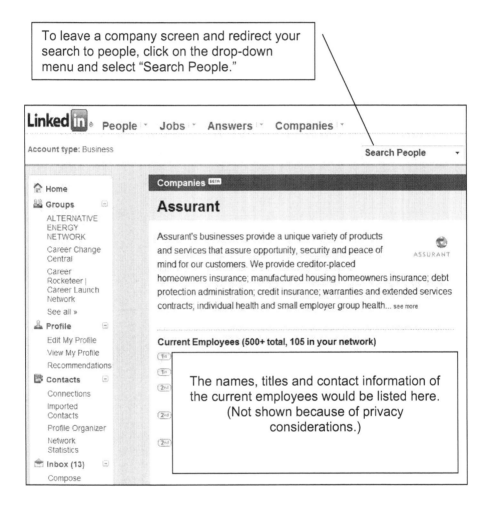

This is the next screen you will taken to in LinkedIn, where you can begin your search for people. Use Boolean search strings. (See table at the end of this section for tips on using Boolean Logic for keyword searching.)

First, do a Keyword search and then, as a separate search, use Titles and Companies. Do *not* use both together because you will restrict your search too tightly. When searching, you can search for current and past employees, just current, just past, within industries and groups—virtually any meaningful combination.

Use the "Advanced Search" option to get started finding people.

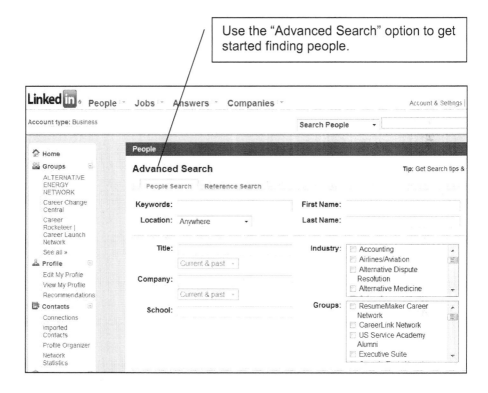

So, for example, (using Boolean) enter your list of possible titles and possible companies, e.g., Titles: (Director or VP or "vice president" or manager) AND (QA or Quality). If you want people who just currently have one of those titles, use the "drop down" and choose "current." Then enter your list of companies if you want to narrow your focus. Otherwise, click "search" and you will come up with people in your network in all companies with those titles.

BUILD AN ORGANIZATION CHART

By using the company search, advanced people search and by looking to see who recommended people, you can build an organizational chart of many companies. For example, many people will have bosses and colleagues recommend them so it enables you to begin to "connect the dots," i.e., "who reports to whom."

You now know the name of someone, and you know their company, CALL THEM. Google their company and ask for them. Use the techniques in Phase Three, **Selling**, on how to get past the gatekeeper.

THE LINKEDIN X-RAY SEARCH ON GOOGLE (WWW.LINKEDIN.COM)

The "site:" command "looks into," or *x-rays*, a website to find the *specific* information you are looking for. For example, if you want to research a company and find just the pages on that company's website that deal with a particular technology (water treatment, for example), you could go to Google and enter the following command: **Site:company.com "water treatment"** and all of the pages with that phrase on it from that company's website will be returned. (**Example**: site:kemira.com "water treatment")

You may want to try to find a sales director or sales manager within a company. X-ray the site as follows:

> **Site:company.com sales AND (manager or VP or director or "vice president")**

Using the same site command, you can find people on LinkedIn who may not be in your network:

> **site:www.linkedin.com intitle:linkedin KEYWORDS**
> **-intitle:profile -intitle:updated -intitle:blog -intitle:directory**
> **-intitle:jobs -intitle:groups -intitle:events -intitle:answers**

Where KEYWORDS is, put in titles, company names, locations, etc., that you are interested in including in the Boolean Logic. Do *not* use the AND operator.

The "-" phrases need to be in the search string in order to cull out non-relevant information that otherwise would be returned.

Example:

site:www.linkedin.com intitle:linkedin (director OR vp OR vice) (IT or "information technology") ("greater charlotte area" OR "charlotte, NC area") -intitle:profile -intitle:updated -intitle:blog -intitle:directory -intitle:jobs -intitle:groups -intitle:events -intitle:answers

This will return all the profiles of people with this title in the Charlotte, NC, area who have chosen not to make their profile private, even if they are not within your own "3 degrees of separation" network.

So, even if you do not yet have a large LinkedIn network, you can reach out to many people.

SUGGESTIONS ON HOW TO NETWORK WITH OTHER LINKEDIN PROFESSIONALS

People normally love to give their advice and opinions! If you found them on LinkedIn, most people are open to communicating with you.

If someone is a first-degree connection in your network, or in one of your groups, you can communicate directly with them. If they are a second- or third-degree connection, you can send them an InMail (for a cost), use the "Get Introduced" function, or use the **site:www.linkedin.com** search discussed earlier and the investigative techniques I will show you for finding their phone number and/or their email address.

You can say, either in an email or on the phone,

"Jim, I found you on LinkedIn and I see that . . ."

And then give them a tidbit . . .

"I see that you are at xyz company"

- OR -

"I see that you are a journalist . . ."

Then give a call to action . . .

"I was hoping that you might be able to give me some advice. Do you have a moment?"

Here is an example of how you might conduct this networking contact on the phone:

"Jim, my name is Skip Freeman. I found you on LinkedIn and I noticed that you have a degree in polymer science. Do you have a moment to speak?

"Thank you. As a thought leader within polymer science, I was hoping that you might be able to give me some advice. I am in a career transition and have a proven track record of developing and bringing new resins to market that have taken market share from the competition and increased profits. What advice do you have for someone like me in terms of getting the word out to companies regarding how I can help them develop new income streams from resins in this challenging economy?"

Then shut up and listen! They may know someone or be able to tell you something. If they say, "I really don't know," you can ask,

"As a polymer scientist, what would you recommend to someone like me?"

— OR —

"As a polymer scientist, what would you do if you were in my shoes?"

— OR —

"As a polymer scientist, I am sure you are well networked. With whom should I speak just to further network as we are doing now?"

At the end of the conversation thank them and ask,

"Is there anything I can do for you to return the favor of your time and expertise?"

Remember to keep networking conversations brief, ideally, under five minutes.

Also, notice that I do not use the phrase that so many of us frequently use when someone answers our telephone calls—"How are you today?" There is a very good reason for this. It tends to put people "on guard" rather than opening them up.

SOLICITING A CURRENT COMPANY EMPLOYEE TO REPRESENT YOU

Now, let's take a look at networking with someone from within a company who could possibly sponsor you regarding an open position. You have found the name of a person at MNO Company, Valerie, who might be able to fill this role. You call her up and guide the conversation along these lines:

(YOU)

"Valerie, this is Jim Smith and I found you on LinkedIn. I know your time is valuable and this will only take three minutes. Do you have three minutes, or should we schedule a time to speak?"

(VALERIE)

"I have three minutes but that's it. What is this about?"

(YOU)

"I noticed that your company has an opening for a mechanical engineer at its Chicago facility. Now, I know that, theoretically, since the position is posted, I either need to go to HR or apply online. However, I have one important question for you. Many large companies like yours have employee referral programs, where if someone is referred and hired the referring employee gets paid a couple of thousand dollars.

"Valerie, if I were to send you my résumé, and indeed you felt that I was 'MNO Company quality material' and a 'right fit' for this position, would you be willing to introduce me into the company? The value of your doing so ensures that I get reviewed by a real person and not a computer, and the value to you is that you might get the referral fee. Would you be open to me sending my information to you for review?"

If you are networking and the company *doesn't* have a position posted, you can approach it like this:

(YOU)

"Valerie, I am a mechanical engineer with extensive experience in reliability engineering. I have always been interested in MNO Company. Now, I know the typical approach is to 'go to HR.' However, before I do that, would you be so kind as to share with me some thoughts on maybe how I could get my information in front of the right person without having to go through HR to begin with?"

147

(VALERIE)

"No, I really don't know. Let me give you HR's phone number."

(YOU)

"Sure, I can take that down. By the way, may I ask how you came to be employed with MNO Company?" (And now, by getting them talking, they may acquiesce and take your résumé for review without sending you to HR.)

SALESPEOPLE ARE 'WALKING, TALKING' COMPANY SOURCES

As you're doing your networking, in an attempt to get a company "insider" to represent you, don't overlook the salespeople. Typically, salespeople are literally "walking talking" sources for a company. Let's say, for example, that you are a chemist specializing in protein research. Using LinkedIn, you find a company that sells laboratory supplies to companies that do protein research. Call the laboratory supply company and ask for the name of the sales representative for the geographic area you're interested in. Assume that salesperson's name is Robert and you call him:

(YOU)

"Robert, this is Skip Freeman. I understand you are the sales person for the Southeast, is that correct?"

(ROBERT)

"Yes it is. How may I help you?"

(YOU)

"Robert, I am a chemist with a background in protein synthesis, and I am in the career search mode right now. I was hoping that you, as a networked leader within the industry, would be able to share with me some names of laboratory managers you know that I could network with?"

(ROBERT)

"Well, I don't know anything about who is hiring and I don't want my customers getting phone calls from complete strangers."

(YOU)

"Robert, I understand completely what you are saying, which is why I can assure you that your name will never come up. I am sure, as a salesperson, you know the value of networking. All I need are some names of people I can network with. I am sure you know how hard it is to get names from the receptionist. Just a half dozen names and that will keep me busy for weeks."

(ROBERT)

"OK, but you won't use my name, will you?"

(YOU)

"No, that's a given. I won't use your name."

And at the end, thank Robert and say something along these lines,

"Robert, if one of these leads takes me into a new opportunity, I will do everything I can to make sure we get to do business together in the future. Thank you."

Will people hang up on you when you're doing your telephone networking? Of course! Will some people be rude to you? Yes, they will! Just remember, though, that is *their* problem, not yours. As we recruiters say, NEXT! and move on! What is the worst thing that can happen to you? They hang up on you. They're rude. What is the *best* that can happen to you? You win your dream job!

NETWORKING WITH *FORMER* COMPANY EMPLOYEES

Another very powerful networking technique is to find someone on LinkedIn who worked for a company in the past. Tell them you are networking, and that their former company is one of your target companies. Then, ask them how they liked working there in the past. Your conversation may go something like this:

(YOU)

"Jim, my name is Skip Freeman and I found you on LinkedIn. I am doing some research on MNO Company, and I believe you worked there in the past. Is that correct?"

(JIM)

"Yes, it is."

(YOU)

"Jim, I am in the process of a career search and MNO is one of my target companies. Could you please tell me a little bit about what it was like working there?"

Then, listen very carefully to how they respond. Is it with enthusiasm, or hesitation? Do they speak openly and confidently, or are they "picking and choosing" their words carefully (which suggests they are trying to not say something bad).

As is the case with all networking calls, don't take up more than five minutes of the person's time, but try to get the name of their former boss and any other people in the company who are hiring influencers. Ask if the company has a good reputation. What is the culture like? Ask if you can use their name if you speak to his old boss. (Now it is easier to reach the old boss.)

OTHER QUESTIONS TO USE IN YOUR TELEPHONE NETWORKING

There are, of course, many, many questions you could ask during your telephone networking. Here are some other great questions I use all the time as a recruiter. I am rewording them for your use:

"As a thought leader in the industry, I was hoping you could give me some advice on. . ."

"If you were in my shoes, what would you do if you were me?"

"Are there any publications I should subscribe to or organizations I should belong to?'

"Who else should I be talking to?"

Remember, when all is said and done, having an internal contact at a company (one that you have developed through networking) who will hand carry your résumé to a hiring manager is the best possible outcome!

GROUPS, DISCUSSIONS AND JOBS

Within each LinkedIn group that you join, there are several tabs at the top that you can use to send information, as well as to review relevant information.

Shown below is the screen from clicking the "Jobs" tab in the **Alternative Energy Network** group.

Use these tabs to join discussions, get the latest news about the group, etc.

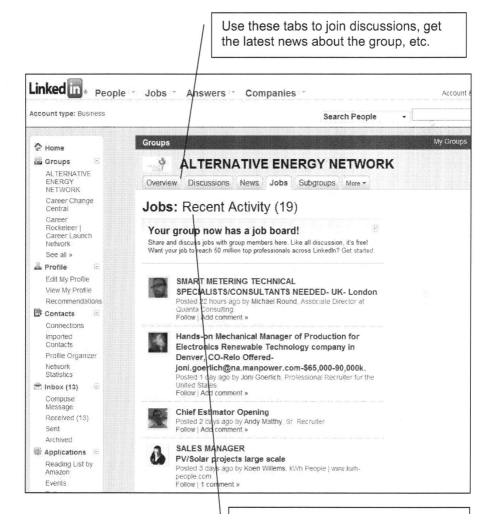

You'll also see recent job activity that has taken place within the group.

Need to ask a question? Can you *answer* someone else's question? LinkedIn features a special "question and answer" section where you can do just that. You can also send out information on your career search.

Post your question here. Then, by checking the box below, you can limit who sees it.

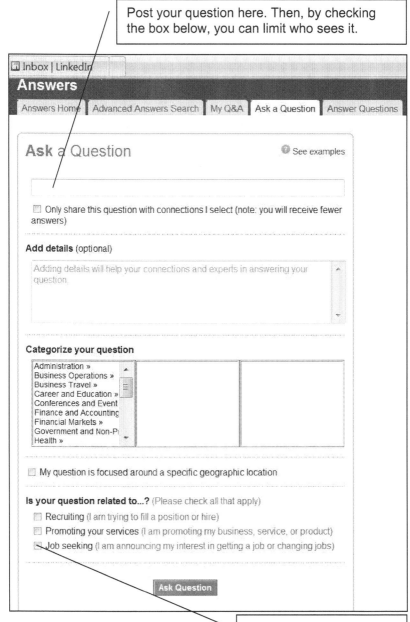

Check here if currently searching for a job.

152

OTHER WAYS TO FIND COMPANIES AND NAMES

As powerful as LinkedIn is, obviously, it is not Utopia. There are other tools that you need to incorporate into your Web research tool box. We have already discussed getting your information into ZoomInfo. Let's now study it as a research tool.

There are two tabs on the opening page: **Find People** and **Find Companies.** Let's choose the "Find Companies" tab and enter the keywords "drug delivery."

Since ZoomInfo indexes companies by their websites, the search will return companies that have the words "drug delivery" on one of their website pages.

Enter your search criteria in this box. In this case we are going to be searching companies that have the words "drug delivery" on any page(s) within their websites.

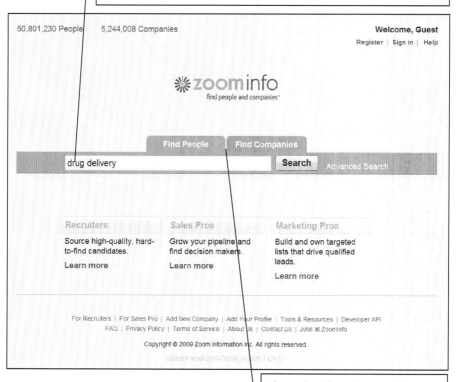

Search either for people or companies by choosing one of these tabs.

If your search didn't return exactly what you were looking for, you can further refine the search here.

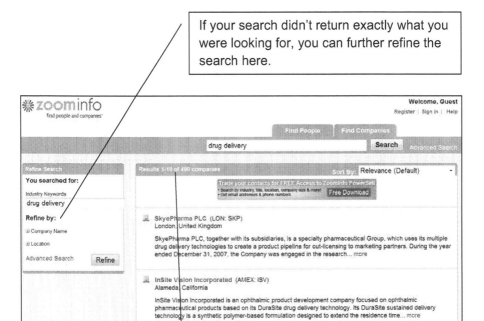

This search returned 490 companies that met the search criteria.

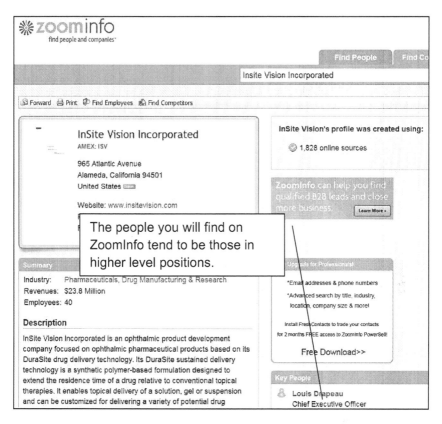

ZoomInfo will help you find additional companies and people, but often the people are in high-level positions. Many times, you will want to find lower level people whom you can contact or network with. If you aren't successful using a Boolean search in one of the search engines or in LinkedIn, you can try Jigsaw.

Jigsaw (www.jigsaw.com)

This excellent site consists of a database that is built from the "field." People enter information and obtain information. If you enter a contact, you can extract a contact. You can also purchase information. This is a great tool that we use in our recruiting firm for finding hiring managers below the executive level. Jigsaw currently has over 12 million contacts from 2 million companies.

Company Reach (www.companyreach.com)

This site is one of the best fee-based databases available. It is a Dunn & Bradstreet product and is excellent for finding office locations, plant sites, satellite offices, etc.

155

In Company Reach you can search companies by SIC code, NAICS code or keywords and target your search specifically by state or city or ZIP code. You can even specify that the company should have revenues above a certain amount or employees above a certain number.

For a fee, using Company Reach, you can build targeted mailing lists or call lists. As an example, we had a candidate that our search firm was marketing who had a mechanical engineering degree, had been a maintenance engineer within a chemical plant and was moving back to Houston. He met the majority of the MPC criteria, thus we agreed to represent him.

Using Company Reach, we identified 347 chemical, petrochemical and refining facilities within a 50-mile radius of Houston, each having 25 or more employees. Quite a nice prospecting list to start from, wouldn't you say?

Let's take another example. If you look up Clorox® on the Web and enter www.clorox.com, you discover that the site tells you all about Clorox® products. You have to root around a little bit to even find that the website with company information is actually www.thecloroxcompany.com. When you go to that site, you find that the individual locations are not revealed to you, only corporate information. If you look at their careers section, you discover that you have to apply online and it therefore goes through Human Resources. This is where the elimination game is at its peak—going through Human Resources at corporate headquarters!

If you research Clorox® on www.companyreach.com, you quickly find that there are 32 locations, along with names listed for each location. Thus, if you are an engineer, for example, you can contact a plant site directly. Still, in a major company like this one, you may end up having little choice but to deal with Human Resources. However, in medium to small companies, you can have great success going directly to the hiring managers.

Two Additional Sites – (www.manta.com and www.thomasnet.com.) These sites are extremely useful for identifying relevant companies for your career search. Manta is particularly useful for finding small companies.

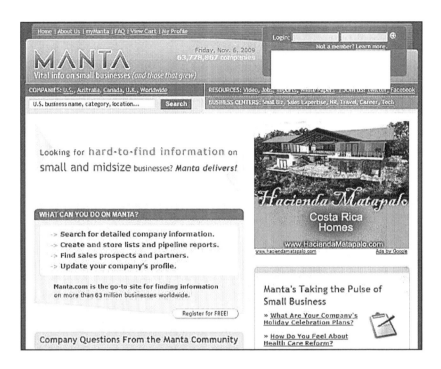

ASSOCIATIONS AND ORGANIZATIONS

Another extremely powerful networking tool is to join associations and organizations that are relevant to your skill set and interests. You may already know the ones that you need to join. An excellent link is www.weddles.com/associations, where you will find links for many of the professional organizations that could be relevant to you. Also, don't forget about your Alumni Association(s), as well as local community groups and various church groups that provide job seeker support. If looking for a job is your full-time job, don't sit at home behind the computer all day. Get out and interact with others.

THE GOOGLE 'RELATED' COMMAND

An additional, very powerful search engine technique is the Google "related" command.

Related:company.com

If you find the website of the "perfect" company, you can use the related command in Google to find companies that have the same keywords in their websites. For example, let's say that, through my research, I have discovered that www.bakerhughes.com is exactly the type of company I would love to work for. I can go to Google and enter this command:

Related:bakerhughes.com

Websites with the same keywords as Baker Hughes's site will be returned to me. This enables me to have a very focused search without the need for complex Boolean search strings.

Also, when doing Boolean searches, use more than one search engine. Each engine indexes differently, so the results will not be the same. Do the Boolean search on Google, Yahoo and Bing at least. That will cover 80-90% of the results.

GETTING IN TOUCH WITH PEOPLE

The resources we have reviewed thus far do not always provide the information needed in order to get in touch with people.

The top Internet sites, by the way, for finding information on how to get in touch with people are the following:

- www.zabasearch.com
- www.pipl.com
- www.whitepages.com
- http://people.yahoo.com
- www.switchboard.com
- www.argali.com

If you haven't found someone's contact information by the time you go through these six sites, it probably isn't to be found on the Internet. Sometimes you just have to "get on the phone" and become an "investigative reporter" and do some additional research and snooping around by calling into the company.

KEEP UP WITH THE NEWS

Keeping abreast of news on companies will also provide you with ideas for additional companies to call and people to reach out to. Once you have joined some organizations and have bookmarked some favorite Web pages, you can use www.watchthatpage.com to notify you if something changes on a page in a site you're monitoring regularly. This will help you better manage your time during your career search, rather than spending hour upon hour in front of your computer doing "research." Certainly, you have to do research, but obviously, there is considerably more involved in a job search.

By finding articles of interest regarding the companies you are targeting, you have a powerful opportunity to reach out to that company and hiring manager in a manner that can set you apart from the "generic" job seeker. Here are some websites that can assist you in that effort:

- www.bizjournals.com
- http://news.google.com
- http://biz.yahoo.com

Use these sites to sign up for "News Alerts" on companies you are targeting to optimize and leverage your time.

- http://www.google.com/alerts
- http://alerts.yahoo.com

If something happens in the company you are following, the information will be sent to you automatically. This gives you the powerful reason you need to contact the company or a powerful reason to follow-up.

Examples include a new contract the company was awarded, a new product, an award or recognition for the company or the hiring manager you are planning to contact.

You can use Boolean in the news sections for finding companies that are growing and expanding or companies that have just been awarded new business.

Examples: In Google News, use the following: **(grow or expands) AND (operations or facilities or plants)**

Or you could use: **(wins or awarded or receives) AND (contract or deal or business)**

Also, do an Internet search (search engines and LinkedIn) on the hiring manager you are going to reach out to. Anything you can find that is positive and unique on the company or the person will significantly set you apart from all others.

Simply using the correct search criteria in Google can return a tremendous amount of information and "news" about companies you may be targeting in your job search.

Google   Intel AND "new product development"   Search   Advanced Search

Web ⊞ Show options...   Results 1 - 10 of about

New Product Innovation
www.strategyn.com   Find hidden opportunities. Download our free white paper to learn more.

[PDF] Course Title: Managing the **New Product Development** Process: Design ...
File Format: PDF/Adobe Acrobat - Quick View
new product development is such a critical process to manage and what the key ... for
linking its strategy to its **new product development** process. ...
download.intel.com/education/.../New_Product_Development.pdf - Similar - ⊙ ✦ ⊠

Driving Innovation
Speeding **new product development** by up to 25 percent. Using **Intel** processors ...
download.intel.com/design/embedded/infotainment/docs/320591.pdf

Intelo Technology Journal
accelerating **new product development**. Historically, **Intel** ...
download.intel.com/technology/itj/2004/.../art06.../vol8iss1_art06.pdf

More results from download.intel.com »

Frost & Sullivan Names **Intel**® Health Guide Home Health Device ...
Intel Recognized for Innovation in Health Care and the Advancement of Better ... in **new**
product development and introductions within its industry. ...
www.**intel**.com/pressroom/archive/.../20090318corp.htm - Cached - Similar - ⊙ ✦ ⊠

Jobs at **Intel**, Careers, Sales and Marketing
In Sales and Marketing at **Intel**, there are excellent opportunities for both the ... **New product**
development; Evangelism to industry groups; Direct sales ...
www.**intel**.com/jobs/careers/Marketing/ - Cached - Similar - ⊙ ✦ ⊠

New product development: managing and forecasting for strategic ... - Google Books Result
by Robert J. Thomas - 1993 - Business & Economics - 352 pages
4 Preparing the Organization for **New Product Development** Facing turbulent and ... **Intel**
microprocessors were used in IBM PCs and in IBM-compatible PCs, ...
books.google.com/books?isbn=0471572268... - ⊙ ✦ ⊠

FACEBOOK AND MYSPACE – (DANGER!)

If you are a member of the younger generation, you probably already have a Facebook or MySpace page. Use these sites for what they are designed to do—be *social* networking sites. If you are in a job/career search, set  everything to be private. If you don't, then any photos of you being yourself could very well be the photos that eliminate you from consideration. If you are drunk in a photo, the future boss will have visions of you being hung over while visiting a client or not showing up for work. If you have just updated your status with, "I can't stand my job today," and your potential new boss reads that, what will she think? If you don't control yourself, others will control you.

Candidates have been eliminated due to racial slurs. One candidate was eliminated when she listed her sex as "yes, please." Then there was the picture of the woman with several others out surfing and the caption read, "We should call in sick more often."

 Though she didn't post the picture, her boss happened to see the photo posted on someone else's site. In social networking you may not even have control over what information is put out there.

This is not to diminish the value of these types of social media. Real friends are the best networking contacts available. Just be aware that, if you have anything unprofessional on these sites and you are looking for a job, it may surface.

One "app" that is very useful on Facebook is the Advanced Search app. You can download it and add it to your Facebook home page from http://apps.facebook.com/advancedsearch. Using this app, you can find people who work for a certain company (or used to), went to the same school as you, find people by location, as well as some other very useful search criteria. While not nearly as powerful as LinkedIn and the Google LinkedIn site search, this app will allow you to search Facebook beyond your own network to establish new contacts.

TWITTER

Create both a Twitter account and a TweetMyJobs.com account, but be sure to observe these considerations:

- Use your real name
- Write a *very brief* biography

- Over time, create a blog, as it shows your personality to a potential employer. Put a link to it in your biography, too. This will allow employers to see what interests you, *vis-à-vis* what you write about, and it will reveal a lot more than a résumé ever could. Do NOT, however, write about things you don't know anything about or say you can do things you can't. Once the truth comes out, you are eliminated.

- Be professional . . . otherwise you will be eliminated. Remember, the idea here is to keep from being eliminated.

- Make sure any "tweets" are professional . . . otherwise you will be eliminated.

The young lady shown here learned that the hard way and was quickly eliminated from further consideration for a very good job with Silicon Valley giant Cisco Systems, as the result of just *one* ill-timed, ill-advised "Tweet."

"Cisco just offered me a job!" she Tweeted. "Now I have to weigh the utility of a fatty paycheck against the daily commute to San Jose and hating the work."

Before the airwaves stopped vibrating with her Tweet, a manager at Cisco sent her one of his own: "Who is the hiring manager? I'll bet they would love to know how much you're going to hate working for us. Hey, we at Cisco do pay attention to what's on the Web."

Needless to say, the young lady no longer had to worry about working for Cisco, the "fatty" paycheck, or for that matter, the "commute." The job offer was immediately withdrawn.

DIRECT MAIL

In the previous sections we have studied how to properly apply to posted positions, find someone to sponsor you internally within a company, what a recruiter can and cannot do for you plus the powerful tools available for your networking activities. We also discussed how to properly reach out and effectively make networking contacts.

The next level of your search involves the so-called "hidden" job market, and a principal tool for cultivating this job market segment is going to involve direct mail. At any given time, depending upon the level of the position, as many as 50% to 80% of the jobs available are *not* advertised, i.e., they are "hidden."

DIRECT MAIL AND THE 'HIDDEN' JOB MARKET

Let's say that a Regional Sales Manager has ten sales professionals on her team. As a sales manager, one's income is, to a large extent, dependent upon the performance of the ten sales professionals. And the reality is, no matter what, the sales manager will automatically (even if it is only mentally) rank the ten people from Number One to Number Ten! And when someone better comes along, that sales manager will think seriously about "upgrading" the sales staff.

By the time a position is posted on a corporate website or any one of the job boards, it is too late to "beat the crowd." This position is now "approved" by Human Resources. The company has to look at internal candidates, they also look into their database, they receive hundreds of résumés from the postings they put out there, and this is when it becomes equivalent to high school football tryouts—it becomes a process of *elimination*, not inclusion.

But, if you can get on that hiring manager's radar while he or she is still thinking about "upgrading," and before it gets pushed out to Human Resources, you have a far better chance of competing against a much smaller pool of candidates.

Another scenario—a person has just resigned. The "boss" makes a few phone calls to trusted friends and colleagues asking, "Whom do you know?" They may just happen to know you. Or, say a person in a role isn't performing too well. The "boss" is thinking, "I have to do something about this, but I can't let them go just yet." A "secret" quest begins to quietly see who might be available.

In all of these cases, the competition will be significantly reduced, as compared to the "advertised" job market where hundreds will apply for positions. In the "hidden" market, hiring managers will still compare and contrast candidates and the rule of exclusion applies, but the field of competition will be much smaller, thereby increasing your odds for success.

How do you find opportunities in the 'hidden job market'? You must prospect! They will not just come to you. You must go out and *find* them!

Getting your résumé on the hiring manger's desk just at the moment when he/she decides to hire someone, and prior to the position becoming advertised, is clearly the ideal scenario. But how do you accomplish this feat if your networking efforts fail to produce that result? The next best approach is your direct mail campaign. By now, you have gathered that your résumé cover letter is *critically* important. Your words are what sell. Your words are what catch someone's attention. Your words are what draws them in. Your words are what keeps them reading.

But unlike applying for a posted, advertised position, **in a direct mail campaign, you do *not* send a résumé.** You only send a well-crafted cover letter that illustrates the value you can bring to a company and a hiring manager.

Do *not* become discouraged if you are not contacted by the company/hiring manager from your direct mail campaign, however. It is *your* responsibility to follow up the letter with a phone call. The goal is for the person to at least somewhat remember you when you call. Even if they don't remember you consciously, if you have written a powerful cover letter or letter of introduction, they may remember you subconsciously.

We discussed in the section on cover letters how to write a powerful letter with IMPACT! Here, we are going to overlay a few additional thoughts.

The first person to send a letter to is the potential hiring manager whose name you obtained from research or from your networking efforts. Do *not* send the letter to Human Resources. If you do that, you might as well wait on a position to be posted and just apply online.

Remember, hiring managers may be on the verge of letting someone go. Someone may have just resigned. They want to hire but can't yet. Thus, they put your letter in a special folder waiting for the hiring freeze to thaw a little and you will be the first one to be called. Top clients tell me all of the time, "Skip, keep me informed of top talent. We always want to be kept abreast of top professionals with whom we can connect at the right time."

Let's look at two examples of value proposition cover letters that could be used in a direct mail campaign.

First, let's say you have researched a company and learned from a news release that they were just awarded a contract for the construction of a new hydrogen generating facility at a refinery. You do names research using the techniques taught in the section on Placement and learn who the Vice President of Engineering is for the hydrogen business unit. Then, you construct and send a letter like the one shown on the next page.

**Companies DO read direct mail ('snail mail')
because it is so seldom received.**

> Let the hiring manager know right up front that you have been following developments in his company.

> Since this is a *formal* letter, notice that I use a colon, *not* a comma, in the salutation line.

May 1, 2009

Mr. Jim Smith
Vice President of Engineering
MNO Company
1234 Industrial Way
Houston, TX 77010

Dear Mr. Smith:

> These three bullet points represent the "value proposition" that is so integral to the success of this direct mail letter. It's the "What I can do for you" statement that the hiring manager will want to know *immediately*!

I recently read the news release regarding construction of the new hydrogen generating facility for MNO Refinery in Houston. Many congratulations on this new opportunity for you, your team and your company!

My experience as a chemical engineer revolves around developing processes that make cleaner burning fuels. My value to you could be:

➢ 8 years experience with system reformers
➢ Both process and project engineering
➢ Extensive trouble-shooting experience, Six Sigma Black Belt and process optimization

As an example, in 2008, a process optimization study, coupled with a small capital equipment upgrade, enabled us to decrease energy costs 2%, while increasing output 8% on a steam reforming unit, resulting in an additional $350,000 to the plant's bottom line.

Mr. Smith, I will call you on Friday, May 8, 2009, at 8:00 a.m. CT to arrange a mutually convenient time to exchange some ideas.

Sincerely,

Skip Freeman

Skip Freeman

> Considerable research has shown the power of using a "P.S." It gets read! Here, you are setting the stage for the critical follow-up phone call.

P.S. If the 8th isn't convenient for you, please have Jennifer call me at 678-123-4567, or email me at skip.freeman@hiretowin.com and suggest a time that is more convenient for you.

> Through your research you discovered that Jennifer is Mr. Smith's administrative assistant.

165

Here is another example of an attention-getting direct mail letter:

May 1, 2009

Mr. Tom Jones
Vice President of Engineering
XYZ Corporation
412 Industrial Parkway
Atlanta, GA 30045

> Inserting a "headline" at the beginning of this letter focuses immediate attention on the "value proposition" outlined in the body of the letter.

Why I can reduce your utility system's energy costs and ensure that your utility system doesn't keep you awake at night.

Dear Mr. Jones:

I have a proven track record of:

> Here's what you've done for your current company and what, by implication, you can also do for the hiring manager/company.

- Reducing utility system energy costs
- Effectively implementing preventive maintenance programs to avoid unexpected downtime

The utility system of a plant is its "heartbeat." As an experienced utility engineer, I understand the criticality of:

> This is what you "bring to the ballgame," i.e., a thorough understanding of and appreciation for how critical this factor is to a plant.

- ✓ Preventive maintenance
- ✓ No unexpected downtime
- ✓ Reduced energy costs
- ✓ Reduced emissions
- ✓ And no lost time due to health and safety issues

Over the past year, we have **reduced energy costs 12%** and **reduced effluent discharge by 15%** because of our focused water reuse/recycling program.

Mr. Jones, my mission is to ensure that you don't get a phone call at midnight because something went down due to utilities.

References are available upon request.

> This last sentence is setting the stage for the vital follow-up phone call.

Sincerely,

Skip Freeman

Skip Freeman

P.S. I will call you on Thursday, May 7th, 2009, at 8:00 a.m. ET to discuss how I can be of value to you at any of your facilities in the Midwest.

While both of the direct mail letters shown on the preceding pages are engineering examples, the same concept applies whether you're an accountant, computer programmer, architect, customer service manager. . . .

PHONE CALLS

There are really three types of phone calls you'll use during your job search.

- The networking phone call (a "warm call").
- The phone call as a follow-up to direct mail (a "warm call").
- The prospecting "cold call" phone call.

(Earlier in this section we addressed the networking phone call and we will cover the prospecting "cold call" phone contact in the **Selling** phase.)

Here, we want to examine the powerful techniques for using the telephone to follow up your direct mail campaign.

The only way for this to work is that you must absolutely, positively call the people to whom you sent a direct mail letter. If you do not follow up with a phone call, the direct mail campaign is not effective. In the letter you set the stage for the follow-up call and you must call exactly when you said you would call. If you fail to do that, you will lose any and all chance you might otherwise have had at a career opportunity with that company.

Failure to make the follow-up phone call on the date and time you indicated in your direct mail letter will effectively eliminate you from any opportunity you might otherwise have had with the hiring manager or company.

Let's examine how you might handle the follow-up call to the **first** direct mail letter, the one regarding the hydrogen generating facility.

(You)

"Mr. Smith, this is Skip Freeman calling you this morning at 8 AM CT, as I indicated I would in the letter that I sent to you. Is now a good time to speak for a moment or should we compare calendars and schedule a time?"

(Mr. Smith)

"Now is good, but what is this about?"

167

(You)

"Mr. Smith, I am a chemical engineer with eight years of experience in hydrogen steam reformers. I have a proven track record in process optimization leading to reduced energy usage and increased throughput. I read with interest about the new contract for the hydrogen plant being built at the refinery. Congratulations! I bet that is an excellent opportunity for you and MNO company."

(Mr. Smith)

"Yes, it is."

(Now, Mr. Smith may continue and start talking or he may say "yes, it is" and nothing more.)

(You)

"The purpose of my call, Mr. Smith, is to ask your advice. As a thought leader in the area of steam reformation and hydrogen generation, what advice would you give someone like me, someone with a proven track record in hydrogen steam reformer process optimization, who is looking for the next step in their career?"

(Note, you are not asking for a job! You are merely asking for *advice,* just as in networking. Hopefully, Mr. Smith will give you some useful advice or refer you to someone else to contact. If so, get that information and follow up with this question, if appropriate. If the advice is non-existent or vague, also follow up with this question.)

"How best can I keep my information and name in front of you so that when you do have a critical hiring need, you have my information available? What would you suggest?"

And then *get his email address* "in order to maintain an open network with you."

What if Mr. Smith doesn't answer the phone? Call his administrative assistant and tell him/her that Mr. Smith was expecting your call today at 8 a.m. and find out when you can reschedule the call.

What if you can't get the administrative assistant? Call Mr. Smith back and leave a voice mail message along these lines:

> "Mr. Smith, this is Skip Freeman calling you today at 8 a.m. CT, as I stated I would in the letter I sent to you. I have a proven track record of process engineering in hydrogen steam reformation. I will call you back on Monday, May 11th at 8:30 a.m. My number is 678-123-4567."

Provide him your phone number as in the example, but do *not* ask him to call you back. He simply will not do it. You call him back. You are the one who must take the initiative. It can sometimes take calling seven or eight times before you are able to speak with a person. So, if he doesn't answer on Monday, May 11th, hit "0" and exit the call. Do **NOT** leave another voice mail at this time. Try to reach his administrative assistant and then keep dialing both Mr. Smith *and* the administrative assistant back until you get one of them. Do NOT leave any more voice mail messages for three days. If you do, you will fatigue them. In fact, that is precisely the term used for receiving too many voice mails from the same person—"voice mail fatigue."

Never, never start out your follow-up phone call to your direct mail letter by saying, 'Mr. Smith, this is Skip Freeman. I sent you a letter. Did you receive it?'

Now, let's examine how a follow-up call might go for the **second** direct mail letter example, the utility engineer.

You would, of course, begin this call in much the same way as you did for the first direct mail letter example:

> "Mr. Jones, this is Skip Freeman. I am calling today, May 7th, as I indicated I would in the letter I sent to you. I have a proven track record of reducing energy costs within utility systems. Is now a convenient time to speak or should we compare calendars and set up an appointment time?"

Unlike in the previous example (where he proved to be a "push over"), however, Mr. Jones could give a wide variety of answers to your lead-in question ("Is now a convenient time to speak. . . ?") He could, for example, say . . .

- Now is *not* a good time to speak and you need to set up a better time.
- "No, I don't recall a letter. What is this about?"
- "I got your letter but you have to speak to Human Resources."
- "Yes, I was impressed by your letter but we aren't hiring right now."

How would you deal with responses like these? My advice? Dive in!

Mentally, never put yourself in the same league as 'telemarketers' when calling prospects. Remember, BTB ('Business to Business') phone calls are not only legitimate, they are expected!

But, you are probably saying, What if someone is rude to me? What if they hang up on me? So what? It is their loss, not yours. They are the ones who will be missing out on the value that you can bring to them!

So what if you "intrude" on their day? Two comments here: First, they shouldn't have picked up the phone. They should have let it go into voice mail. Second, you can prevent your call appearing as an "intrusion" by asking, "Is this a good time to speak?" If it isn't, they will say so! If it is, they will say that, too.

But let's assume that the response you actually receive from the hiring manager when you call is this:

"This is fine. What is this about?"

Then, you simply proceed with your "script," which is an excerpt from the direct mail letter you sent the hiring manager.

"Mr. Jones, as a utility engineer, I know that the 'heartbeat' of a plant is the utility system. I have a proven track record of reducing energy costs, reducing emissions and, through effective preventative maintenance programs, reducing unexpected downtime and those pesky phone calls in the middle of the night that can happen when something breaks.

"I simply wanted to call and introduce myself so that when you have a critical hiring need in the utility area in any of your plants, you will know that you have someone available who can do the job. What are your thoughts, Mr. Jones?"

Notice that you are asking a question to get Mr. Jones talking. You aren't coming out directly asking for a job.

How would you deal with the response of . . .

"I was impressed with your letter, but we aren't hiring right now."

170

(You)

"Mr. Jones, I wasn't calling with the expectation that you were hiring. What I was hoping is that you could tell me how best I can keep my information and name in front of you, so that when you *do* have a critical hiring need, you have my information available. What would you suggest?"

If he offers something vague, then suggest . . .

"May I send you an email on a monthly basis, in order to maintain an open network with you?"

(Get his email address, then proceed to your second question.)

"Mr. Jones, my last question: Whom do you know that I could network with, or what would you suggest that someone in my position do?"

Thank him and hang up. Now that you have his email address, send him a follow-up "Thank You" note. Finally, using your notebook and Outlook® calendar, keep tabs of to whom you need to send an email on a monthly basis.

Let's briefly look at how you might handle the *"You need to call HR"* response. First, don't fight it, roll with it, and respond like this:

"Mr. Jones, no problem. I can call HR and I would like to get the HR point of contact from you. May I ask you a question? (pause) "When one of your facilities has a need for a utility engineer, are you involved in the decision making process?" (Yes, I am, he says) Then, you say, "In order to help you the next time you have a critical hiring need, how best can I keep my information and name in front of you so that you will have my information readily available? What would you suggest?"

If he says that he isn't involved in the process, thank him and ask for the Human Resources contact. Do *not* contact Human Resources, though. Work on finding another person in the company, one who would be involved in utilities.

The purpose of the phrase in your script, "...so that you will have my information available" is to try to get him to commit that he will keep your information handy. This, of course, will *only* work if you have created a value proposition. Otherwise, there is no compelling reason for anyone to keep your information—or do anything else for you, for that matter.

CAREER FAIRS/JOB FAIRS

In today's job market, attending a career fair/ job fair is a lot like mass emailing your résumé to every opening you can find. You may get lucky and stumble onto something, but I wouldn't count too heavily upon that occurrence, if I were you. Still, should you go to these events? I would answer that with a qualified "yes," but keep things in proper perspective, too.

The odds of your finding your next career at a job fair are extremely low in a down economy. Of course, your odds greatly improve in a rising economy. In Atlanta, a job fair was recently hosted at a downtown hotel. Over 150 employers were present for about 500 different openings. Over 9,000 people showed up! The line was over three hours long—just to get inside the building! Job seekers would wait another one to two hours in line leading up to the employer's table. Most people got to make their "90-second pitch" to, maybe, five or six employers, maximum.

After giving their "90-second pitch," they would hand their résumé (and, perhaps, a networking business card) and move on. A depressing exercise no matter how one looks at it.

So why should you go? If you have been stuck behind the computer you need to get out. Personally, I would recommend association meetings, civic clubs, alumni groups, etc. But career fairs at least get you out among people and put you in a position to meet others. You dress up. You get the chance to perfect your "90-second elevator speech."

And, of course, you could always get lucky! (With a heavy emphasis on "lucky.")

Also, remember that a job fair is normally for entry level to mid-level positions. You will probably never see a job fair catering to someone above junior management.

And only go to a career fair IF there are companies and positions being advertised in your niche. If you are a civil engineer attending an IT job fair, you will be wasting your time. No, they won't think, "This is a great engineer. We have to get his information in front of our engineering department." They will eliminate you on the spot, as we have discussed time and time again.

So, once you know that the career fair is within your niche and within your level of expertise, rehearse. Have your "90-second elevator speech" down pat.

Have at least 30 high-quality résumés and your networking business cards with you. Dress professionally. Show up early and be near the front of the line. That is the only way to have even a shot at more employers. Plus, they love to see the early arrivals. By the end of the day, the recruiters at the job fair are themselves exhausted and you have to be that much more on top of your game to impress them.

Get the business card of every person you meet with (potential employers, that is). Other business cards might be nice, but those folks probably aren't going to help you too much.

Follow up the next day with a "Thank You" to every employer you visited with at the fair. A typed business letter via snail mail sent the same day (or next day at the latest) is the best here. Overnight is a waste of money. Once you have sent the snail mail, an email follow-up is appropriate also. Don't make the two identical, however. Thank them for their time, restate your value, and strongly express your interest once again. Honestly, that is about all you can do.

SOME ADVANCED TOOLS TO CONSIDER FOR PROPER PLACEMENT

After you have started implementing elements of ALL of the previous "channels to market," then you can circle back and create a website using, for example, www.weebly.com.

You might also consider creating a blog on your website (or on one of the other networking sites previously mentioned in this section). If you do decide to create your own blog, be sure it is about areas within your own expertise. A good place to review how to start a blog is www.problogger.net/blog. Before ever launching a blog, or even considering launching one, though, make absolutely sure that all of the other elements in your marketing plan that we have studied are firmly in place!

Tips on Boolean Keyword Searches

Boolean Operators	Examples	What it Does/Returns
AND	Insurance AND Sales	Web pages containing both words, although not in any particular order.
OR	IT OR "Information Technology"	Will find Web pages containing "IT" OR "Information Technology," but not necessarily both.
No Boolean operator used	Insurance Sales	Automatically adds "AND" between the two words. Both words must appear in the Web page, but in no particular order.
Quotation Marks " "	"Pharmaceutical Sales Representative"	ALL of the words must be in the exact order given before a search result is returned.
Wild Card *	Program*	Searches for spelling variations within the same or related terms. Example: Program* will return program, programming, programmers, etc.
NOT	"Insurance Sales" NOT Life NOT Medical	Web pages containing "Insurance Sales" but NOT the words "Life" or "Medical."
Parentheses ( )	(Web OR Internet) AND (Programmer OR Developer) AND (Tampa OR Miami)	Parentheses are used to separate phrases using the OR operator from the words or phrases using the AND operator. It ensures the computer knows how to find the information.
Using ALL of the Above	("Mechanical Engineer*" OR "Automotive Engineer*") AND "Plant Manager" AND (Ford OR Chrysler) NOT Honda	Mixture of quotes, AND, OR, parentheses, NOT and the wildcard.

PHASE THREE
SELLING YOURSELF

In the **Marketing** phase you learned the critical factors in getting your "product"—YOU!—ready to go to market. You now understand your pricing (value to the marketplace), you developed your promotional literature and you are now placing yourself in front of your target audience.

This next phase, **Selling Yourself**, is about understanding your "prospects'" needs and positioning yourself as the solution of choice.

The majority of people are not salespeople and the majority of jobs are not sales positions. But, one of the main secrets, one of the rules of the game, is that you approach everything in your job hunt as if it were a sales call! This section teaches you how to accomplish that.

In this phase, we cover three methods for accomplishing your "sales" task:

- Telephone marketing
- The telephone interview
- The face-to-face interview

In order to ensure that you are among the TOP candidates to be considered for a job today, it is imperative that you master these three approaches.

> "Marketing is about 'filling up the funnel'; selling is about 'executing' at the narrow end."

175

YOUR JOB HUNT MUST BE APPROACHED LIKE A 'SALES CALL'

One of the universal truths about job hunting, but also one that is almost universally not understood, is that job hunting is a sales campaign. "But I am not a salesperson!" you say. "Oh, yes, you are!" is my response, and that's precisely how you *must* treat job hunting!

Whether you are an accountant, a chemist, an engineer, a project manager, a computer programmer, or an assembly line worker, if you have ever presented a solution to someone, you were, in fact, acting in the capacity of a salesperson. Sales is nothing more, or less, than providing a solution to a need or problem. And, that is exactly what you are doing in a job search— uncovering the prospects' needs, i.e., what they need done to make 'em money or to save 'em money, and positioning yourself as being THE solution of choice.

If you understand that sales is the process of identifying needs and presenting solutions, then you will be able to approach your job search as a sales campaign and, armed with the secrets presented in this section, you will dramatically increase your probability of success.

If you are already in some type of sales position, don't stop reading because you think you "know what to do." Let me provide an example: I have asked many professional salespeople to give me their definition of sales, and even among "sales professionals," some of the definitions given are the following (and none are correct, by the way):

- Being able to talk people into anything.
- Getting people to buy something they don't need.
- The proverbial "selling ice to Eskimos."
- Someone who is a "fast talker."
- Talking to people you don't know and trying to take their money.

Because so many people do not understand what sales really is (even salespeople), they don't take a "sales" approach to their career search.

Now, here are some responses that are more in line with what sales really is:

- Helping to solve a problem.
- Providing someone with a solution.
- Looking for prospective buyers who have the need, want or desire for your product or service and helping them make a decision.
- Exchanging goods or services.

Succinctly put, sales is **"finding a need and filling it,"** and if you likewise embrace that idea, **you will see that you** *are* **a salesperson, have always been a salesperson and** *must* **continue to** *view* **yourself in your career search as a salesperson.**

The concept we have actually been developing from the beginning of this book is that, in every single step in the job hunting process, you need to put yourself in the mind, heart, soul and shoes of the hiring manager or recipient of your communications. Figuring out what will make it easy for the hiring manager (or reader of your communications) to know, without question or doubt, that what you are trying to accomplish is of definite benefit to them and their company is what will keep them from excluding you.

Remember the radio station "call letters" mentioned earlier? You know, WIIFM, that station *everybody* listens to regularly (including you!)? "What's In It For Me?" Every communication, both written and verbal (résumé, cover letter, reference letters, email, telephone interview, face-to-face interview, etc.), initiated during your job search, must be approached with the realization that the hiring manager is listening to WIIFM radio! Turn *your* "radio station" off! Let theirs play, and then you deliver the message to them as to why you are their solution. The moment it becomes about you, instead of them, you get excluded!

I want to share with you an example of a cover letter I recently received from a candidate while writing this very section of *"Headhunter" Hiring Secrets*. He was responding to one of our postings and this is the approach he took:

Dear Hiring Manager:

Currently, I am looking for a mechanical engineering or related role. I feel my sales background will benefit me when facing customers and working with individuals on all levels.

I am looking forward to moving back into an inside sales role, so that I can gain a more challenging career.

As I said in the previous section on résumé cover letters, this type of cover letter is very, very typical of the ones I (and scores of hiring managers!) receive virtually every business day.

What's wrong with this candidate's approach?

- First, if the person would have spent just a moment researching our firm (our website address is on this posting), he would have known that we are a recruiting firm and that I am therefore *not* a "hiring manager."

- Second, notice how the entire focus of the letter is on the candidate himself! Notice how many times this candidate refers to himself ("I"). *Everything* in the cover letter is about him!

- There is not one single thing mentioned about what he can do for a prospective hiring company! And, I would overlook the fact that he addresses the cover letter incorrectly if he proved his value—but he doesn't.

It's obvious that this candidate is listening to his *own* WIIFM station, certainly not to the recruiter's or hiring manager's station. Don't you make this same mistake!

You must make sure you're always 'broadcasting' on the *hiring manager's* WIIFM 'radio station,' not on your own!

SELLING IS NOT TELLING—IT'S ASKING!

Many people, and even many salespeople, think that "fast-talking" is the way to be successful in sales. Actually, nothing could be further from the truth. Rarely are the "fast-talkers" the leading salespeople for any product or service. Salespeople who ask intelligent, probing questions designed to get the "prospect" to tell them, in his or her own words, what they want, need or desire, are among the most successful people in sales.

And, somewhat surprisingly, when successful salespeople *do* talk about the product or service they are selling, they keep their sales "pitch" low-key and succinct, periodically reinforcing in the "prospect's" mind what the product or service can *do* for them, and how they can *benefit* the prospect and the company he or she represents. In other words, they are "broadcasting" the message through the *prospect's* WIIFM radio station, not their own.

> **In the simplest terms, then, Selling is NOT Telling—It is ASKING!**

Committing this basic principle to memory, and then exercising it faithfully during your entire job search, will pay substantial dividends and likely put you among the top candidates vying for the same positions.

But obviously, before you can *sell* an authentic product or service to anyone, you must first prospect in your target market, make your presentation, and finally, close the deal. Until this process, which involves . . .

Prospecting → Presenting → Closing

is initiated and completed, nothing is going to happen. Certainly, no one is going to make any money.

Prospecting is the research we discussed earlier in the **Placement** section of the **Developing Your Marketing Plan** Phase. Find the companies and hiring managers in your niche. Find the open positions. Find the associations and networking contacts.

Now you must *present* the product, which is you.

Until you PRESENT the PRODUCT to a real PROSPECT, nothing, and I mean *nothing*, will move the sale forward, i.e., move you closer to finding your next career opportunity.

Prospecting and presenting are 65% of the sales process.

That means, of course, that the same is true for the **job hunting process**, since it is, essentially, a *sales* process—65% of the process consists of **prospecting** and **presenting**!

Let's get back to a truism. Companies are in the business of making money. Very few companies are charities. If you can't make 'em money or save 'em money, you will be let go. If you can't make 'em money or save 'em money, you will not be hired. FACT. Period. End of story.

I don't care how badly YOU need a job, if you can't present your value to a hiring manager who can make a hiring decision, you won't get the job.

The best way to understand how you can present value to the hiring manager is to show how you can *benefit* the prospect, followed by asking well-thought-out questions. This will be illustrated in the pages ahead, as we discuss:

- Telephone marketing
- The telephone interview
- The face-to-face interview

Sales & Job Hunting are Both 'Numbers' and 'Skills' Games

THE STORY OF THE STREET VENDOR

I heard an interesting story about a street vendor in New York City that captured, at least for me, the very heart and soul of the importance of good **prospecting** and **presenting** skills. This man, a very normal-looking man, dressed in casual, clean clothes, stands on a busy street corner each and every business day of the year selling "business card holders"!

Millions of businesspeople pass by this corner every work day, so these are obviously a properly identified "target market," i.e. his prospects.

The man's "presentation" could hardly be referred to as "sophisticated." As a matter of fact, it's downright mundane and (you should pardon the pun) "pedestrian." But it works!

"Wanna buy? Wanna buy? Wanna buy?" is his "sales pitch." Simple, yet quite effective. It turns out that many of the passersby, businesspeople all, do indeed "wanna buy" and do!

The street vendor had very basic presentation skills. His 'sales pitch' was 'Wanna buy? Wanna buy?' But he was successful because he kept at it day after day, week after week, and aimed his efforts at the right prospect population.

From time to time, the man stops and takes a sip of water from the bottle he always carries with him, to keep his voice in good timbre, his throat from becoming dry.

At the end of each day, a Rolls Royce limousine pulls up to the curb next to the man, he hops in it and off he goes to his multi-million dollar home in the suburbs!

The point is this: If you *present* your value to enough *prospects* (among the right target market), you will eventually overcome every hurdle, every objection and every problem—including even a bad economy!

But to dramatically improve your odds, you also have to improve your presentation skills.

181

Back to the man selling business card holders for just a moment.

Despite his best efforts with the water bottle, his voice sometimes does give out and he is forced to stand, mute, on the street corner by his display of business card holders. Unfortunately, when this occurs, his sales literally plummet. Businesspeople pass him by without giving him a second look, and certainly without acknowledging his presence. (After all, this is New York City!)

Why is this? Simple. He is still located among his target market—businesspeople on their way to work—but he is no longer *presenting*, so his "prospects" no longer pay any attention to him whatsoever! Their minds are perhaps too filled with upcoming activities of the day, concerns and anxieties they themselves have, you name it. Unless the street vendor can interrupt such thoughts and concerns with his "Wanna Buy?" presentation, they will remain in their respective "shells."

This is exactly analogous to sitting at your computer hour after hour and doing the following:

- Sending out résumé after résumé, none of which is "targeted."
- Not properly following up.
- Not picking up the telephone and making a phone call.

It's simply a fact of life in the business world, or in most parts of our world, for that matter: "The squeaky wheel gets the grease"! It's certainly like that in the recruiting world. As professional recruiters, if we don't reach out to prospective client companies *proactively*, only in the rarest of circumstances do the companies contact us. If we had not *proactively* reached out to prospects, in sufficient numbers, and used our very best presentation skills, our company, The HTW Group, would not have become one of the Top 200 offices (out of 800) in the MRI Network of recruiting firms.

You've undoubtedly heard this many, many times before: Successfully attaining any goal is, more often than not, both a *numbers* and *skills* game. Do the right things often enough, exercise the *right* skills and talents, and you will ultimately be successful. Certainly it's true when it comes to a job search.

Recall the résumé cover letter mentioned earlier, the one in which it was obvious that the candidate was listening to his *own* WIIFM station, not to the recruiter's or hiring manager's "station." Note that the writer of that cover letter made no effort to "target" his communication, nor was there any evidence that he was qualified for any particular job!

Imagine the kinds of numbers this candidate would have to generate to even come close to getting an *interview*, let alone a job, with this kind of approach! The numbers, of course, are astronomical!

By applying the right skills, such as crafting a résumé and cover letter that align with specific job requirements, and positioning yourself in terms of the value you can bring to a company, the numbers required to be successful go down dramatically.

So, what exactly are the numbers? Let's examine them.

SO WHAT *ARE* 'THE NUMBERS'?

The most important thing for you to understand in this section is just how very, very *critical* "the numbers" are to a *successful* job search in *any* job market. Understanding, and then applying, the *realistic* numbers involved in a job search will help you in three key ways:

- You won't get discouraged.
- You can keep yourself focused.
- You won't let your emotions rule your actions.

There are TWO key numbers that you need to know, measure and work toward each and every day:

- Connects
- First time face-to-face interviews

Effort (Connects) → Activity (Face-to-Face Interviews) → Results (Job Offer)

It's important to also keep in mind that the *only* activity that ultimately leads to an offer is the **face-to-face interview**. Unless you get these interviews, there can be no job offers.

WHAT IS A CONNECT?

A "connect," or more accurately, a "targeted connect," is defined as one of the following: applying to a position for which you are qualified; calling a company that is in your area of focus or interest; discussing your background with a recruiter who serves your industry niche; networking with people in the right industries at the right levels; and, properly targeting emails and direct mail letters and appropriate follow-up communications. In order to be successful in your job search, you need to make . . .

50 Targeted Connects per Day
(on days that you do not have face-to-face interviews)

Indiscriminately "blasting" your résumé to 3,000 recruiters does *not* count as a "connect," by the way. Randomly applying to as many jobs online as possible doesn't count, either. Going to a networking event and meeting 75 people who in no way can be helpful to you (or vice versa) doesn't count.

I point this out because people in a career search all too often *think* they are doing a lot of productive work toward finding a new job, when, in reality, they aren't doing anything at all of value, anything that will truly move their career along. Let me give you an example of what I'm talking about here.

I had a conversation recently with a friend who commented that his wife had been out of work for six months and both of them were getting desperate. They needed both of their incomes to make ends meet. I asked him to describe her job search methodology to me. He said, "Every morning and every evening, she goes online and responds to every new job that has been posted in the Charlotte, NC, area."

As I dug deeper, I learned that she applies for *every* position—whether she is qualified or not! She sends out the *same* résumé to *every* position. That's it. That's the extent of her "job search" activities. She is not contacting companies directly, either through direct mail or by telephone prospecting. She is not networking nor is she using the assistance of a recruiter. In other words, she does not have a focused plan. And she doesn't understand why she is having such a hard time finding a new job!

If you will diligently make 50 targeted connects per day, you will find that you will make significantly more progress than if you simply "stumble" along day after day with a *non-targeted* approach such as that being used by my friend's wife. (**NOTE:** When measuring connects, we actually count a phone conversation *or* a face-to-face meeting as **three** connects. Voice mail, email, direct mail letters, responding to a position on-line count as one each.)

THE FIRST TIME FACE-TO-FACE INTERVIEW

A **first time face-to-face interview** is defined as the "first time" you meet with a prospective employer company, regardless of how many people you actually meet at the company. Since different companies have different processes, we measure only the "first time" interviews. Some companies can make a hiring decision after just one interview, but most require two such interviews. In today's market we have seen some companies actually have a person come in *five* times before making a decision!

So, in order to standardize the measure, we (and you) should count just **first time face-to-face interviews**. (We will use the symbol **1FTF** to represent the first time face-to-face interview.)

From thousands of interviews throughout the recruiting industry, a generally accepted metric is that it takes **six (6) 1FTF** to make a placement, i.e., to get a candidate hired. Yes, it can take fewer, but by knowing the *average* across the nation, you won't lose focus or become discouraged if you don't get an offer after your first interview with the first company. Plus, it gives you a gauge for knowing how much more work you need to do, which will also help you stay focused.

6 1FTF ~ 1 Offer

As an example, right now, the 52-week average for our recruiting firm is five (5) 1FTF = 1 Placement. We have to send five people to interviews (or the same person to five different first-time interviews) in order to get a placement.

The "6 1FTF ~ 1 Offer" is a little known number outside of the recruiting industry and is extremely important for you to know as a job seeker. By knowing this number you can manage your job search. Not knowing it means you are guessing, wondering if you are making progress or not, and you can become emotional instead of remaining focused and logical.

But remember, it is an average. Our firm recently represented a candidate who received an offer from a company after just *one* 1FTF! That's a 1:1 ratio of 1FTF to Offer and, of course, is certainly an unusual occurrence.

Another job seeker with whom we were talking had been on 35 1FTF and received four offers, basically, a 9:1 ratio. This candidate had choices, as well as the luxury of taking the position she most desired.

I read an article in the newspaper recently with this headline: "After a year and a half, HIRED!" The article pointed out that the person had interviewed with five different companies and had *finally* been made an offer. This person, of course, had a 5:1 "1FTF to Offer" ratio, about the average.

The article went on to say that this person had sent out 200 résumés. That right there made it very clear to me why it took this person so long to be made an offer! Their "1FTF to Offer" ratio was right in line with the average, but the weak link was their number of *targeted* "connects." If you want to speed up the process, you have to have enough daily effort to make the 1FTF happen in a timely manner.

By knowing the 6 1FTF~1 Offer ratio, you won't get discouraged. If you have your first interview and never hear back, you still have five more to go! OR, if you're on your ninth 1FTF, anticipate something good happening soon!

Of course, the "**6 1FTF ~ 1 Offer**" ratio assumes you are doing the right things right. That is, you have properly identified your target market, you prospect well, you interview well and you follow up properly. Otherwise, the ratio will not hold true for you. If anything, it will end up being much higher.

HOW DO YOU GET THE 6 1FTFs?

So how, exactly, do you go about getting the **6 1FTFs**? You do it through your daily activities.

Let's review the channels to market (i.e., **placement**, mentioned in the section on Marketing):

- Properly applying to positions online
- Recruiters
- Networking
- Direct mail
- Phone calls
- Career Fairs

And within each of these activities, of course, are such follow-up activities as sending a "Thank You" note/letter after an interview, making that second call to try to get a hiring manager's attention, sending an article of interest to someone as a follow-up methodology, etc.

DEVELOPING A 'DAILY PLAN'

You may have heard the saying about "Planning your work and working your plan." Certainly this approach is necessary if you want to become successful in your job search. You must make a plan and then *work* that plan, faithfully and diligently, day-in and day-out, until you are offered, and then accept, a position that is exciting to you.

Here is the sequence of questions you should ask yourself each and everyday until you have a new position. These questions enable you to assess where you are in your job search process and help you determine what you need to do to move the process forward. Also, by measuring your daily connects, you will be able to determine what areas need additional effort and focus.

186

Ask yourself these questions, *in this order*, each and every day:

Do I have an offer on the table that I can consider?
What 2nd, 3rd or final interviews do I need to follow up on?
What 2nd, 3rd or final interviews do I need to prepare for?
What 1FTF do I need to follow up on?
What 1FTF do I need to prepare for?
What telephone interviews do I need to follow up on?
What telephone interviews do I need to prepare for?
What prospecting voice mails, emails and direct mail letters do I need to follow up on?
What NEW voice mails, emails and direct mail campaign pieces do I need to send out?
What networking contacts do I need to follow up with?
What NEW networking contacts do I need to make?
What recruiters do I need to follow up with?
What NEW recruiters do I need to develop relationships with?
What positions have I applied to online that I need to follow up with?
What NEW positions are online that I need to apply for?
How many connects did I make today in each area, and what is my total?

After reviewing the answers to these questions, you can then develop a solid plan for the next day. On days that you do not have face-to-face interviews scheduled, remember, your mission is to get **50 targeted connects**.

So, let's assess a theoretical job seeker's efforts at the end of the day and see how many actual "connects" this person made on this particular day:

- Applied to nine positions online from Indeed, SimplyHired, Hound and a niche site (9 connects).
- Sent eight direct mail letters (8 connects).
- Attended a networking meeting at lunch sponsored by a university alumni association. Spoke to twenty or so people. Four indicated they might be able to provide additional information, an introduction to a company or a referral (4 connects).
- Made phone calls to companies and, in the process, left fifteen voice mails (15 connects).
- Sent 3 follow-up emails (3 connects)
- In making the phone calls to companies, also spoke to four hiring managers (12 connects).*

Remember, a phone conversation with a hiring manager is equivalent to **three** *connects.*

TOTAL CONNECTS = 51

The target of 50 was exceeded by applying the concepts discussed and remaining focused. This person had a far more productive day than if he or she had spent $79 dollars "blasting" their résumé to 5,000 recruiters and companies using a résumé blasting service, followed by just sitting in front of a computer applying for position after position online that may or may not be relevant, while using the same "non-tweaked" résumé for each and every one of those positions.

Is making **50 connects a day** hard work? Sure it is! No one said it was going to be easy. Knowing that the job search process is a "game" of *exclusion*, you have to develop a campaign that is based upon both improving your skills and having enough "numbers." There simply is no way around this fact!

WHY ALL OF THIS IS IMPORTANT

Keep in mind, there will be many days that you receive no feedback from your efforts. Or, if you do get to speak to a hiring manager (or a representative), you may be told, "We are not hiring." Or, you may have gone to that interview for your "dream job" and never heard another thing back! Certainly, you will encounter many similar occurrences that simply will be beyond your control. Under the circumstances, it is easy to get discouraged. However, if you know you have a *mission* to make **50 connects** a day, in order to ultimately get to **6 1FTF** interviews (which, on average, just might lead to an offer), and you are indeed accomplishing that mission each and every day, you will know that you had a great day, no matter what!

If you are not a full-time job seeker, then you must decide what you need to do in terms of pacing yourself on a weekly basis to achieve the desired outcome based upon these metrics. Depending upon your schedule and your internal motivation toward finding a new position, you will be able to establish a weekly target for the number of connects you need to make.

By making 50 NEW connects a day in your target market, you won't get discouraged when you don't hear back from previous connects. You will know that you had a great day no matter what!

Below is a table that you can use to measure your daily connects. Each recruiter at The HTW Group uses a similar table each day. We have some different areas we measure, but the concept is identical.

Your Daily Connect Log Sheet

Date:	1st FTF	2nd, 3rd or Other FTF	Phone Interviews	Hiring Manager Connections	Networking Connections	Jobs Applied for Online
In person (X3 if w/Hiring Manager)	(3X)	(3X)				
Phone Conversations (X3 if w/Hiring Manager)			(3X)	(3X)		
Voice Mail						
Email						
Direct Mail						
Total Connects						

THE 'STATUS QUO': YOUR FIERCEST COMPETITOR IN *ANY* JOB MARKET

You will of course encounter many obstacles when you are prospecting and presenting during your job search. A major obstacle, if not *the* major obstacle, you're likely to encounter in today's job market is the company that itself is in a state of inertia. (If you remember from your high school or college physics classes, the Law of Inertia, in part, states that "a body at rest tends to stay at rest," or, in other words, it maintains the status quo.) This is a characteristic of many companies today, primarily because of the dismal state of the current economy.

A company has a critical hiring need. The economy is down. They would like to fill the position, and, in fact, they know if they *did* fill the position, they quite likely would make more money. Still, there is a risk, or at least the *perception* of risk, which normally is one and the same thing. If they fill the position, they will have to pay that person. So, the dilemma becomes this: Do we fill the position and have to pay the person, in *hopes* of making more money? Or, do we *not* fill the position, and therefore *not* make any more money, but know at least that we will not be *spending* any more money? (Or even worse, could we actually end up *losing* more money if we fill the position?)

Certainly, anyone who has ever owned or managed a business can easily understand this feeling. There is an old saying that applies well here: *"The fear of loss is greater than the desire for gain."*

But being in a perpetual (or at least what sometimes seems to be *perpetual*) state of inertia hardly is limited to hiring companies. I've seen many great candidates, who absolutely hated their jobs, their bosses (or both!) but who still would not make any moves to explore new positions and opportunities—despite actually interviewing for, and being offered, marvelous positions and opportunities! Why? Because the fear of making a move was greater than the desire to gain a new and better job, as well as a new and better boss! In other words, at the end of the process, the candidate felt the "best" choice was to make *no* choice, or at least no choice that resulted in change.

And companies do the same thing. Many often are literally *paralyzed* in fear, even in a good economy. It will therefore become your job, using your presentation and sales skills, to overcome their fear. You will have to prove, among other things, that you can make 'em money or save 'em money, preferably, that you can accomplish both of these things. You have to move them off "dead center" because they often feel the safest choice is not to make a choice, i.e., to maintain the status quo.

DON'T *YOU* FALL VICTIM TO THE STATUS QUO, YOUR FEARS & DOUBTS

To successfully be able to move a company, of course, you have to be moving yourself as well. Not only can the desire to maintain the status quo have adverse effects for a company, it can also have equally adverse effects on you, the job seeker.

So, how do you keep from "freezing up"? How do you avoid falling victim to the status quo? First, practice The Daily Misogi. Think. Use the creative power of your mind to develop solutions to problems and learn to overcome any and all obstacles thrown in your path.

Also, remember what we learned in the previous section: Job hunting is both a "numbers" *and* "skills" game! By setting daily targets for *effort* focused on the right *activities*, you WILL get *results*!

Effort ⇨ Activity ⇨ Results

As a recruiter, I am constantly reaching out to people, both client companies and candidates (job seekers). As a result, I experience the same things, both good and bad, that you will undoubtedly experience during *your* prospecting efforts and activities. Let me share the results I get day in and day out.

- Yes, people hang up on me.
- Yes, people are sometimes unprofessional, bordering on being rude.

A more typical response, however, is simply to be told "No, thanks." Or, "No, thanks, we're not hiring now." Or, in the case of a candidate, "No, thanks, I'm really not interested in considering a move at this time."

I have yet to be threatened with physical harm for calling. No one has ever shown up at my office door and told me, "If you ever call me again I'm going to 'key your car.'" And they won't do that to you, either.

Is there any "upside" to my daily prospecting efforts? You better believe it!

- I find GREAT people GREAT jobs in GREAT companies.
- I get HUGE checks in the mail for my efforts.

Let me assure you, then, there is absolutely no question whatsoever in my mind that my efforts are richly rewarded, and I'm not just talking financially, either. Let me further assure you, that, once you land the position you're seeking, you will feel exactly the same way, too. Believe that!

Do you know what *actually* is the worst thing that can happen to me as a recruiter (and, by logical extension, to you as a job seeker)? As I've shown you, it's certainly not the reception I sometimes get when I am prospecting and presenting. It's when I defeat myself! It's when I allow myself to become paralyzed.

When is this most likely to happen to you as a job seeker? When you lose sight of the end goal—the new job, the new career, the better boss, an opportunity to live in a more preferred geographic locale, doing the things you really want to do. It's when you don't do the things you know you need to do because you are afraid that someone will say, "No!" or you stop doing the right things right because no one has yet said "Yes!" Either can be paralyzing. Don't let that happen to you.

WHAT WEARS DOWN SALESPEOPLE (AND JOB SEEKERS!)

Salespeople get worn down primarily because of three basic factors:

- They don't know how long it will take for them to achieve their goal, i.e., they can't clearly see the "end of the tunnel," and may not believe that there actually *is* an "end" to the "tunnel."

- They are sometimes overwhelmed by the sheer numbers involved in making meaningful contacts with qualified prospects.

- They constantly feel the pressure of others who are (or at least seem to be) performing at a level perceived to be far higher and better than they themselves are performing. (Example: You are on your 7th 1FTF and don't have an offer; a colleague gets an offer after 3 1FTF.)

All of these feelings, and yes, fears, are certainly understandable. But put them into proper perspective and keep your eye constantly "on the ball," on your ultimate career goal. In the final analysis, you'll certainly be glad you did!

DON'T OVERLOOK THE POWER OF A COACH

N o one knows it all. No one can even *learn* it all. We all need the input from others. There is an old Romanian saying:

**"Only the foolish learn from experience. The wise
learn from the experience of others."**

The primary intent of *"Headhunter" Hiring Secrets,* of course, is to help you learn from the experiences of others, mine and the many job seekers and client companies mentioned in this book. Now might be a good time for you to take a break from the book and spend 15 minutes viewing the 2005 commencement address to the Stanford graduating class from Steve Jobs, co-founder of Apple Computer.

"Remembering that you are going to die is the best way I know to avoid the trap of thinking that you have something to lose," states Steve. (Meaning that you should have NO FEAR going after the job of your dreams.) Here is the link to the complete address:

YouTube: Steve Jobs's 2005 Stanford Commencement Address

(http://www.youtube.com/watch?v=UF8uR6Z6KLc)

There are essentially two types of coaches: The indirect coach and the direct coach. After listening to Jobs's commencement address, you should understand how some of the characteristics he has shown throughout his life, plus the trials and tribulations that he has faced, have a direct bearing on you and your job search activities. For example . . .

- He used (and uses) creativity.
- He had (and has) an entrepreneurial spirit.
- He has been fired.
- He was diagnosed with cancer.

And there is much all of us can learn from people like Jobs. Great leaders, businesspeople and people within your own circle who have overcome adversity, can therefore serve as solid, *indirect* coaches for you.

Other examples of indirect coaching come from joining networking groups and job search support groups. They can help you keep a tight focus and maintain a single-minded pursuit. Here is how:

- Coaches help you not lose faith that you can achieve what you set out to achieve.

- Coaches help you understand that you must be ready to pursue your dream, your goal at any opportune moment, not just 9 to 5.

- Coaches help you understand that a single-minded pursuit is not the same thing as a *closed-minded* pursuit.

- Coaches help you recharge and avoid getting worn down.

The *direct* coach is someone who works with you personally, one-on-one. This individual provides you with awareness, education, and accountability through regularly scheduled coaching sessions and other means. They challenge you and help you close the gaps. They provide information that enables you to implement best practices and meet your objectives. A coach is someone to role play with, bounce ideas off and debrief with after an interview. A coach will help you think through the issues of offer negotiation. A good coach will never tell you what to do, but rather, will engage with you to help you make the best decisions for yourself.

We all need coaches. As mentioned in the section on Misogi, I have a mentor/coach. I don't have time to learn how to build a successful recruiting firm by constantly reinventing the wheel and constantly learning from my mistakes. The only way I can get there faster is not only to learn from my own mistakes, but to learn from the mistakes—and successes—of others and be guided through that process by a coach.

I therefore strongly encourage you to engage a coach, someone who understands the ins and outs of a successful job search and works with you on an on-going basis.

In the near future, I will be working with a small group of professionals on a select basis as a coach. Contact me through my book website, www.headhunterhiringsecrets.com, if you have an interest in learning more.

PUTT! (PICK UP THE TELEPHONE)

You have been applying to appropriate online positions the correct way, networking and sending out direct mail letters and email communications. The next powerful step that will take you to the next level more quickly than anything else, i.e., position you above your competitors, the other job seekers, is to PUTT—Pick Up The Telephone.

This phase of prospecting and presenting can strike fear in the hearts of many men and women. But like most things that we fear in life, if we merely learn the "tricks of the trade," our fear can be brought under control. Thus, in this section, we are going to teach you what to say and what not say, during your telephone prospecting, in order to greatly reduce any fear you might have.

So pick up this frightful instrument and start calling prospects! Don't wait for them to call *you*! Because they won't. You need to adopt this method and level of commitment if you want to *significantly* speed up your career search.

Remember, your correspondence can get lost in the in-box, or in the paper shuffle, or even end up in the trash can (accidentally *or* on purpose). Computers don't hire people. People hire people, so get out from behind the computer and PUTT! Until you begin connecting with *real* people, you are not going to significantly progress ahead of other job seekers. Most times, the initial contact is made on the telephone, and you can bet your life that, nine times out of ten, it won't be a prospective employer initiating the call.

In my experience, the principal reason most people are literally terrified of "cold calling," either on the telephone or in person, is usually because they:

- Don't know *how* to approach a prospect; or

- Don't know what to *say* to a prospect once they do make contact with them; or

- Both of these.

There is no "magic" method for totally eliminating these fears, but they *can* be significantly reduced, so that you can *successfully* prospect via telephone. Let's take a look at how the "typical" job seeker approaches the telephone "cold call." (I have actually seen this very approach touted in a book recently as *the* way to telephone prospect. . . .)

195

THE 'TYPICAL' TELEPHONE APPROACHES . . . THAT TYPICALLY DON'T WORK!

RING! RING! RING!

"ABC Company, James Smith speaking."

(Since this is your first "cold call" of the day, you immediately break out in a cold sweat.)

"Jim, hi! My name is Skip Freeman. I was referred to you by Tom Jones, and I am interested in speaking to you about employment opportunities with your company."

(*James—not* "Jim"!—rolls his eyes and answers the 27th such phone call today.)

"You'll have to call Human Resources."

(James hangs up. You sweat even more profusely, if that is possible.)

Even though this, your first "cold call" of the day, didn't turn out to be all that spectacular (to put it mildly), guess what you have to do next? Right! You guessed it! PUTT! Pick Up The Telephone—again!

So, here you go again.

RING! RING! RING!

(You're immediately sent to the dreaded voice mail of the prospect. You're somewhat ashamed to admit it, but you're

THE DREADED VOICE MAIL!

Eight out of ten calls to a business today will *automatically* go to "voice mail."

I'm not a big fan of leaving voice mail messages when telephone prospecting because you actually want to talk to the person. If you don't leave a voice mail message, you can still keep calling back. *You* are in control. Once you leave a message, you have put the *recipient* in control.

Still, If you DO decide to leave a VM, one of the approaches I have found that results in a call back about half the time is called the "advice" or "project" message:

"Bob, this is Skip Freeman. My phone number is 678-123-4567. I am working on a project that I would really like to get your opinion and advice on. I will be in my office all day today, April 27th. Again, Skip Freeman. 678-123-4567."

Another message that often works is the "referral" message:

"Bob, this is Skip Freeman. My phone number is 678-123-4567. Jim Rogers suggested that you and I should visit soon. I will be in the office all day today, April 27th. Again, Skip Freeman, 678-123-4567."

These approaches don't work all of the time, and certainly not on everyone you call. But they work often enough to consider using them.

If you do leave a voice mail message:

➤ Keep your message short and simple.

➤ Leave your name and telephone number at the beginning *and* end of the message.

➤ Clearly state the purpose of your call without "giving everything away"!

almost glad you don't have to actually *talk* to this prospect. But, hey, this call will count in the "numbers" you need to hit each day, right?)

(You, leaving a voice mail message. Sweating not quite so pronounced this time.)

"Mr. Jones, this is Skip Freeman. F – R – E – E – M – A – N. It is Monday, April 27th at 9:30 a.m. I am a chemical engineer and I am thinking of relocating to Atlanta. I would like to discuss any possible positions you and your company might have for me."

What do you suppose the chances are that Mr. Jones will actually call you back? Well, probably about the same chance you have of becoming a crew member on the next space shot. But who knows, you might get lucky.

OK, PUTT, again! You've still got a l – o – n – g way to go to make your "numbers" for the day!

RING! RING! RING!

(Since is your *third* "cold call" of the day, you're getting yourself somewhat under control. Sweating is held to a minimum. You're literally "on a roll" now!)

(Prospect picks up and answers phone.)

"ABC Company, James Smith speaking."

(It suddenly occurred to you not to address this hiring manager as "Jim.")

"Hello, James. My name is Skip Freeman. I emailed my résumé to you yesterday regarding the job you had posted and I just wanted to follow up and make sure you received it."

(James rolls his eyes again, looking up at the ceiling in his office, continuing to ask for strength to overcome what has become his daily burden ever since he advertised some positions that need to be filled in his division.)

"Well, Mr. . . . . uh, what was your name again . . . ?"

"Skip Freeman."

(Regaining some control over his emotions and using his most professional voice and tone, the hiring manager decides to humor you.)

"Well, Mr. Freeman, I have five jobs currently posted on the Internet, which job are you referring to specifically?"

(Thinking fast, you respond in the following manner:)

"The chemical engineer position."

(Still continuing to "humor" you, the hiring manager goes on.)

"Well, Mr.—Freeman, wasn't it?— of the five posted, three are chemical engineering positions. Which one of these positions are you *specifically* referring to?"

Well, you get the point by this time. On this contact you have quickly painted yourself into the proverbial "corner" with your prospecting approach. There is no way to exit gracefully, and the impression you have obviously made is not the one you intended.

Now that I've shown you how *not* to be very effective in your telephone "cold call" prospecting, obviously, it's time to show you an example of an approach that *can* work, not every single time, nor with every single hiring manager, but frequently enough to get you where you want to go—to an interview!— provided you keep plugging away at your telephone prospecting.

RING! RING! RING!

(You picked up the phone, dialed it and you're very confident in your approach. This confidence will come through "loud and clear" once you have a hiring manager on the phone, too.)

(Hiring manager answers the phone.)

"ABC Company, James Smith speaking."

(Now, with controlled enthusiasm and a high level of confidence, you respond.)

"Good morning, Mr. Smith, my name is Skip Freeman. I know your time is quite valuable, so I will get right to the point. I know that, with my experience and unique skill set as a chemical engineer, I can offer you and your company substantial value in a very competitive marketplace. I sincerely believe it would be in both of our interests to schedule a few minutes to speak as soon as possible to discuss this further. I hope you will feel the same. When would be a good time this week to meet? Is either Wednesday or Thursday morning good for you?"

(Now, if this hiring manager has even one degree of curiosity in his body, he is going to respond with something like the following.)

"What did you say your name was?"

(Still confident and continuing to project that confidence.)

"Skip Freeman."

(Hiring manager is thinking something like this, to himself, of course. *Boy, this guy's got some "chutzpah"! Let me feel him out a little.*)

"So, Mr. Freeman, what is so unique about your experience and skill set?"

(You, still exuding confidence.)

"I have been in the chemical engineering profession for 15 years now, and have been involved in virtually every phase of the business. The teams I have led during the last seven years have produced five award-winning products that resulted in increased revenues of nearly 45% for the company during that time. I can make this same kind of contribution for you and your company."

Well, I'm sure that you get the idea. Can you clearly see why an approach such as this just might work, while the first two examples clearly are quite problematic for most job seekers *and* hiring managers? In the example above, you are beginning to discuss "WIIFM" in terms of what could be of value to the hiring manager, versus what is of value to you.

You exude confidence and when the hiring manager asks you, "What is so unique about your experience and skill set?" you are able to deliver a specific value equation that has made a company money. From a hiring manager perspective, the WIIFM is what you can do to make 'em money or save 'em money.

Also, it's important to keep this in mind when making your calls: If you don't *feel* confident, or are clearly nervous, anxious or otherwise uneasy, that attitude and tone are going to be clearly communicated in your voice over the telephone.

Additionally, the last approach shows a lot of "chutzpah." But, hey, if you don't think you're among the very best at what you do, and unashamedly project and communicate that attitude to others, why should they think you're anything other than "ordinary"?

THE PHONE ENVIRONMENT – THE PROPER ATTITUDE

Getting Ready. Before beginning with your phone calls, make sure you are in a relatively quiet room. Remove all distractions—kids, TV, loud radio, dishwasher, etc.—and get in the right frame of mind. Rather than projecting *dread* at having to make prospecting phone calls, make sure you instead project enthusiasm and confidence by keeping a "smile" in your voice. Also, make sure you have your prospecting (or marketing) plan and your notebook in front of you, so that you can keep track of your progress.

Put a 'smile' in your voice when telephone prospecting. It definitely will come through to the recipient! (It will also come through if you *don't* put a 'smile' in your voice.)

Telephone calls are just one part of your daily plan, but a very critical part that will set you apart from most other job seekers. Let's say that you have set a target of 20 phone calls as part of your 50 connects for the day. Once you do, set a "dials-per-hour" objective. Ideally, you should shoot for doing the entire 20 dials in one hour and you will hit that if you get voice mail but don't leave any messages. (Remember, if you do not leave voice mail messages, you can always call back!) The moment you leave a message and they don't call you back, then what do you do? When do you call back? What do you say the second time?

If you aim for making 20 calls an hour, you should expect to end up with **two to four conversations**, which, of course, is the real goal, not just dialing the phone! On the other hand, if one call ends up being a half hour in length, then obviously, you shouldn't be too concerned that you are not on target for your 20 dials in the hour! The real objective is to get the live conversation, not the "dial."

My recommendation is to leave voice mail messages only after you have made repeated attempts over seven days to reach a real person. When you do leave a message, be sure to say your phone number clearly and slowly, so that the intended recipient will have time to write it down! If the hiring manager you are trying to reach cannot clearly understand the phone number you leave because you said it too fast, he or she will quickly hit the DELETE key on the voice mail and you will be *excluded*!

Stand up for yourself. I stand up a lot when I am on the phone. It helps me keep the energy going, the blood flowing and my enthusiasm at its peak. It might work for you, too. I also use a headset. You can get a good head set at Radio Shack® or most quality electronics stores for about $100. It will keep your hands free and your neck "crick free," something that can certainly become an issue after several hours on the phone!

PHONE SCRIPTS

Prior to making *any* phone calls, of course, make sure you have carefully prepared scripts.

"Scripts?!" you might be asking. "A script doesn't feel 'natural.' I want to be real, not fake," some say. Others say, "I just 'wing it' when I'm on the telephone." Let me put this issue into perspective for you.

You've probably been to a professional play, correct? If not, you've certainly gone to a movie or two. Think about it—all the dialogue in a play or movie is carefully *scripted*, isn't it? But you can't tell it, can you? That's because the actors and actresses are professionals and have learned how to deliver their lines with natural ease and a high degree of believability! Am I saying, then, that you should become an actor or actress when doing your telephone prospecting? Absolutely! That's precisely what I am saying.

Just as actors and actresses rehearse their 'lines" for hours and hours before performing, that's what you must do, too, when preparing your phone scripts. Not necessarily hours and hours, but you *must* practice your scripts with your spouse or older children, a friend or a neighbor. The idea is to get some feedback from people whose opinions you trust, as well as from people who will tell you the truth if you are really rough around the edges. Again, **the job seekers we coach** have a **50% - 60% greater probability of success** versus their competitors. That is because most of them are willing to adopt this practice.

GETTING AROUND THE GATEKEEPER

Since I am a recruiter and am on the phone all day, I have learned that the fastest way to get off on the wrong foot is to trip coming out of the starting gate, i.e., take the gatekeeper for granted. (This includes not only the person answering the phone at the company's main switchboard, but also someone's administrative assistant.) Treated properly, they actually can become your ally. Maybe not at first, but possibly . . . just don't make them your enemy!

Remember, if the person who answers the phone is other than the hiring manager you're trying to connect with, it is his or her *job* to screen you (and everybody else possible!) out, to keep you from "bothering" "the boss." In other words, it is their job to exclude you—as soon as possible.

Using the tips we share with you next, you should be able to "get through the gate" and moved on to the person who has decision-making power, i.e., a hiring manager. If you do get stopped at the gate, no problem! Just place your future calls either *before* or *after* hours, when the designated gatekeeper is less likely to answer the phone, and the hiring manager is *more* likely to answer it.

When you do have to speak with the gatekeeper, here are some proven techniques for dramatically increasing your probability of getting through. First, make sure you know the name of the hiring manager you are attempting to contact. (We discussed earlier the ways to find names through Internet research. Another method is to call the company before or after hours and "mine" names from the company's voice mail directory.) Once you have the correct name, try this approach:

(Gatekeeper answers phone.)

"This is Skip Freeman calling for Jim Smith." **(Say it just like this and with confidence.)**

(Gatekeeper is somewhat "thrown off script," not sure if you are a friend, colleague, customer, an old Army buddy or just another "cold call." Calls such as, "May I speak to Mr. Smith please?" or "Could you please connect me to the person in charge of the IT department?" are usually the types of calls a gatekeeper gets, and thus, knows how to screen you out. And if you say the latter, the response usually is, "Sir, unless you have a name, I cannot put you through.")

But let's continue with the script started above. The gatekeeper responds:

"And the purpose of your call is?"

(You, remaining confident, assured but respectfully insistent.)

"Yes, certainly, I am looking to do some business with your company and I want to make sure I have the right information first. I was told Jim is the person I should speak with. Could you connect me, please?"

(Now, the gatekeeper is *really* conflicted. "Business?" Hey, that's what the company is all about, right? That's how he or she gets a paycheck! And you're implying some degree of familiarity with Mr. Smith by using his first name. It is likely, then, that the gatekeeper will immediately put you through to good old "Jim.")

Now, you may even be asking, "Business?" Yes. No one owns anyone. So if you provide services to a company and they pay you, you are doing business together. An employee/employer relationship is indeed a business relationship.

HOW TO HANDLE A TENACIOUS GATEKEEPER

If you encounter a really tenacious gatekeeper—and a good one is really tenacious!—they may say,

"I can try to help ensure that you have the right information. What is it you're looking for?"

Here is how you keep the conversation going. What you want to do is "mine" for some names in the area in which you want to become employed. Let's say, for example, that Jim is the Director of IT. Here is how you continue:

"We are doing some 'due diligence.' I understand Jim is the Director of IT. In that role, he would have some direct reports. In order to provide everyone the correct information, I need to get the names of his direct reports and their correct titles. Are you able to provide this information?"

(Gatekeeper remains suspicious, continues to resist.)

"And why do you need this information?

(You continue with confidence and a sense of purpose.)

"As I mentioned, we are doing some 'due diligence' so that we can provide the right people in your company the correct information. If it's easier for you, I can just get that information from Jim."

Again, at this point, there remains a high probability that the gatekeeper will put you through to "Jim." She simply won't want to be the one providing you this information! On the other hand, there is a chance she just might provide you the information! Now you have additional names of people you can contact in the company.

The key operative words that get action are **due diligence**. I have found those two words get me past more gatekeepers than any other phrase! Why? Because most people don't have a clue what the term means and they are hesitant to admit that!

However, if the gatekeeper still refuses to put you through, or provide you the information you seek, then simply end the call, politely and professionally.

As "headhunters," we have to get by gatekeepers all the time. Using these techniques can also get *you* by them.

So, if you aren't put through, what do you do? Call back later and ask for "accounts payable" or "shipping and receiving."

You will be transferred there. Then, when someone answers the phone, "Accounts payable, may I help you?" you respond, "Oh, I'm sorry. I was trying to reach Jim Smith in the IT department. Could you transfer me, please?"

And off you go to Jim Smith's phone . . .

These techniques for getting around gatekeepers are for the *main* gatekeeper at the switchboard. If you get the administrative assistant of the person you are calling, here is how to handle the call. (Let's say Jim's administrative assistant is named Gary.)

(Gary)

"Jim Smith's office."

(You)

"This is Skip Freeman. Is Jim in?"

(Gary, using a "standard" line.)

"He is in a meeting. May I help you?"

(You)

"Are you Jim's assistant?"

(Gary)

"Yes, I'm Gary."

(You're setting out to make Gary your *new, best friend*! or at least not your enemy.)

"Gary, it is nice to meet you over the phone! I know your time is quite valuable, so I'll get right to the point. I know that, with my experience and unique skill set as a systems engineer, I can offer your company substantial value in a very competitive marketplace. Now, I know your initial reaction will most likely be to tell me to contact HR, and I can appreciate that. But may I ask you a question?"

(Gary, sufficiently flattered by your approach.)

"Sure."

(You again.)

"How can I get my information directly in front of Jim? Is that something you can help me with?" **(Say it exactly like this.)**

(About half the time the administrative assistant will offer to help you. The other half will still insist on putting you through to HR.)

(Gary, now getting noticeably nervous and somewhat uncomfortable.)

"No, really, I can't help you. You need to contact HR."

(You, forging ahead.)

"Gary, thank you very much. Who in HR would you recommend I contact?"

At this point, there is little else to do but to "back off" gracefully. Now that doesn't mean you do what he says and "call HR." What you do is call the hiring manager back, early or late, before the administrative assistant gets to the office or after he leaves the office. If, after numerous attempts, you still are unable to reach the hiring manager, then simply leave the "project" or "referral" voice mail message discussed earlier and move on.

MARKET YOURSELF LIKE A 'HEADHUNTER' WOULD MARKET YOU

Sales of any kind, including selling yourself and your abilities during a job search, is both a numbers game and a skills game. Do enough of the right things right often enough and, ultimately, you will be successful.

In this section, I am going to show you how to market yourself the way a 'headhunter' would market you. You will *not* have seen this technique revealed *anywhere* to a job seeker!

'Hello, I recently applied for a position in your company. Did you get my résumé?' is a typical telephone prospecting approach used by job seekers. It does NOT work!

As a recruiter, let me first show you an approach that does NOT work:

"Hello, my name is Skip Freeman and I am an executive recruiter. Do you have any job openings I can help you fill?"

Likewise, here is a "typical" approach used on the telephone by many job seekers (It doesn't work, either.):

"Hello, do you have any positions I can apply for?" ("You will have to call HR." Or, "You need to go to our website and apply for anything that is open that you are qualified for," are the usual responses to this approach.)

— OR —

"Hello, I recently applied for "such and such" a position. Did you get my résumé?" ("If you sent it in, I am sure we have it. If we are interested, someone from HR will get in touch with you," is the usual response.)

You see, this is one of the rules of the game a job seeker *thinks* a company plays by. "They have an opening, I applied to the opening, I want to follow up and make sure they received my résumé. They should be interested in me and in reviewing my résumé, right?" That is not the rule the companies play by. Their rule is, "Yes, we want to hire, but don't bother us with such a mundane approach. If you do, you have made our job easier because we can now eliminate you."

SOME POWERFUL TELEPHONE SCRIPTS THAT WORK!

Let me share with you a couple of **powerful** telephone prospecting scripts that we use effectively as recruiters to market candidates. Then, I'll show you how to adapt these scripts to use with hiring managers, when you finally are on the telephone with them. Here is the first sample *recruiter's* script:

The Recruiter version:

"Mr. Jones, my name is Skip Freeman. We don't know each other yet and I know your time is valuable. I need just 75 seconds. At the end of that time, you can tell me if it is worth continuing the conversation. Are you OK with that?

(Let's assume that I caught Mr. Jones at the right time, so he says, "OK, I'm listening.")

"My colleagues and I have been in the chemical industry for nearly a quarter of a century. Some of the companies we work with are Air Products, The Linde Group and Clorox, to name just a few. What we do is comb the landscape looking for talent that truly stands out as a rarity among their peers and that is why I am calling you today.

"Mr. Jones, as you may have guessed by now, I am a headhunter and I promise you, I wouldn't be calling you if I only had the 'run of the mill' candidate to talk to you about because you can find those easily enough.

"In these turbulent economic times, many of our client's have hiring freezes and some are even downsizing. But, in parallel, these very same clients are telling us that they are still looking for the freshness, eagerness and work ethic that an infusion of new talent can bring them, new talent that not only improves processes and reduces costs but also stimulates the thinking of those around them, which moves everyone to a higher gear of renewed intensity.

"The professional I am representing has FOUR unique things about him that truly set him apart from many other candidates.

"May I share those with you?"

(Let's further assume, for the sake of illustration, that I have Mr. Jones's complete attention now. He says, "I'm still listening. Go on.")

"Great! I think you will be as impressed with this candidate as I am.

- In 2005, he received his BS in Mechanical Engineering Technology from the University of Houston and joined the U.S. Army Corps of Engineers soon thereafter. He has served in Iraq and is currently the Executive Officer of an engineering brigade headquarters. He will be honorably discharged from the Army in May.

- "Prior to attending the university, he worked in the chemical industry for nine years, moving up from labor positions unloading rail cars and packaging products to a lead process operator. Ultimately, he became the plant Mechanical Maintenance Engineer, upon completion of his degree.

- "So, unlike most engineers, this candidate has been on both sides of the business, the 'blue collar' and the 'white collar.' He has experience with batch operations, packaging, sampling and all maintenance issues within a chemical plant.

- "His industry experience is complemented and strengthened by the strong leadership skills, honed under some of the most demanding environments imaginable, that he acquired as an Army officer.

"Upon his discharge from the Army, he is eager to renew his career in the chemical industry. He has a very high degree of self-discipline, offers fresh ideas and is ready to begin making a positive impact for your company immediately upon joining it.

"How shall I go about getting this individual with you so that you can see the tremendous benefit he offers to you and your company?"

Is it quite as easy as I've portrayed it here? Not usually. Oftentimes I am interrupted in my script by the manager asking questions, seeking clarification, etc. You will be too. Sometimes I am flat "shut out" with a comment like, "Just send me a résumé." You will be too. Still, more often than not, I receive comments such as, "Tell me more" or "That certainly is a different approach, one I don't hear from recruiters very often."

What was the result of this campaign? We started marketing this candidate in early 2009 and six weeks later he accepted a position that offered him an outstanding career opportunity!

ADAPTING THIS SCRIPT FOR YOUR USE

Here is how **this same script could be adapted for this individual's personal use**, if he had decided to conduct his job search without the help of a professional "headhunter":

"Mr. Jones, my name is (your name). I know we don't know each other yet and I know your time is valuable. I need just 75 seconds. At the end of that time, you can tell me if it is worth continuing the conversation. ARE YOU OK WITH THAT?"

(Let's again assume that you caught Mr. Jones at the right time and he says, "OK, I'm listening.")

"I have been in the chemical industry for several years and understand that, in these turbulent economic times, many companies have hiring freezes and some are even downsizing. But, I also know that many companies are actually looking for the freshness, eagerness and work ethic that an infusion of new talent can bring them, new talent that not only improves processes and reduces costs but, in parallel, stimulates the thinking of those around them, which moves everyone to a higher gear of renewed intensity.

"I am representing an individual who has FIVE unique things about him that I believe truly set him apart as someone who can make a positive, immediate impact on your company, especially in these turbulent times. MAY I SHARE THESE UNIQUE THINGS WITH YOU?"

(Just for the sake of illustration, let's further assume that you now have Mr. Jones's complete attention. He tells you, "OK, I'll listen to what you have to say for a few minutes. Go ahead.")

- "In 2005, this individual, who has a BS in Mechanical Engineering Technology from the University of Houston, joined the U.S. Army Corps of Engineers. He has served in Iraq and is currently the Executive Officer of an engineering brigade headquarters. He gets out of the Army in May.

- "But here is the extraordinary uniqueness. Prior to the Corps of Engineers, he worked nine years in the chemical industry, moving up from labor positions unloading rail cars and packaging products to a lead process operator. Ultimately, he became the plant Mechanical Maintenance Engineer, upon completion of his degree.

- "So, unlike most engineers, this professional has been on both sides of the business, the 'blue collar' *and* the 'white collar.'

- "He has experience with batch operations, packaging, sampling and all maintenance issues within a chemical plant.

- "This is coupled with the strong leadership skills honed as an Army officer, in some of the most demanding environments imaginable. When he gets out of the Army, he is indeed eager, disciplined, fresh and full of energy and ready to make a positive impact for any company he joins."

COMMON RESPONSES FROM HIRING MANAGERS

So, let's think through some of the possible questions/comments the hiring manager may have at this point. All of the following are quite common ones:

(Hiring Manager)

"Just email me the résumé."

(You)

"I can do that. May I confirm your email address, please? **(After getting his email address, continue.)** Would calling you back Tuesday afternoon at 2 p.m., Eastern Time, or Thursday afternoon at 4 p.m., Eastern Time, be the best time for us to follow up together?"

- OR -

(Hiring Manager)

"Are you a recruiter?" Or, they may say, "We can't pay any recruiting fees for anyone."

(You)

> (If asked if you're a recruiter, admit that you are not and then add the comment that you are "actually representing myself." If *not* asked this question, *don't* admit to representing yourself.)

"That is exactly the best thing about this individual. He won't cost you a cent in recruiter's fees because the individual I am representing is actually myself."

- OR -

(Hiring Manager)

"Well, you need to contact HR."

(You)

"I certainly can do that. Before we do that, though, can you see someone like this having a positive impact on your team's performance?"

- OR -

(Hiring Manager)

"We're not hiring right now."

(You)

"I didn't call necessarily expecting that you were. Sometime between now and the end of the year, however, due to unforeseen circumstances, you might need to hire an individual. Could someone with this background ever be of interest to you or your company?"

- OR -

(Hiring Manager)

"This individual sounds interesting, but we don't need anyone like that right now."

(You)

"I would imagine that you are well-connected in the industry. Whom do you know who would appreciate hearing about someone like this?"

- OR -

(Hiring Manager)

"How did you get my name?"

(You)

"I was able to get your information through some research. Is someone like this an individual who could have a positive impact on your team or your company?"

- OR -

(Hiring Manager)

"You probably are not on our approved vendor list."

(You)

"That is actually the best thing about this individual. I am not a recruiter or a vendor, so this person won't cost you a cent in recruiter's fees because *I am actually representing myself.*"

(Hiring Manager, suddenly realizing your unique approach could say . . .)

"You're a little full of yourself, calling in like this, aren't you?"

(You)

"If my method was a little forward, I certainly do apologize. One of my strengths is finding unique solutions to problems to help companies *make money* or *save money.* That is why I was looking for a unique way to get my information in front of you."

- AND/OR -

(Hiring Manager)

"By the way, you said this would only take 75 seconds. It sure took a lot longer."

(You)

"Well, overall it did and you are right in that regard. I did, however, mention that I would take only 75 seconds of your time and proceed only if you told me it was worth continuing the conversation. That is why I asked if it was OK to share this person's five unique things with you. I hope that you are glad that I did."

Every once in awhile, a hiring manager may also say . . .

"We only accept candidates who have applied to a position through our website or one of our postings."

(You)

"May I ask you a question? (Normally, they will say, "Sure.")

"Do you ever look for unique solutions to problems? (Obviously, this will be perceived as a rhetorical question.)

"That is why I was contacting you directly . . . to be your unique solution."

Does an approach like this work every single time? Of course not, nothing does, but it is so unique that it works often enough to use it! And, to the best of my knowledge, no other book or recruiter is coaching job seekers in the proper use of this approach.

ANOTHER POWERFUL TELEPHONE SCRIPT

So that you have another powerful example, let's take the same technique and adapt it to a position for industrial sales. In this case you received Mr. Smith's name from a networking contact.

"Mr. Smith, my name is (your name). We haven't met yet but your name came up in a conversation today and the person I was talking to thought it might be a good thing if we spoke together. DO YOU HAVE A MOMENT? (If you were not referred to this individual, use the introduction from the previous sample script.)

213

"In this turbulent economy, many companies are not hiring and some are downsizing. But, in parallel, many companies are using this time to add some top sales talent to their team, particularly if that individual has a proven track record of taking business from the heart of the competition. I am representing an individual who has just this track record. MAY I TELL YOU ABOUT HER?" (The second paragraph is where you craft a message that is unique and sets the stage for the hiring manager to want to hear about your key points.)

KEYS TO SUCCESS IN USING THIS APPROACH

Make sure you don't reveal that you are representing yourself too early because you will be cut off and told, "Call HR." Remember, you aren't asking for a job. You are using an *indirect* approach enabling you to position yourself in terms of *value* to the hiring manager and the company he or she represents.

NEVER REBUT AN OBJECTION—ROLL WITH IT!

There is always a natural tendency to attempt to rebut each and every objection you might receive when conducting your telephone prospecting (or while interviewing). The secret to handling objections, though, is simply to "roll with them"! Get a dialogue going! Rebutting an objection causes tension and anxiety, and seldom gets you anywhere.

In wrestling, martial arts and hand-to-hand combat, the easiest way to deflect the opponent is to "roll with them," not block them. Someone is coming at you, use their momentum to keep them going past you.

Let's review some common objections and how to roll with them.

For example, get prepared for this **Number One** objection:

"You need to call HR."

The best way to handle this objection, which will occur often enough to become an issue, is by using a response like this:

"Sure, I can call HR. But before I do, may I ask if I am the type of individual you could see making a contribution to your team?" (You didn't try to block the objection. You "rolled with it" by saying, "Sure I can call HR." You have agreed with them, which they weren't expecting. Now, when you ask the follow-up question, they are more apt to work with you.)

Another, very common objection you will encounter when telephone prospecting:

"We are not hiring."

Here is how you might handle this response:

"I didn't necessarily think you were at this point. If someone were to resign, or when business increases at some point in the near future, am I the type of individual you would be interested in speaking with?" (Assuming you have laid out your credentials. Otherwise you can say/ask, "I didn't necessarily call thinking you were hiring right now. What is the best way for me to get my information in front of you, so that if someone were to resign, or when business increases at some

215

point in time, I will be 'top of mind' in terms of being able to bring value to you in a position?")

Let me give you an example of an objection I, as a recruiter, hear virtually every day:

"We don't use recruiters."

My response is always something like this:

"I understand. Please tell me, when you have a very difficult position to fill, how do you go about filling it?"

Notice, I don't "push back"—I merely "roll with it," and you should too. What do I mean by pushing back? If I responded something like this, "The reason you should use recruiters is. . . ." I would be pushing back.

Let me share with you one more instructive example:

Someone tells you:

"You need to go to our website, see what positions are open and apply online."

(You)

"Certainly, I can do that. By the way, may I ask you a question? (Remember, selling is *not* telling, it is asking.)

(Their response)

"Sure."

(You)

"What do you feel makes your company a unique place to work?"

Assume they respond with something positive. Then, you could say,

"Wow, that sounds interesting and it sounds like you enjoy working there?"

(Their response)

"Yes, I do."

(You)

"May I send my information to you? I would like to be able to stay in touch with someone who is as excited about his work and company as you are. That is somewhat rare these days."

Now, she may or may not agree to do that, but it is a way to again develop an insider who might ultimately sponsor you. You didn't debate why you shouldn't apply online, you didn't whine (spew venom) about how you have applied online six times and have never heard from someone.

Though there are no "magic words" for overcoming objections, there is a "magic formula," and this is it:

- Don't push back. Do not become (or appear) argumentative.

- Ask questions. Get a dialogue going.

- As you will learn further on in the face-to-face section, "lead the witness." Implement that here.

TRIPLE VOICE MAIL RESPONSE RATE
WITH PROPER USE OF EMAIL

As stated several times, I am not a big advocate of leaving voice mails when conducting telephone prospecting. Still, I am a realist and know that, at least sometimes, voice mail might be the only "contact" you're likely to be able to make with some hiring managers. I've also pointed out that the odds aren't all that great that a hiring manager will actually call you back. "So what is a job seeker to do?" you probably are asking.

Recent studies indicate that people typically respond to voice mails (if they respond at all!) in *three* days. The same study shows that they will respond to an email within *one* day. Following up voice mails with an email can *double* the response rate. However, sending an email two to three days *before* making the call, and then following up with another email, if you get voice mail, can actually *triple* your response rate! Obviously, the latter approach is best, but taking either approach can turn "cold calls" into warm calls.

Using the ideas presented in a previous section, **"Market Yourself Like a 'Headhunter' Would Market You,"** let's look at an example of the email-voice mail-email approach. The initial email sent twenty-four to forty-eight hours in advance could be worded as follows:

> **Mr. Smith,**
>
> **My name is Skip Freeman. Though we don't know each other yet, I have some information that I think you will find extremely helpful in today's competitive global marketplace. I will call you on Tuesday, June 9th, at 9:00 a.m. I will be brief in my call.**
>
> **Sincerely,**
>
> **Skip Freeman**

When you call, be prepared to deliver your marketing message. If you get voice mail, leave the "project voice mail":

> "Mr. Smith, this is Skip Freeman calling you today at 9:00 a.m., as I indicated I would in my email message. I am working on a project that deals with beating the competition in today's marketplace. I can be reached today, Tuesday, June 9th, between 10:00 a.m. and 6:00

p.m. My phone number is 678-123-4567. Again, this is Skip Freeman."

And then send an immediate follow-up email phrased in this manner:

Mr. Smith,

I wasn't sure which you would have access to first, voice mail or email. Thus, out of professional courtesy, and in order to make it easier for you, I am also sending you this email, in addition to the voice mail I left.

I called you this morning at 9:00 a.m., as I indicated I would a couple of days ago. I am working on a project that deals with beating the competition in today's marketplace. I can be reached today, Tuesday, June 9th between 10:00 a.m. and 6:00 p.m. at 678-123-4567. If you prefer to respond via email, please advise a time and phone number when I may call you. The call shouldn't take more than three minutes.

Regards,

Skip Freeman

Remember, the **seven touch points** we discussed earlier? This just gave you **three** of them.

> **Caution:** Do not email and leave voice mails for any individual hiring manager more than THREE times (combined total) in a week. Exceeding this limit doesn't make you look aggressive, it labels you as a pest!

The fact is, many businesspeople today, me included, use voice mail to "screen" all incoming calls. By the end of the day, the voice mailbox may well be full and, to the extent that one answers *any* voice mail message, they are going to be very, very selective. On the other hand, since most job seekers do *not* send follow-up emails, when the manager is checking emails at the end of the day, or perhaps while on the road on business, you at least get another "shot" at him or her.

HOW TO FIND EMAIL ADDRESSES FOR HIRING MANAGERS

Admittedly, it can be difficult, but certainly not impossible, to get an email address for a hiring manager. A good place to start is LinkedIn, where many professionals today have their profiles posted. ZoomInfo also is a good place to check. And, of course, you should always check the website of the company employing the hiring manager.

Here is the stepwise approach for deducing a hiring manager's email address:

STEP ONE

Determine the suffix (what follows after the @ symbol). This information is usually found at the company's website. For example, you click on the "Contact Us" section of MNO, Incorporated, and you may see an email address along these lines:

customerservice@mnoinc.com

Now you know that the suffix is "mnoinc.com." (Versus "mno.com" or "mnoinc.net", etc.)

STEP TWO

Now, **determine the prefix**, i.e., that which goes before the @ symbol.

- Occasionally, you will actually find the email address of the person you're trying to reach. More often, however, you need to deduce the prefix format. Let's say, for example, the website has a news release that states, "For additional information, email lsmith@mnoinc.com. You can then logically infer that this email format, i.e., first initial, last name, is one convention used by the company. Be careful, though, because there may be some other conventions that you find.

- Also, research **LinkedIn** and **ZoomInfo**

- **Research Google, Yahoo and Bing using the Boolean search string:** First name Last name Company.com

    Example: Skip Freeman headhunterhiringsecrets.com
    (With this search string, you will discover that my email address is skip@headhunterhiringsecrets.com)

STEP THREE

Validate the possible email addresses

- Go to www.mailtester.com, enter the email address and it will let you know if the address is valid.

STEP FOUR

Send the email using both the "To:" line and the "Bcc:" lines:

- Put the email address on the "To:" line that you believe is the most likely address. If you found additional formatting conventions, put the other addresses on the "Bcc" line.
  - Example: To: lsmith@mnoinc.com; Bcc: lindasmith@mnoinc.com; linda.smith@mnoinc.com; linda@mnoinc.com.

Linda will get the email at whichever address is valid, and because you used the "Bcc" line, she will *not* see the other e-mail addresses. (The invalid email addresses will bounce back to you as undeliverable.) The one that does not bounce back is obviously the correct address and update that in your notebook or records for future reference.

CREATE AN EMAIL THAT WILL GET READ

Regarding the email that you send as a follow up to your voice mail message, the "Subject" line is critical. It needs to be written in such a manner that it will not get knocked out by the spam filters nor get deleted by the reader because he/she thinks it is spam!

The "Subject" Line. Arguably, the "subject" line is the most important component of your follow-up email. Looking for some "guarantees" during your job search? I'll give you one. I'll absolutely *guarantee* that your email will quickly be deleted if you use a subject line like the ones below:

Trying to reach you
Can we talk?
A moment of your time

On the other hand, using a subject line like the following can *substantially* increase the odds that your email will at least get a glance:

Referred by Bob Jones (assuming that you were, of course, referred by Bob and that you are reasonably sure that the email recipient will know who he is!)

Re: Your article in Finance and Accounting News (you did research and discovered an article, news release, etc., that the hiring manager wrote, or he/she was promoted, given a new project or assignment, etc.)

Follow up to voice mail

Also, be aware that the use of certain typographic symbols ($,-,+,&, =) can cause spam filters to identify your email as . . . well, spam!

One more thing regarding the "subject" line of your email: Do NOT mention "résumé," "job," "position," or similar words. Nine times out of ten, emails with such subject lines are deleted without further ado, or the "forward" button is hit and your email is sent to HR without the hiring manager ever having looked at it.

The Body of the email. The most important consideration when it comes to writing the body of your follow-up email is to keep your message "short and sweet." I will provide one more example. Let's say that you used the subject line "Referred by Bob Jones." Here is how you might write the body copy:

> **Mr. Smith:** (notice that I used the *formal* form of address; you should too!)
>
> **Bob Jones suggested that I give you a call. You may reach me any afternoon after 3 p.m., ET, at 678-123-4567. Or, if it would be more convenient for you, please email me and suggest a day and time when I can call you.**
>
> **Thank you very much!**
>
> **Skip Freeman**
> **Cell: 678-123-4567**

And finally, as with ALL written communications used in your job search, carefully proofread it *before* hitting the "send" key! Remember, if you spot a major error in your email *after* you have sent it, you can't recall it! Also, avoid abbreviations and acronyms, unless you are absolutely *positive* that they will be clearly and easily understood by the recipient.

THE BEST TIMES TO SEND AN EMAIL

If you choose to follow up with an email be aware that there are good times and bad times to send emails to businesses. For example, it is almost never a good idea to send emails on Mondays or Fridays. On Mondays people are just getting back into work and deleting all of the "spam" from the weekend. Fridays, they want to get out of there! Never send an email at night, either. There is a high degree of probability that it will be overlooked and viewed as "spam." **Tuesdays, Wednesdays** or **Thursdays** are the *best* days to send an email to a business. The best *time* to send the email is from **9 a.m.** to **10 a.m.** and from **2 p.m. to 3 p.m.** (in the time zone of the recipient). That way they have cleared out their inbox for the morning or right after lunch and now your email is right on top.

NOTE: In Microsoft® Outlook® you can schedule when emails are to be sent. Therefore, you can write the email at anytime and then schedule it to be sent at these times and on these days.

NEVER ANSWER YOUR PHONE!
USE VOICE MAIL
TO 'SCREEN' CALLS

Positions are posted. Job seekers apply. Job seekers are being screened out. At some point, the company is left with a pool of candidates to further screen. At this point, you may be sent an email with a form or application to fill out, or you may even receive a call from the company.

We have already discussed how critical it is to have a professional voice mail greeting.

If you receive a phone call and do happen to answer your phone, make sure you answer it in a very professional manner. My recommendation is to use your full name, followed by, "speaking." For example, I answer my phone by saying, "Skip Freeman speaking."

Since this is a business line, or a dedicated line for your career search, don't just answer with the old, run-of-the-mill, "Hello?" (However, 90% of the people I call do just that.) For example, just recently, Craig (I won't mention his last name) called me one morning and left me a voice mail message. His voice mail intrigued me enough to motivate me to action and call him back that afternoon. He answered "Hello?" I asked, "Is this Craig?" His response, "Yes." (Now there is a long pause . . . so I pick up and carry the conversation.) "This is Skip Freeman, I am returning your call." Again, silence. So after about 15 to 20 seconds I continue, "You called me this morning. You said you were a chemical engineer and you were responding to my posting." And his response was, "I did?" (With his voice inflection clearly being on the question mark.) As you can imagine, by now I am pretty frustrated. I just work to politely end the phone call and move on. Much to my continued and shocking surprise, this type of dialogue happens every single week. I will show you how to avoid this mistake.

Similarly, I have known people to get calls while they are driving, in the grocery store, or even while picking up a child from day care. They receive THE call they have been waiting on. Yet, they handle the call much like I described above. Furthermore, they can't focus on the call because they are in rush hour traffic, or their child is screaming, or there is so much noise in the grocery store or at the soccer game no one can hear. Why on earth did they answer the phone? I wonder. As another example, I returned a person's call recently one evening. She was at a soccer game and here is what she said, "I can't hear you. I am at a soccer game. Whoever you are, call back tomorrow." (No, I did not call back and neither will a hiring manager.)

My professional advice: **Do not answer the phone**. The fact of the matter is, oftentimes, hiring managers, Human Resources professionals—and, yes, even we recruiters!—deliberately call at unexpected times to see how a candidate will react in such a situation. And, yes, if you don't handle it correctly we will exclude you.

And, by the way, if you put your home phone number down as your primary point of contact, I strongly encourage you to make sure your family members know that (1) you have put your résumé out and (2) that they, too, answer the phone professionally. I called a job seeker who was employed and had a particularly impressive résumé. They had responded to one of our postings. The wife answered the phone. After I introduced myself, her response was, "My husband is not looking for a new job and don't call back again." And once I tried a job seeker three times before I gave up. Their young child would answer the phone each time. I would implore, "Please give the phone to your mommy or daddy" and ultimately would get hung up on each time. (Yes, I moved on.)

The main reason for letting the call go into voice mail is so that you can screen the call and be prepared for an appropriate response. Let's say, for example, you get a call from someone named Sue Jones of XYZ Company. She tells you she is responding to the résumé you sent her company for a marketing position. If you answered the call, and you don't even remember applying for such a position (like the job seeker I described earlier), you quite likely will end up fumbling around, thinking to yourself, "I did? What marketing position? Who is XYZ Company?" You can now scratch any further chance you might have had for *that* position. You are excluded.

Had you used voice mail to screen this call, you would have had time to quickly check your notebook (where you have been *religiously* keeping a record of companies you have contacted, etc.), look up the marketing position you applied for, and do three minutes of Googling. Then, you can call Ms. Jones back, thank her for calling, express your interest in the position and schedule a time to talk—just like you knew what you were doing!

THE 'SHADOWS ON THE WALL' SYNDROME
('ANYTHING YOU SAY CAN AND WILL BE USED AGAINST YOU!')

You have been prospecting and presenting and now you finally have the opportunity for an interview. Whether it is a telephone or a face-to-face interview, remember, the primary purpose of the interview is to find a reason to screen you *out*, not in!

It's time to restate, yet again, what I have been emphasizing over and over in this book: The entire hiring process is designed to *exclude* as many candidates as possible, so the hiring company can get the "pool" down to a very select few. And, of course, it's out of this much smaller "pool" that the successful candidate is selected. In 80% of the cases (the great majority), hiring managers and Human Resources professionals want to pick the *safest* person for the company, not the *best* person. Not a very pleasant thought to entertain, I grant you, but it's nonetheless true.

Anybody who watches *Law and Order* on TV (and there are legions who do!) knows the familiar Miranda warning read to alleged wrongdoers: "You have the right to remain silent, anything you say can and will be used against you."

The smart "criminal" would be very wise to either keep his or her mouth shut, or at least not to volunteer information that ultimately could come back to really haunt him or her! You should adopt this same cautious approach when talking to, or dealing with, hiring managers and/or Human Resources professionals.

Remember when you were a small child (or now have small children of your own) and Mom was getting you ready for bed? She would tuck you in, perhaps read a short bedtime story, and once she was certain that you were getting sufficiently drowsy, she would tip-toe out of your bedroom. Normally, she didn't make it five feet, however, before you said something like, "Mommy, I'm thirsty. May I have a glass of water?" Were you (or are *your* children) really thirsty? Of course not. You were simply scared and needed a little more comforting before finally going to sleep. What were you scared of? Maybe it was simply because there was a full moon out and it created shadows to be cast upon the wall by the gently swaying trees outside your bedroom window. In truth, there never was anything "real" to cause your fear. Still, that fear was there because there actually *were* shadows on the wall!

This same phenomenon occurs during both phone and face-to-face interviews with a hiring manager or Human Resources professional. Something you say without thinking it completely through suddenly causes "shadows" to appear on the walls of the screener. As a result, they get frightened that you may be the wrong candidate for the position, which would reflect poorly on *them,* so they mentally *exclude* you early in the interview. Most times you make these "slip ups" because the interviewer has made you feel so very, very comfortable, and you merely let down your guard! Or, you simply didn't know this "Headhunter Hiring Secret," and thus, were trying to be as "open" as possible!

Let me give you a couple of examples from my professional experience of how easily such a "shadow" can be cast upon the wall and cause one to be excluded.

HAVE A 'SECRET' CAREER DESIRE? KEEP IT TO YOURSELF!

A friend of mine is a Human Resources screener, a position he has held for nearly thirty years. He has an uncanny knack for immediately putting a candidate at ease during an interview.

I sent my friend a candidate for a technical sales position his company had open, and my friend said he would like to conduct a telephone interview with the candidate.

It just so happened that my friend had been in the candidate's hometown once for a baseball game, so he and the candidate chatted briefly about their mutual love of the game. Then, the Human Resources screener asked a typical, "warm and fuzzy" question:

Got a 'secret desire' to be an artist and just bum around Europe? Keep it to yourself!

"If you could wave a magic wand and be anything you wanted to be, what would that be?" he asked the candidate.

By this time, the candidate was feeling very comfortable with his "new buddy," so he responded, quite honestly, with this response (remember the candidate was interviewing for a *technical sales position*):

"If I could wave that magic wand and be anything I wanted to be, I would want to be in *product marketing,*" the young candidate said.

"Why would you want to do that?" the HR screener asked the candidate.

The candidate then went on for at least another five minutes about his deep interest in marketing. How he wanted to get an MBA in marketing. How he felt he would like to be able to position products strongly through well-done sales literature, creative training materials, etc.

Typically, a phone interview with this company would last about an hour. This one lasted just 20 minutes.

Soon after the telephone interview, the candidate called me and said, "Skip, the interview went GREAT! I think I nailed it and I am so excited."

Upon learning from the candidate that the phone interview had lasted only 20 minutes, instead of the typical hour, I knew, instinctively, that the only thing the candidate could possibly have "nailed" was his own foot to the floor! The evidence that I was correct came very shortly thereafter when the screener called me.

"Skip, your candidate doesn't even want to *be* in technical sales," he said. **"He wants to be a product marketer, so that's the type of job he really needs to find."**

In other words, this candidate cast a "shadow" on the screener's "wall"!

If you are interviewing for a sales position, you want to be in sales more than anything else in your life. If you are interviewing for an accountant's position, you want to be an accountant more than anything else in your life. During an interview, you want to be in that particular role more than anything else in your life. (And this is true, at least during the interview, right??!!)

KEEP *PERSONAL* BUSINESS STRICTLY *PERSONAL*

I presented another candidate for a marketing position in Denver. The candidate lived in Dallas. She was a high-quality, very-qualified candidate, too, just like the candidate previously mentioned. Still, she also managed to cast a "shadow on the wall" and exclude herself during her phone interview. About 45 minutes into the interview, which had gone rather well up to that point, the screener simply asked,

"Why would you want to leave Dallas and move to Denver?"

This was the answer the candidate gave to the question:

"My husband is running around on me, so I am going to divorce him. I don't care where I go, just as long as it gets me out of Dallas."

Talk about "shadows on the wall"! And that "shadow" got even bigger in the hiring manager's mind.

"Skip," the hiring manager told me over the phone, **"If she can't keep her personal information confidential, then how do we know she would keep company information confidential? We just can't take that risk."**

THINK YOU'RE BEING 'DISCRIMINATED' AGAINST?
MAYBE YOU ARE: IF YOU VOLUNTEER THE *WRONG* INFORMATION

In the previous examples were the hiring manager's fears legitimate or imagined? It really doesn't matter. You still will be excluded. Cast a "shadow on the wall" and you will have quickly given the hiring manager or Human Resources professional reason to *exclude* you. You simply will no longer be considered a "safe" candidate!

Remember, a company essentially wants to know just TWO things about candidates it interviews for open positions: Can they make 'em money or save 'em money, preferably both. Any other kind of information presented by the job seeker, either knowingly or unknowingly, normally results in the candidate being summarily *excluded* from further consideration. Children who are ill, or spouses who are ill or otherwise unable to care for themselves, marital difficulties, aging parents requiring care from their own children, are certainly all facts of life for many people. Job seekers all too often *voluntarily* provide such information, and that gets them excluded.

Another example: If an interviewer asks a job seeker, "Are you able to perform the specific duties of the position?" think through the duties of the position. If you have diabetes and the position requires that you lift boxes weighing up to 30 pounds, unless you have a back problem or some other muscular/skeletal problem, being a diabetic generally won't affect your ability to lift 30 pounds. So your answer can be:

"I can't think of anything that would prevent me from performing the duties of the position and performing them well."

There is absolutely no reason to voluntarily disclose the fact that you have diabetes, or any other chronic affliction that doesn't affect your ability to lift 30 pounds.

ARE THE QUESTIONS 'LEGAL'?

To the layperson (i.e., most interviewers and most job seekers), there is a fine line between questions that are *illegal* to ask and those that are perfectly legal to be asked, and it is sometimes difficult to know exactly where that line is. Generally, no one is going to come right out and ask you direct questions dealing with most EEO issues.

Since I am not a lawyer, I am not going to spend time here defining legal and illegal questions. If you need legal advice or have a question in this area, my recommendation is that you seek the counsel and advice of an attorney.

If you do feel that you were asked illegal questions and were discriminated against, again, only you can decide what to do in consultation with an attorney. What you've got to ask yourself is this: Is it worth the time, energy, trouble and effort? I would imagine that if you are reading this, your primary concern is getting a job, not trying to determine the legality (or illegality) of this or that question asked of you in a job interview.

On the other hand, if you are asked questions during a job interview that really offend your sense of right or wrong, or ones you feel unnecessarily invade your privacy, you should ask yourself if you would really want to work for a company that asks such questions of job candidates. If, in rare circumstances, that happens to the job seekers we coach, we simply move on together and work to find the right companies.

For coaching purposes, let's look at a few more examples.

We had a job seeker interviewing for a position in St. Louis. The interviewer asked the following question, "Is there anyone who would be negatively affected by a move to St. Louis"? The job seeker's response was, "My wife isn't too excited about moving to St. Louis, but I will be able to talk her into it."

He was excluded. Most companies know that the spouse is 60% of a decision in any family move. If the spouse isn't for it, either the relocation won't happen or the hired job seeker ultimately ends up quitting and moving within the first year. Thus, the "shadow on the wall" for the company was this: "If we hire him and train him, there is a greater than 50% probability that he will quit within one year due to an unhappy spouse and we will have to start over."

What should the candidate have said? "No, no one will be affected negatively by a move to St. Louis. Only positively." Remember, you can't turn down an offer you don't have. If you believe your spouse will "buy in" to the career opportunity you are interviewing for, then work toward obtaining the offer and turn it down later if it isn't going to work out.

AGE DISCRIMINATION

You may recall that, when it came to your résumé, you should always include the year you graduated from college, if in fact you are a college graduate. (Note: Research has shown that 33% of people who *don't* put the year they supposedly graduated from college didn't actually graduate!) Sure, this can help screeners rather quickly "place" you in the age spectrum, but unfortunately, there is no getting around that here.

The sad fact of the matter is, if you are going to be screened out because of age, you are going to be screened out because of age. Sure, you have legal options, and only you can decide if it's worth exercising them. My advice? Just play the "numbers game" longer and harder and you'll WIN!

However, if you do secure an interview, again keep the "shadows on the wall" under check. Don't talk about "kids today," or about how you can't "keep up with technology," the absurdity of "text messaging" or anything similar that could give an interviewer the impression that you are resistant to anything "new," or that you are not comfortable with any kind of change. Such comments can quickly "date" you and will definitely get you screened out of most opportunities almost immediately.

Just remember this: Steve Jobs, the co-founder of Apple, was born in 1955. Yet, he is the continuing creator of most of the technology that is used today. (iPhone, iPod, iTunes, to name just a few.)

BEWARE OF 'GREEKS' (OR ANYONE ELSE!) 'BEARING GIFTS'

I hope this doesn't come as any kind of surprise to you, but keep in mind that interviewers will trick you, or at least *try* and trick you. This happens all the time. Say, for example, while waiting to go into your face-to-face interview with a hiring manager, you sit and "shoot the breeze" with the department receptionist.

During this conversation, you want to be friendly, so you spill some confidential information. Then, at the first opportunity, he or she fills in the boss and you're *excluded* as a candidate.

Interviewers are certainly not above trying to 'trick' you into revealing information that will not be in your best interest and quickly end your candidacy.

Or, say, during your face-to-face interview, the hiring manager complains about his or her knee hurting, and tells you that soon he or she will have to undergo surgery to correct the problem. Sensing an opportunity to build some "rapport" with the manager, you confess that you are having problems with your shoulder and that you, too, probably will have to have surgery within a couple of months.

About a thousand "alarms" can—and usually do!—go off in the hiring manager's head, as a result of your volunteering such information. "Why would I want to hire this person over someone who is also fully qualified but who doesn't face being off work for what may be weeks because of surgery?" the manager asks himself/herself. The "shadows on the wall" begin instantly appearing for the hiring manager.

Even though most professional job candidate screeners, hiring managers and Human Resources professionals are *supposed* to be well-versed in all the applicable Equal Employment Opportunity Commission (EEOC) rules and regulations regarding employment, that doesn't mean that they all necessarily are. In my experience, many continue to ask questions of candidates that aren't strictly "by the book." However, it has also been my experience that most "sins" committed by such folks are more often those of *omission* rather than *commission*. In other words, they all make mistakes from time to time, but I've found that, usually, they are honest mistakes and the person committing them meant no harm or disrespect to candidates.

OTHER QUESTIONS YOU MAY BE ASKED

There are, of course, a number of other types of questions you might be asked during an interview. Some may *seem* to you to have little to no bearing on your ability to do the job. Upon closer examination, however, you'll find that most are perfectly legitimate, pertinent questions, even though that might not be readily apparent to you. The point is, always be on guard as to *how* you answer these—and all—questions during the interview. Otherwise, you'll risk creating "shadows on the wall" for the screener or hiring manager. Following are some additional categories of these "other" questions you should anticipate.

Asking you if you've ever been convicted of a felony is a perfectly legal question when interviewing for a job.

Criminal Background. Nearly all employers today query their potential employees about any criminal activity or behavior that may have occurred in their past. (If you become a *serious* candidate for a position, the employer, regardless of size, will almost always order an official criminal background check on you.)

Questions regarding this area of your background typically are phrased in this way:

Question: *"Have you ever been convicted of a felony?"*

Suggested Answer: *"No, I have not."* (If this is an accurate answer, of course.)

Even though by this day and age most interviewers know that the foregoing question is the *correct* way of asking a question to assess a candidate's criminal background, some still will pose the question this way:

Question: *"Have you ever been arrested?"*

Your answer to such a question, even though it's not recognized as the "correct" way to phrase it, can unnecessarily cast "shadows on the wall." Let's say you answer the question in this way:

Answer: *"I was late for a sales call and got arrested last year for driving 90 miles per hour in a 55 mile per hour zone, but I got a good lawyer and we beat the case in court because they forgot to properly calibrate the radar gun."*

Here come the "shadows," here come the "shadows"!

Think such things don't happen? Think again. I sometimes shudder when I think of some of the candidates I've represented over the years who were absolutely great candidates, soundly coached and then, out of the blue, provided such self-defeating answers to such "innocent" questions asked during interviews.

HOW TO ANSWER THE 'HAVE YOU EVER BEEN ARRESTED?' QUESTION

The way I recommend you answer the "Have you ever been arrested?" question is merely to come back with the answer you would give if the question had been phrased in the appropriate, generally accepted manner:

Answer: "I have never been convicted of a felony."

What if you have been convicted of a felony sometime in your past? Can companies really exclude you because of that? Even though you've paid your "debt to society"? You bet they can, and they do! As long as the company is consistent in its policy addressing this it is perfectly legal. It is any variability in this policy that can be considered discriminatory. For example, if the company policy is not to hire a person who has been convicted of a felony in the last ten years, they are fine—as long as they are *consistent* in the implementation and application of that policy.

QUESTIONS ABOUT TRAVEL

While virtually all questions you may be asked during an interview can be "loaded," the travel question can be particularly so, even though many times travel questions seem "innocent" and merely "routine." Here is how the question usually begins:

Question: "Are you willing to travel?"

Answer: "Oh, yes, that won't be a problem at all."

So far, so good. But there's more.

Question: "So, if you are the successful candidate for this position, and the boss told you that you need to be on a plane to Omaha in three hours to visit a disgruntled client, you would be able to do that?"

Didn't expect that question, did you? And, if you hadn't prepared for such an "off the wall" question prior to doing the interview, chances are, the answer you will come up with will risk getting you *excluded* from further consideration. Your answer could quickly cast the old "shadows on the wall." Caught unaware, it would be easy to respond with the following answer:

Answer: "Well, I sure would try, but I probably would need just a little more time to get prepared. I would have to arrange for someone to pick the kids up from school, go home and pack, that type of thing."

While such an answer certainly would seem to be appropriate and quite understandable, at least from a human standpoint, the answer also could easily cast "shadows on the wall" for the screener. He or she will immediately start asking, *Will this candidate really be able to deliver when a crisis occurs? Maybe, maybe not. That candidate I interviewed yesterday is single and she probably could jump on a plane at a moment's notice.*

So, how do you answer the question? Remember, earlier we learned that "selling is not telling, it's *asking.*" Therefore, you could first ask,

"Does a situation often arise in which you have to hop a plane in three hours?"

Then, if the hiring manager responds,

"It's rare, but sometimes once or twice a year."

If you have no problem with that, simply state,

"I would have no problem hopping a plane with three hours' notice." (Do NOT, however, add the caveat, "As long as it only happens a couple of times a year.")

If the hiring manager responded with, "It happens about once a month," just remember, you can't turn down an offer you don't yet have! So don't say *anything* that could cast a "shadow on the wall" and get you *excluded!* You can later do "due diligence" and find out just how often that scenario occurs if you are made an offer. Then you can decide if that is the type of job you want. Why exclude yourself prior to an offer?

Remember, the screener's fear of possibly hiring the "wrong" person for the position more than likely will get you *excluded.* Fair? Of course not, but "fair" has absolutely nothing to do with it, either. Keep that in mind. Always.

RELOCATION QUESTIONS

Unless you literally live right down the street from the company you're interviewing with, relocation definitely will become a relevant issue, provided you are the successful job candidate. Here is a typical question about relocation:

Question: "Are you willing to relocate?" (As if you wouldn't be, since the job is in San Diego and you now live in Houston!)

Again, this question simply seems "routine," but be careful how you answer it nonetheless. It can be yet another "trap" being set for you by the person conducting the interview. The typical candidate will almost immediately reply with an answer like this:

Answer: "Oh, that will be no problem."

Now, the screener begins to dig deeper.

Question: "What about your family, are they going to be comfortable with relocating to San Diego?"

Since the screener has put you so at ease by this point in the interview, you quickly respond, without giving your answer any additional thought, in the following manner:

Answer: "Well, our seventeen-year-old daughter probably will want to kill me and her mother because she won't want to leave her boyfriend, but we'll just have to deal with that, I suppose."

An innocent and very human response, correct? Yes, but you may have just cast the old "shadows on the wall" for the screener with your answer. Should she consider you further, knowing that any move is going to cause possibly deep divisions and discontent in your family? And, could that have a very negative impact on your job performance if she chooses you as her candidate of choice? Maybe she should just go with one of the "safer" candidates in the running.

Now, I'm not suggesting that you respond to such questions with outright lies, but remember, the time to reveal intimate details about your personal or family life is *not* during a job interview. If you think there are going to be "issues" with your family if you relocate (and in what family wouldn't there be, particularly those with teen-age children?), keep it to yourself and deal with it privately. My recommendation would be to answer the relocation question in this fashion:

Answer: "My family completely understands that my job sometimes requires moving to another part of the country, and they have always been very supportive."

The types of questions featured above are by no means *all* of the questions you should anticipate—and prepare for!—in a job interview. These are just some of the more common types of questions you'll be asked. There probably is no realistic way you (or anyone, including me!) could anticipate each and every question a screener might hit you with. The point is, regardless of questions you'll be asked, stop and THINK before answering each and every one of them.

PEOPLE HIRE PEOPLE THEY LIKE

Now, it is a fact that, generally, people hire people they like. So it is critically important to build rapport with the hiring manager, receptionist, assistant, other interviewers, etc. What all too often happens is, in the spirit of building rapport, many job seekers say too much or don't stop to really think about the implications of their answers because they have never been coached in this area.

Only by avoiding casting "shadows on the wall" for a hiring manager, Human Resources professional or other screener can you ever hope to be among the top candidates to be considered for jobs in the highly competitive job market. This is the only way you can keep from being *excluded* from further candidacy!

Remember, **"Everything you say can and will be used against you"**! Believe that with all your heart and soul when it comes to interviewing during your job search.

THE TELEPHONE INTERVIEW: BE ON 'HIGH ALERT'!

Great news! All your prospecting and presenting activities have paid off and you've landed a telephone interview with a prospective employer. This is an opportunity, correct? Well, yes and no. You have made it all the way to "round one," and that's certainly something positive, something to celebrate. But wait! You still have to go into "round two," either another telephone interview, or perhaps, the all-important "face-to-face" interview, which, of course, is the *only* goal you should have for the outcome of phone interview.

Don't be fooled about the *real* purpose of a telephone interview. It is just another step in the hiring process in which hiring managers are looking for reasons to *exclude* you from further consideration!

It's important to keep in mind what hiring managers are attempting to do. Remember how we have already compared job hunting to high school football "try outs"? Coaches are not looking for whom to include on the team, rather, they are looking to see whom they can *exclude*! It's the same with hiring managers.

Prior to the telephone interview, you'll likely be sent an email containing a form or application to fill out and return *before* the hiring manager calls you. Obviously, you'll want to take considerable care in completing this form and returning it to the hiring manager as soon as possible. Make sure there are no misspelled words and that you use proper punctuation and grammar. Whereas your résumé is *not* a *legal document*, an *application* is! Any incorrect information on an application, such as improper dates, leaving companies that you have worked for off the application and the like are immediate grounds for excluding you from the process, if they find out (and in most cases today a background check is done prior to your start date and it generally will be found out).

WARNING! THE INITIAL PHONE INTERVIEW IS USUALLY A TRAP!

On rare occasions you'll encounter a hiring manager who has a genuine interest in speaking with you (or having one of his screeners speak with you) on the telephone. Maybe your résumé got the hiring manager's attention. Maybe the professional manner in which you conducted your telephone prospecting impressed the manager. In any case, *something* caught the manager's attention, so either he or she personally calls you, or has one of the screeners in the department (or sometimes in Human Resources) give you a call.

While not true in every case, many times these phone calls are a trap, especially if they come from a large corporation or from the Human Resources department. Why? These screeners are trained to sound upbeat, enthusiastic and friendly, but the fact of the matter is, their job is actually to *exclude* as many candidates as possible. It's just another installment of the "winnowing down" process that occurs day in and day out in the job market.

After receiving one of these screening calls, you quite likely will be on cloud nine, thinking you just made a new, best friend of the person calling you. Not only are you absolutely sure that you will be getting a face-to-face interview, **you feel the job is practically yours**! Nothing could be further from the truth. No one is ever hired as the result of a telephone interview. It bears repeating: Your sole objective on the telephone interview is to get the face-to-face interview!

Because you have followed our coaching up to this point, you let any phone calls from companies go into voice mail so you aren't caught off guard and "pushed" into a phone interview. You also know to return any call as soon as possible and **schedule** the phone interview so that you are able to fully and properly prepare.

PREPARATIONS FOR THE PHONE INTERVIEW

- **Research the company and the position.** Learn the employer's "hot buttons" and then *sell* them what you know they need, i.e., tell them how you can either make 'em money, save 'em money, or both.

- **Review news releases and other public information about the company,** as well as quarterly and annual reports. Pay particular attention to such communications as the CEO letter to shareholders. Learn about any new product releases, any awards or special recognition received by the company, etc.

- If you can, **learn in advance who is interviewing you,** and then check for that person's LinkedIn profile and/or ZoomInfo profile. You can also "Google" them to learn more information.

- **Do not bring up compensation, benefits or vacation!** If you are asked your current salary or what salary you expect, state what we have discussed earlier. "Susan, the most important goal is the opportunity. If I am the right person for this job from your perspective, and indeed your company is the right company for me, then I know an offer will be more than fair."

- **Have questions written down** that you would like answered before a face-to-face interview.

- Use **positive** phrases, such as "I know," and avoid passive phrases such as "I think."

- **Never speak negatively of *anyone* or *anything*—**a former boss, co-worker or company.

- **Always emphasize *why* you want to go to work for the company** you are interviewing with and *not* why you want to leave your current employer.

- **Do not try to evade any question.** If you don't know the answer to any particular question, say so, and then say you'll get the answer and call back.

- **If things sound good to you, say so!** Don't play "poker." Remember, the interviewer can't SEE you, so verbalize your reactions/feelings.

- If something *doesn't* sound good to you, take note of it. **Do NOT confront the interviewer!**

- **"Close" at the end of the interview.** Here is how: "Jim, I really appreciate your time today, and I am genuinely excited about and interested in this opportunity. Based upon our conversation, is there anything that will keep us from moving to the next step?"

- **Avoid mention of *anything* personal,** e.g., marital status, sexual orientation, state of your health (or even the state of health of any of your family members), etc.

'TELL ME ABOUT YOURSELF' DOES **NOT** MEAN, 'TELL ME ABOUT YOURSELF'!

Usually, one of the first questions a job candidate screener will ask goes something like this: "Tell me about yourself." (The answer to this question is also known as "the 90-second elevator speech.") Beware! The "trap door" has just been sprung and the screener is merely waiting for you to walk in—*fall* in would probably be a better way to describe it.

While you may not be aware of it, the reason screeners begin with such "soft" questions is to get you relaxed right from the start of the call. Warning: Put your guard up and *keep* it up from this point forward during the conversation! Even if you have to write it down to remember it, always have in the back of your mind that, through the entire process, *every* contact you have with a prospective employer is intended to *exclude* you from the final list of candidates.

Back to the typical opening question: "Tell me about yourself." In no way, shape, form or fashion is the screener actually asking you to . . . well, tell him or her about yourself. What?! Bear with me for a moment. Besides simply being a "warm up" question to get the interview rolling, what the screener is actually seeking to learn is how well you speak, i.e., do you use proper grammar, do you have a pleasant voice, do you "hem and haw," etc., as well as to begin analyzing how you think. Even more important, the screener is attempting to determine, as quickly and as efficiently as possible, precisely what, if anything, you can offer the hiring manager and the company. They want to make sure that they don't hire the *wrong* person for the position under consideration, so—surprise!—they continually look for reasons to *exclude* you from further consideration.

So, how should you handle the old "tell me about yourself" question? A job seeker not well versed in the "rules of the game" might respond with something similar to the following:

"I am one of three kids. I grew up in the foothills of the North Carolina mountains. I played football and baseball in high school. I took music lessons for two years but got tired of it so that is when I decided to try out for baseball . . . I worked the summer between my 10th grade and 11th grade as a life guard . . . blah . . . blah . . . blah. . . ."

If *you* respond in this same, or similar, manner, the screener quite likely will stop listening to anything further you might have to say and conclude the interview as soon as possible—in order to *exclude* you and move on to the next candidate, also looking for ways to *exclude* that candidate as well!

The *correct* way to answer the "Tell me about yourself" question is to break it down into **three distinct parts**. Parts one and two can more or less be "recycled" from interview to interview, while Part three will need to be "customized" for each job opportunity and prospective employer. A graphic illustration of this concept, along with sample responses, is featured on the next page.

HOW TO ANSWER THE 'TELL ME ABOUT YOURSELF' QUESTION

	PART ONE (can be "recycled" for use with numerous job opportunities)	PART TWO (can be "recycled" for use with numerous job opportunities)	PART THREE (Must be company and/or position specific)
	Use a *one-* or *two-*sentence statement of your career history, i.e., condense your entire career into one pithy sentence!	Use just a few sentences to summarize a single accomplishment that you are proud of, and one that will capture the potential employer's attention. It must be one that is easily explained or illustrated and MUST highlight a "bottom line" impact.	The final part is the most fluid and is the one that varies from interview to interview. It needs to be a few sentences summary of *specifically* what you want to do in your next career move AND it must be relevant to what the company is interviewing you for.
EXAMPLES:	"I am a chemical engineer with eleven years of experience, six of which were in process engineering at Clorox, where I worked on improving plant productivity, and five were in specialty resin chemical sales. In this last capacity, I assisted our customers in developing new products to improve their competitiveness in the marketplace."	"Recently, through networking, I learned of a company that had great products except for their concrete coating line. I knew that we had a resin that would enable them to develop a faster drying concrete coating, thereby improving their ability to compete more effectively in their marketplace. I identified and called on the decision makers, got their interest, worked with R&D and helped them develop a product line that resulted in $2 million in new sales for them in the first year, which meant $400K in new sales for us."	"For the next step in my career, I would like to be with a larger firm with more resources, so that I can continue to drive business and grow sales for both the company and my customers in a wider variety of applications. Once I have proven myself and earned the right to get promoted, I would like to use my skills to lead and develop a sales team." - OR - "For the next step in my career, I prefer to be with a smaller, more entrepreneurial firm. That way, I can focus on a niche, drive business and increase sales for both my company and my customers. I love technical sales and would like to be able to focus in this area for the next ten years. I want to be a career sales professional."

THE FACE-TO-FACE INTERVIEW:
STAY IN THE GAME
BY 'LEADING THE WITNESS'

You have prospected, both by various written communications and by telephone. You have survived the telephone interview. Now, you have—finally!—been invited for the all-important face-to-face interview! You're practically "home free," right? Well, not quite yet. How you handle the face-to-face interview will ultimately determine if you succeed (or fail) in your job candidacy.

As you are preparing for the face-to-face interview, I strongly recommend that you go back and review how to properly "package" and present the "product" you are selling—you—in the **Developing Your Marketing Plan** section.

HOW COMPANIES VIEW THE FACE-TO-FACE INTERVIEW, THE HIRING PROCESS

You should pay particular attention to such key considerations as dress, hairstyle, and overall grooming and hygiene, i.e.. how you are "packaging" yourself. Keep in mind that this interview is yet another step in the entire hiring process when hiring managers are primarily interested in one thing—"thinning the herd," as it were. At this stage of the game—and that's the way you should continue to look at a job search, as a "game"—they are now looking for even *more* ways to *exclude you* from further consideration.

Let me reinforce this point by briefly quoting from the hiring guidelines manual used by a major corporation. The language and approaches used in this manual, by the way, are *very* typical in corporate America.

"The purpose of the face-to-face interview is to further narrow your initial group of applicants by learning as much about them as you can in a relatively limited time."

Notice that this "purpose statement" doesn't say one single word about "determining the best candidate for the job"! The emphasis is on *excluding* as many candidates as possible, in order to "narrow" the initial group of applicants.

Let me share just a few more *direct* quotes from this manual, so that you will see, *in writing,* the "rules" that companies play by:

> **"Some job seekers are very well rehearsed. They know how to anticipate or deflect difficult questions. Therefore, try to formulate questions that cannot be anticipated in advance by the candidate. Make sure your questions get them to do 70% of the talking."**

But there's more:

> **"Be sure to look for and ask question about:**
>
> **"Gaps in employment (do not assume they were due to negative situations. Ask about them.) Words used by applicants, such as 'assisted,' 'arranged,' or 'responsible for.' These words don't mean they actually accomplished anything. You'll need to explore this further.**
>
> **"Many short-term jobs, i.e., job longevity. This is an indication of one's loyalty to his/her employer."**

This, ladies and gentlemen, is how corporate America views the "game," and this is how it is played, so you need to be prepared!

Of course, this is part of the reason I am teaching you the concepts featured in *"Headhunter" Hiring Secrets.* That's why I am providing you with as many specific examples as possible to illustrate the tactics and strategies recommended in this book. I want you to be well trained and very well prepared going into the interview.

Keep in mind, the *well-rehearsed* job seeker will be far less likely to be excluded than is the case with those job seekers who are either ill prepared or not prepared at all. (This is why the HR department of this company "warns" the reader of their manual to be aware of the "well-rehearsed" job seeker. But not being rehearsed means you will probably be the first to get excluded.)

WATCH YOUR 'BODY LANGUAGE' AND MANNERS

Bad breath, wearing inappropriate clothing to the interview (men or women can never go wrong wearing stylish, well-cared-for business suits), outrageous hair styles, gaudy jewelry, scuffed or unshined footwear—you name it!—these can be (and are) reasons for your face-to-face interview to be derailed. And so can bad manners.

You were more or less "safe" during the telephone interview stage. The hiring manager (or screener) at the other end of the phone line couldn't see you, so there was no way, of course, to evaluate your "body language." Obviously, this safety net is removed when you get to your face-to-face interview.

If you've studied anything about human behavior, you know that body language conveys far more than the actual words a person is speaking. The person might be answering "yes" to a question, while everything about his or her body language is saying "no" (including, sometimes, the actual shaking of the head "no"), for example. Posture is also a dead giveaway to the *real* you, or at least what will be perceived as being the real you. What is your impression of someone who slouches? Probably not someone who can be expected to be a real "hard charger," correct? How about the person who seems unable (or unwilling) to maintain eye contact with you while you are talking to them? Not very trustworthy or self-confident, right? Or how about the "foot-jiggler," the "hair-twirler," the "ear-puller," ad infinitum?

Other mannerisms that you should be on the lookout for, and gain control of, are such things as nail-biting. Loudly blowing your nose. Squinting. And, God forbid, picking your nose. Any and all such mannerisms can get you quickly *excluded* during the face-to-face interview. Happens all the time!

True story: I once ruled out a candidate because we went to lunch and he ordered spaghetti. Now, the fact that he ordered spaghetti wasn't the issue— it was the manner in which he "attacked" the meal. As he ate the spaghetti he had long strands of it literally hanging out of his mouth! To put it bluntly, he "ate like a hog"! Let me tell you, a "shadow on the wall" appeared for me right there in the restaurant. My fear was that this candidate might repeat his meal performance while lunching with a representative of a potential employer, or worse, while in front of customers or prospects, if he were to actually get a position.

Oh, one other thing! **Turn off your cell phone**!

RUNNING LATE FOR THE INTERVIEW? MIGHT AS WELL NOT SHOW UP AT ALL!

Unless your plane is delayed on the way to the interview, and you had to catch another to make it to your face-to-face interview, there will be absolutely no acceptable excuse you can give for being late. There simply is no such thing as being "fashionably late" for a job interview.

As a matter of fact, over the years, I have had three excellent candidates get *excluded* from further consideration because they were late! Each of these candidates, by the way, had good reasons for being late, but you know what? It still didn't matter. Their being late for the interviews was the Number One reason cited by all three hiring managers as the reason they were no longer being considered.

But just being late isn't the only factor to consider with regard to the appointment time. Arriving "just under the gun," out of breath and obviously still somewhat disorganized, can oftentimes be just as egregious in the minds of hiring managers as your actually being late! Plus, allowing yourself absolutely no extra time to "spruce up" in the bathroom before your scheduled appointment, puts you at a disadvantage before you even get started!

I am sure some of you reading this section are saying to yourselves, Oh, I already know this kind of stuff. I would never do such things. I hope you're right, but let me give you an example of how quickly you can eliminate *yourself* by improper or total lack of planning ahead for the very important face-to-face interview.

I "coached" a sales manager just a few months ago. He was flying into a city one evening for an interview the next morning. Also, he was renting a car. I advised him, "Patrick, no matter how late in the evening your plane arrives, drive from the hotel where you are staying to the company office. That way, you'll be certain that you know the way there, plus you can get a pretty accurate gauge of how long the drive will take the next morning." "Skip," he said, "I have been around the block a time or two, you know. You don't need to tell me things like that."

OK, fair enough, I thought.

But, the candidate did not follow my advice, and the next morning he got lost on the way to his face-to-face interview. He ended up being an **hour and fifteen minutes late**! The Human Resources manager called me and said, "Skip, your candidate was an hour and fifteen minutes late. He's 'toast.' Keep on looking for additional candidates. We'll try to get Patrick in and out of here as quickly as possible and back to the airport."

BE FULLY PREPARED FOR THE FACE-TO-FACE INTERVIEW

You should already have done much of the necessary preliminary research on the interviewing company when you prepared for your telephone interview. Go back to your notes and research and review them thoroughly prior to meeting with the hiring manager during the face-to-face interview. During the phone interview, you probably had those notes and that research in front of you to refer to. Obviously, you won't have that luxury when you meet face-to-face with the company representatives. So study up! Go prepared and be as informed as you can about what could end up being your new employer.

Just to briefly review, be sure you are fully conversant (and comfortable) with the following kinds of information about the hiring company:

- The company's relative ranking, reputation and noted accomplishments in the industry it represents.

- Know the company's "hot buttons" forward and backward and be prepared not only to include comments about them in your interview, but also, be prepared to *sell* them what you know from your research that they want and need. (The "hot buttons" can often be found in the annual report and in the company's news releases, as well as from having networked on LinkedIn with people in the company.)

- Be prepared to show the company representative how hiring you will benefit the company and provide significant value to it, in the form of increased revenues, market share gain, increased profits or decreased expenses. (In other words, show them how you can either make 'em money or save 'em money, preferably both.)

- Search and review any current news releases about the company and be prepared to mention anything favorable or noteworthy in them, such as awards, new products or recent accomplishments. Also thoroughly review the company's annual report, paying particular attention to the CEO's letter to shareholders. Review the latest quarterly report of earnings and be prepared to make comments about it, provided it was positive.

- Do your very best to find out in advance of the meeting who is going to be interviewing you. If you can obtain this information, look up this person's (or persons') LinkedIn and/or ZoomInfo profiles. And don't forget to search for their names on Google, Yahoo or Bing, too. You would be surprised at how much information you can get on most anyone these days on the search engines, including *yourself*, by the way!

Also be sure to bring enough copies of your résumé on *high-quality* paper stock, your networking business cards, your "smile file" plus any information you have compiled on the company. For example, print out the latest quarterly report, the CEO letter to shareholders and any recent news releases. Keep all of this type of company information in a professional "portfolio," one that holds 8 ½" x 11" pad of paper. Do

NOT bring a tacky three-ring binder or a big, bulky, clumsy briefcase that has seen better days.

When you open the portfolio, make sure the hiring manager (or other interviewer) can easily see that you obviously have done your "homework" on the company.

Practice, Practice, Practice!

It's often said that the definition of a true professional is someone who can make even the most difficult tasks seem relatively easy. How do they do that? Simple, actually. They practice, practice, practice, and after that, they practice some more! That's how.

I always coach candidates I am preparing for both telephone and face-to-face interviews to **buy (or borrow) a hand-held recorder and practice answering anticipated interview questions out loud**. Playing the recording back to yourself can be sobering! You probably will be surprised, and often not pleasantly, at how many times you hem and haw around, stumble over words and otherwise simply "blow it." If you stick to it, though, you soon will see tremendous improvement in your responses.

Initially, rehearse your answers aloud to yourself whenever you get the chance, e.g., while you're driving, taking a shower, walking the dog, etc. Then, after you gain confidence and the answers begin to actually seem quite "unrehearsed," role play with your spouse, other family members or friends. Soon, you will be able to use proper voice inflection, infuse your answers with the proper emotions (excitement, enthusiasm), exercise appropriate pauses, look people right in the eye and deliver your "lines" perfectly!

And finally, don't go into the face-to-face interview with the intention (or expectation) of getting the job. Rather, go into the interview with the intention of accomplishing just two key things: 1.) Building rapport with the person (or persons) interviewing you; and 2.) Not being *excluded* from the race!

Getting Off 'On the Right Foot' in the face-to-face Interview

You might suppose that most hiring managers would be really good at conducting job candidate interviews. The fact is, though, that is not always the case. Because the typical manager hires relatively few new people over an entire career, they usually just don't have the skills necessary to be great interviewers. Most, though certainly not all, really don't even know where to begin an interview, what to ask of the person being interviewed, or even the direction in which to take the interview. So, as a candidate, you've got to

Most hiring managers aren't 'expert' interviewers, so it is to your advantage to learn how to 'lead the witness,' i.e., the interviewer.

learn how to **"lead the witness."** Now, I caution you here, this is *not* the same thing as taking over (or hogging!) the interview.

Even if they don't actually ask you, hiring managers want to know essentially **four** things from you:

- Can you *do* the job?
- Do you *want* to do the job?
- *Will* you do the job?
- Are you a cultural fit?

So, learn how to craft your answers accordingly!

There is, however, something *every* hiring manager *does* know instinctively—they want to find ways to *exclude* you from further consideration! The faster, and more efficient they are with "winnowing" the candidate "pool," the quicker they can come up with candidates they feel will be the *safest* hires . . . not necessarily the best, but the safest.

(Please note here, however, there are professional interviewers who are quite good at conducting interviews. That's how they can easily "trick" an unsuspecting, relatively naïve candidate into saying things they shouldn't!)

'GET THE BALL ROLLING' WITH 'PLEASANTRIES'

Will you be initially nervous when you go into the face-to-face interview with the hiring manager? Sure you will be. You might be surprised to discover, however, that there may be at least one other person in the room who is also slightly nervous—the hiring manager, for the reasons just mentioned above, i.e., many don't quite know what to ask, how to ask it, or even which direction to take the interview. So, if you're a well-prepared, informed job seeker, as you will be after studying this book, this is your first chance to **"lead the witness."**

A good way to start the process is to be proactive and immediately express a pleasantry:

"Thank you for seeing me today. I know how very busy you must be and I appreciate your setting aside the time to discuss this career opportunity with me."

The hiring manager, in an attempt to get his or her end of the interview underway, may respond with a general comment such as,

"Did you have any trouble finding us?"

"Oh, no, I didn't," you might respond, "the directions you provided were excellent!"

Or, suppose the hiring manager "tests" candidates by not including relevant information in the directions provided, such as the existence of a construction detour. The object is for the hiring manager to evaluate how well the candidate handles being "thrown a curve."

In that case, your response may be something along these lines, "Well, that construction detour caused me a little bit of confusion, but since I drove the route last night after I checked in to the hotel, I was ready for it this morning."

If you think hiring managers don't pull these kinds of "tricks" on job seekers, think again. This very scenario happened to a job seeker I know. When the hiring manager asked the "Did you have any trouble finding us?" question and the candidate answered as described above, the client had a good laugh and said, "That's just my way of seeing how people I work with react to the unexpected."

GETTING DOWN TO BUSINESS

Once you've exchanged a few pleasantries with the hiring manager, it is time to get down to business. Ask permission to take notes during the interview.

"Do you mind if I jot down a few notes while we talk?" you might ask. "I just want to make sure I can later recall all the important details about this opportunity."

Do NOT, however, spend the entire interview writing notes and concentrating heavily upon those notes. That is distracting, annoying and borders on rudeness in the minds of most interviewers. Maintain constant eye contact with the hiring manager, jotting down a note every once in awhile. That will make you look engaged in the interview, but at the same time, give the distinct impression that you are paying careful attention to what is being asked and said.

I know this is going to sound "picky" as the devil, but make sure the pen you bring to take notes isn't one of those 100 for $10 varieties. You don't have to have a $300 pen, of course, just choose something that is professional looking.

EXACTLY HOW SHOULD YOU 'LEAD THE WITNESS'?

Almost all hiring managers use a list of static questions they use on every candidate they interview. This gives the hiring manager a "track" to run on, as well as helps them maintain at least some kind of direction and pacing during the interview.

> **Be advised, however, that a significant number of questions will be designed to get you to give a negative answer of some type. When you do, they are ready to pounce!**

A typical question is one like this:

"Why are you considering leaving your present company?"

An appropriate answer would NOT be,

"Because I just really don't like my boss."

Rather, the kind of answer you should give is geared toward why you want to **move toward something, not away from something**. Here is an example:

"Jim, it isn't so much that I am interested in leaving my current company. It's more a case of my seeing a tremendous opportunity with you and MNO Company. In my current company, I have developed three new products that increased sales 20%. What excites me about this opportunity is that, with the additional resources of a larger company, such as the research capabilities and in-depth database, the opportunity for new product development is significantly accelerated and enhanced. I simply love the challenge of developing new products."

Here is another powerful, perfectly appropriate answer to the question:

"My current company has been a great place to work. I have learned many things about supply chain management, and improvements that I implemented have reduced costs 16% per year, which represents nearly $175,000 in savings. Recent restructuring, however, has made it a little more challenging to keep on track with my career goals. Thus, I am looking for a more progressive company with new opportunities and new challenges."

REMEMBER THE 'SHADOWS ON THE WALL'

Some things you'll definitely want to keep in mind during *any* interview are listed in the table below:

Never say ANYTHING negative about ANYONE or ANY company.
Keep in mind that "anything you say can and will be used against you."
Never admit you were fired. (It was simply time to "move on" is an acceptable answer.)
If the hiring manager doesn't ask the right questions, you have to **"lead the witness,"** i.e., provide answers to his questions that will take him down the path of knowing that you *can* do the job, that you *want* to do the job, that you *will* do the job and that you are a cultural fit.
Avoid directly stating that you were "laid off." (Managers might wonder why you didn't survive. Usually, the first to be laid off are the highly paid or the less than stellar performers. It's better to leave the impression you were cut because you earned too much money. If you survived one or more layoffs before you were finally "chosen," make that point known.)

FIELDING THE 'GOTCHA!' QUESTIONS'

Virtually all hiring managers—actually, I should say virtually *anyone* who conducts job interviews—always ask what are sometimes called "Gotcha!" questions. So be on guard. These are questions purposefully designed to lure you into giving negative answers so they can *exclude* you!

While I am not going to cover each and every "Gotcha!'" question you might be asked, I am going to cover some of the more common ones. Let's begin with the "weaknesses" question. Usually, the question is asked in this form: "Tell me about your weaknesses." Or, "Let's talk a little bit about your weaknesses." Sometimes the hiring manager asks you to address a specific number of weaknesses, say, two or three, sometimes not.

ANSWERING THE 'SHARE YOUR WEAKNESSES' QUESTION

You certainly should be prepared to answer this question, but answer it in such a way as not really to cite weaknesses, while, at the same time, avoiding vague, non-answers. If you suggest that you really have no weaknesses, the "shadows on the wall" will rear their ugly, frightening heads. Let me give you an example of an excellent way to answer this very typical question. This example is from an individual interviewing for a vice president of sales and marketing position:

> "Steve, one of my weaknesses is patience, or actually, the 'lack thereof.' As a salesperson and sales manager, I want new business and I want it NOW. We salespeople are an impatient breed. However, I know that people will buy on their timetable and not mine. So the way I manage that is to ensure that I have enough prospects in the pipeline at any given time. That way if prospect A, B and C aren't closing yet, I have prospects D, E and F who are."

Notice how he readily admitted his "weakness," but also demonstrated how he had turned it around to a *strength*?

Whatever you do, don't feel that you need to "bare your soul" and tell the *absolute* truth when answering the good, old "weaknesses" question. (Regardless of how comfortable you may have become during the face-to-face interview, remember, the hiring manager is *not*—repeat, *not*—your new best friend!) Consider what one job seeker I was working with said when asked about her weaknesses.

> "I need to improve my listening skills," the job seeker said. "I have been told that, when I am asked a question, I really provide an answer that doesn't mean anything, and I think that is because I don't listen well. My mind wanders."

This candidate might as well have said, "You probably wouldn't want to hire me because I really am a person who can't seem to pay attention to anything. Or at least that's what a lot of people have told me." In any case, the result was entirely predictable—the candidate was quickly *excluded* from the "pool" of possible candidates!

Another "truth-telling" candidate provided an equally devastating answer to the question.

> "I have trouble waking up in the mornings," he said. "I don't really become productive until about 10 a.m."

Immediately excluded!

In each of these cases, incidentally, the face-to-face interview was terminated within ten minutes of these answers!

As self-defeating as such answers are to candidates, it can be equally counter-productive to give vague, non-answers to the "weaknesses" question." Here are examples of such vague "non-answers":

> "I am an over-achiever."

> "I am a workaholic."

> "I am a perfectionist."

While such answers may *appear to* be similar to the one the candidate provided to the interviewer when he was applying for the vice president – sales and marketing position, in fact, that's not the case at all. In that response, there at least was an *implied* weakness (his "impatience"), which he then turned into an actual strength by giving specific examples of how this "weakness" manifests itself. Considering the position being applied for, there was absolutely no way the hiring manager would perceive his "weakness" as anything other than a strength.

On the other hand, someone who claims to be an "over-achiever," a "workaholic," or a "perfectionist," easily could cast "shadows on the wall" for the hiring manager, who probably would think, "This candidate will have difficulty getting along with the rest of the team, if they don't 'measure up' to his or her 'standards.'"

Some candidates attempt to get around the weaknesses question simply by saying, "I really don't have any weaknesses." Unfortunately, this doesn't work either. Everyone has weaknesses, and the hiring manager will certainly be aware of that. The impression the candidate will leave is one of attempting to "snow" the hiring manager.

Immediately excluded!

Another example you can use to help you craft your thinking is the second answer the candidate for the vice president position gave to the "weakness" question. (The hiring manager had asked the candidate to cite three weaknesses.)

> "My second weakness, or so I have been told," he continued, "is that I am pretty 'anal' about the numbers. I keep intricate details about the number of sales calls I make and the outcomes. But what I have found is that by knowing my numbers, I have been able to set targets that help me achieve the goals I have set for myself and my company. If I know that 11 sales calls equals a proposal, and three proposals equal a sale, then I know where I stand at any given time and I am able to make an accurate forecast for the company."

In this example, any good manager would love to hear a candidate saying that he was "anal" about the numbers. But other salespeople who aren't that interested in the numbers don't like it, so he "spins" the answer into a weakness by saying that others tell him this is a weakness when, in reality, it really is a strength.

(Oh, by the way, you're probably wondering if this person was indeed offered the position. The answer is, yes!)

By now, I'm sure you understand the coaching point. Anticipate "Gotcha!" questions, such as the "weaknesses" question, and adequately prepare appropriate answers for them *prior* to having your face-to-face interview.

Write down four or five of your own "weaknesses"—too competitive, unable to take "no" for an answer when making a sales call, a perfectionist when it comes to the numbers (if you are an engineer or accountant), etc.—and construct methods of seeming to "admit" your weaknesses, while at the same time "spinning" them into what will clearly be perceived as *strengths* by an astute hiring manager.

Your Biggest Career 'Failures' Question

This is another perennial favorite of interviewers. The question usually is phrased along these lines:

"Thinking back over your entire career, what would you consider to be one of your biggest failures?"

Oh, boy! Another question that you just can't "waltz" around, right? Just as everyone has *weaknesses,* so also has everyone had *failures* in life, particularly when it comes to a career. And the hiring manager knows it! That means you've got to come up with ways of answering the question by "admitting" your past failures, but at the same time, not undermining your candidacy. Tricky, but clearly possible for the job seeker who knows the *"Headhunter" Hiring Secrets*!

Don't try to 'waltz' around the 'tell me about your biggest failures' question by claiming to have had none. The hiring manager won't believe you—everybody has had failures!—and you'll lose all credibility.

Predictably, many candidates try to skirt this question by claiming to have had no failures in their career. They correctly assume that "anything they say can and will be used against them," so they try and bluff their way through the question, hoping the hiring manager will be impressed that he or she is dealing with someone who approaches perfection. This approach is doomed to failure and will quickly get you *excluded* from further consideration. Let me give you an example of how this approach can backfire on a candidate.

When asked the "failure" question by the hiring manager, one candidate I was presenting answered in this way:

"You know, I can't think of any (failures)," he said. "Everything I have done has been a success."

Immediately excluded!

Later, when I talked to the hiring manager on the telephone following the candidate's face-to-face interview, here is what she said:

"Skip, everyone has failures," she told me. **"No one is perfect. The fact that your candidate doesn't recognize that he has any tells me that he won't learn from his mistakes. Often the best lessons**

learned happen to be when you failed at something versus having succeeded at it."

So, how could this candidate have effectively dealt with the question? Here is one way:

Question: "Thinking back on your career, what was one of your biggest failures?"

Answer (after some obvious thought): "One of my biggest failures occurred right after I was first appointed maintenance manager. At that time, we had a six-day turn-around scheduled. It ended up taking us seven and a half days to get the plant back online. That cost us about $600,000 in lost production!

"About day four is when my team and I finally realized the nature of the problem—that we weren't taking one particular area of equipment inspections into proper account. We all agreed to work overtime, without pay, to correct the problem as soon as possible.

"After the turn-around, we spent much time brain-storming in the conference room, checking and rechecking the schedule at least a thousand times to see what happened. Through that process, we ultimately came up with an efficient way to ensure the problem didn't happen again, and going forward, we were able to complete every future turn-around in five days. That was a very valuable lesson, let me assure you."

Again, it's clear to see that the way to handle virtually all of these kinds of "Gotcha!" questions is to, first, be prepared for them, because they *will* be asked, and second, to take a "negative" and "spin" it into a "positive," whenever possible. In this particular situation, the candidate did indeed admit that he had made a mistake, a rather costly mistake at that, but that he and his "team" (something always important to emphasize) learned from the mistake and even ended up benefitting the company in the long run.

THE 'MOST DIFFICULT SITUATION

This question, of course, is somewhat of a variation of the "weaknesses" and "failure" questions, although you should find it much easier to respond to this question. Also, your answer to it may not pose quite as much risk of being *excluded* as the other two questions can.

The hiring manager is seeking to learn essentially two things about you with the "difficult situation" question. First, he or she wants to know what you consider to *be* a "difficult situation." And second, the manager wants to learn how you handled it. Relatively straightforward kind of stuff, but still be on "full alert" when you answer the question because, here again, "anything you say can and will be used against you"! Following is an example of a good way to field and answer this question without casting any "shadows on the wall," something the hiring manager is always hoping you will do when answering these types of questions!

> "Jim, with my previous company, I was part of a five-person team tasked with writing procedures for our new manufacturing line. We each had a particular part of the line and a deadline to meet. I knew that my co-worker wasn't doing his part, and when I approached him about it, he kept telling me he had not had the time to complete his part of the assignment and didn't know when he would have the time to do it.

> "I knew that I could just wait and let him fall on his own sword at the next meeting, but the problem with that was that it would have set the production line start date back and have been bad for the company.

> "I didn't have time to do his job and mine too. I also knew that volunteering to write his procedures wasn't the right thing to do, and neither did I want to 'rat him out' to the boss. So I asked him if it would help him if he just did one section a day and I could get different team members to review the draft sections and offer suggestions. That way he would save time by not having to think back through everything and he could move on to the next section.

> "We got the job done on time and ensured the production line started up on schedule, but I'll admit, there were times when it seemed like 'touch and go.'"

Note that the "secret" we discussed earlier, "telling stories," adds immeasurably to your answers to the "Gotcha!" questions. People not only like to "hear" what you're telling them, they also like to "see" what you're telling them. Using this approach amply accomplishes that desired goal.

THE 'TELL ME ABOUT YOUR WORST BOSS' QUESTION

Another of the perennial favorite "Gotcha!" questions asked by hiring managers and other job interviewers is the one that goes something like this: "Tell me about the worst (or most difficult) boss you've ever had." (Talk about a "loaded" question!) This is really a "heads up" question, so be especially careful how you answer it!

No matter how tempted you might be, don't fall into the 'tell me about the worst boss you ever had' trap! You'll be *immediately excluded* if you spew 'venom'!

As has been illustrated, some interviewers try to lull candidates into a false sense of security during an interview, to make them comfortable enough to cast "shadows on the wall" and/or "spew venom." Well, here is a prime example of how that sometimes is accomplished. In order to "prime the pump" for *your* answer to the old "tell me about your boss question," the hiring manager may even relate his or her own story about a terrible boss they have had—*before* asking you the question. Beware! **More than likely, they are merely setting you up**, and if you aren't very, very careful, you will easily fall into the trap they have so conveniently set for you. No matter what it takes, refrain from reciprocating with your own "boss from hell" story. Rather, here is the *correct* way to answer the question:

> "I have always had bosses with whom I could get along professionally. Every work situation requires that you get along with a wide variety of people, of course, from your boss to your co-workers to people who report to you. Sometimes, you have to share ideas and you may ultimately agree to disagree. However, when you leave the conversation, you need to be 'on task' and ensure that what you are doing is indeed meeting the company goals and objectives. My most challenging boss actually has been my best boss. Under him, I was able to learn different viewpoints and that has expanded my ability to be effective." (Be prepared to give examples of what you mean here, if the hiring manager decides to probe further.)

Another acceptable answer might go like this:

> "Conflict is unavoidable in the workplace, whether it is with a boss, co-worker or someone else. The first thing that is important is to never let anger be an emotion that you feed. If I encounter a difficult situation, I remember that different people have different points of view, and it is important to understand those. So I will ask a question such as, 'That is an interesting perspective and I would like to understand it better.' I always work to ensure that I act with

integrity and keep the best interests of the company in mind at all times."

And since this is a question that is so very, very important to be answered correctly, here is just one more example of how you might address it:

"My most difficult boss was one that I would also readily tell you was my *best* boss. Why? Because he constantly challenged me, on everything! He made me think, to consider other viewpoints, other people's positions. That enabled me to open up my mind to a broader range of thinking, and I was surprised at how many times his challenges to me were spot on. I will always be grateful for that experience."

If you think these answers are "laying it on a little too thick," perhaps you're right. But it's still better to err on the side of remaining totally positive when it comes to talking about a current (or former) boss. Why? Because the hiring manager interviewing you will be your next boss, if you are the successful candidate, and if you freely "bad-mouth" a current or former boss, he or she can easily assume that you wouldn't miss a chance to do the same to him or her, that's why! It's similar to a gossipy person. Don't you ever wonder, after they have told you some scurrilous, outrageous "tidbits" about people you both know, how long it will take before they are talking to others about *you*?

In addition to all of that, of course, the hiring manager also wants to know how you might handle confrontational situations. Will you get angry and throw a tantrum? Will you merely sulk? Will you try to "get even" with whoever gets on your wrong side? Remember, companies almost never want to hire the *best* candidate for a job, they want to hire the *safest*!

BE PREPARED FOR 'OFF THE WALL' QUESTIONS

Before leaving this "boss" question, I simply have to tell you about a twist to this question. Here is how the question was phrased:

"Tell me about a time you had to disagree with your boss in front of others."

Here is how the job seeker deftly answered this question:

"We were in a meeting once and my boss, in his presentation, gave some conclusions that were contrary to the data we had. In the question-and-answer session at the end, I was asked, 'Do you agree?' Whew! I knew that what my boss had said was not correct. This is the way I handled the situation: I said, 'I was just informed that some new studies are in the process of being conducted. The new data will certainly be able to confirm our conclusions or enable us to re-evaluate them.'"

CAN YOU *DO* THE JOB? DO YOU *WANT* TO DO THE JOB? *WILL* YOU DO THE JOB? ARE YOU A CULTURAL FIT?

So, you handled the initial phases of the face-to-face interview with élan, you've satisfactorily fielded and answered a variety of "Gotcha!" questions and now you feel that you are definitely "on a roll." Where do you go from here?

Everyone you meet within a company instinctively wants to know the answer to these FOUR questions:

- Can you do the job?
- Do you want to do the job?
- Will you do the job?
- Are you a cultural fit?

Thus, given the new rules of the hiring game, one of the key secrets to strongly positioning yourself as a TOP candidate in ANY job market is to **memorize these four "leading the witness" questions** and have **well-developed stories prepared and rehearsed that will provide proof.** And proof most often comes through illustrations of past accomplishments and achievements that demonstrate to the hiring manager that you can make 'em money, save 'em money, or both.

About half of the people you interview with are very skilled at asking the right questions within the framework of these four questions. In other words, their questions will be offshoots of these four. Then it is up to you to provide the right answers as previously discussed, i.e., don't cast "shadows on the wall," don't "spew venom," don't ramble, and be able to ask the interviewer good questions. Also, be prepared to review and *stress* every single bullet point on your résumé and have a story ready to back up these points. A good interviewer will pick out relevant points on your resume and ask questions about them along the lines of, "Tell me about . . ." or, "How did you accomplish. . . ." Make sure your answers are subliminally aligned to the four questions above. YOU "lead the witness" by taking him or her down the path you know they need to go in order for you to get hired!

Unfortunately, the other half of the people you interview with have no idea how to effectively interview you. Maybe they were put on the agenda at the last minute, and consequently, have other things on their mind; or, they have never had any training in this area, so they do all of the talking or ask irrelevant questions; or, they simply are nervous. And more often than not, it is this half of the interviewers who sabotage your candidacy. Because they didn't know *how* to interview you, they can't provide feedback to the hiring team as to why you *should* be hired. Thus, it is easier for them to provide a reason why you should *not* be hired (excluded), so that they "look smart" and appear to have effectively interviewed you. This is where the criticality of effectively "leading the witness" vis-à-vis these four questions will separate you from the pack and help you WIN the job and GET HIRED!

Let's examine each of these four "leading the witness" questions in greater detail.

BEING ABLE TO 'DO THE JOB' TAKES MORE THAN TECHNICAL SKILLS

One of the most important things a hiring manager wants to know is whether or not you can actually do the job. And what we're talking about here goes far beyond your simply having the *technical* skills to adequately perform the duties of the job for which you are applying. These skills, sometimes referred to as *hard* skills, are definitely a prerequisite for further consideration, but the so-called "soft" skills are equally important.

"Soft" skills generally are those skills that have to do with personality and human interaction. An example of a soft skill would be *attitude*. Are you a positive or negative person? Do you have the ability (and skill) to lead other people? Do you have good communication skills, both written and verbal? Are you clearly willing to learn new things, or do you come across as someone who already knows everything and doesn't suffer "fools" easily or well? Are you creative, i.e., can you come up with creative, effective ways of handling those challenging situations that are bound to come up from time to time in *any* job? Are you adaptable to unexpected change? Are you honest? Do you maintain a high degree of personal and professional integrity in all that you do? And, extremely important in today's job market, are you able to work well in a "team" environment?

All of these soft skills are highly prized in most organizations today. There are exceptions, of course, but you probably wouldn't want to work for any company that didn't prize such skills. If you, as a job seeker, come across as lacking, or even being somewhat deficient, in any of these soft skills, you will be *excluded* from further consideration today by most hiring managers.

CONTINUE TO 'LEAD THE WITNESS' USING YOUR HARD *AND* SOFT SKILLS

Just as you did on the "Gotcha!" questions and other elements of the face-to-face interview, continue to **"lead the witness,"** aka, the hiring manger or other interviewer, about both your hard *and* soft skills. Weave into every comment you make or answer you give during the interview evidence that you can perform the job in terms of both hard and soft skills. Based upon your earlier research about the company, continue to *sell* what you know they need and want!

You've undoubtedly seen this disclaimer before: "Past performance is no guarantee of future results." Usually, it is printed in prospectuses for various investments. Makes sense, right? Well, maybe, at least where it concerns financial investments. But it actually makes very little sense when it concerns a candidate's perceived ability to do any given job. After all, past performance is the *only* touchstone employers can realistically use as any kind of dependable gauge! You would do well to consider this fact when interviewing for positions.

Let me give you an example of how important this issue can become for a job candidate.

I was interviewing a candidate for one of my client companies. He had an impressive résumé and had increased sales $2 million over the past three years. I asked him the behavioral interview question, "Tell me how you did that?" His response was, "Skip, just plain dumb luck. I happened to call on that client one day and he said, 'We are unhappy with our current supplier. Would you be interested in writing a proposal?' I wrote the proposal and got the business."

Now, that is NOT something that either the candidate or I could sell to the client. How *should* he have answered the question? A properly phrased answer that would **"lead the witness"** and demonstrate that he **could do the job** would be something like this (and we crafted this message after painstakingly dissecting the job seeker's sales process):

"This sales situation demonstrates the power of an organized, consistent approach to prospecting. It is critically important to stay on top of current customers, but it is equally important to continually prospect.

"I have identified all of the potential buyers of my product within my geography and I call on them on a regular basis. With some, you have to make many calls over time, and with others, you just happen to call on them at the right time. The key is that you are calling, so that when they have a 'pain point,' you are there.

"On this particular day, I called on this prospect and he said, 'We are unhappy with our current supplier. Would you be interested in writing a proposal?' I scheduled a time when we could review the key issues that were important to him, so that I would ensure those 'hot buttons' and 'pain points' were integral parts of my proposal. Over the next six months, I organized a sales campaign, making sure I got in front of every decision-maker, so that I could understand everyone's needs. We closed the sale, which has brought in $2 million over the last three years at a 30% margin."

A lot different answer from just "plain dumb luck," wouldn't you say? Now, we had something to "sell" to the client! Something very tangible and very good. In fact, the second answer is *exactly* what had happened to allow this candidate to cultivate the prospect. He just had not thought it through, nor did he understand the critical nature of communicating it properly in an interview.

As the great motivational speaker and author Zig Ziglar advises, "Be a meaningful specific, not a wandering generality." Based upon the first answer, the salesperson is a "wandering generality," cruising around the territory *hoping* to find some new business. Is that the type of person a hiring manager would want on his or her team? Of course not!

In the second answer, the salesperson demonstrates, through telling a story, that he is a "meaningful specific." He shows the hiring manager that he can do the job by illustrating the steps a good salesperson would follow in any sales campaign: Being organized, planning well, prospecting, asking good questions, developing relationships and, even more importantly, showing that he can make 'em money! Past performance is indeed an indicator of future results where this candidate is concerned. He demonstrates unmistakably that he can deliver and he is able to sell his prospective new employer on the fact that his performance can certainly be replicated.

The second answer proves to the hiring manager that he can *do the job*, while the first answer merely shows that he can "roll the dice" and occasionally come up a winner.

Additionally, the comparison between the candidate's first answer and the second answer vividly illustrates several of the "secrets" we have been studying:

> - The impact of stories to paint a picture.
> - The value of being well rehearsed versus "winging it."
> - The power of a coach.
> - The use of "power words."
> - Crafting the message to "lead the witness" and proving that you can do the job.
> - Clearly and effectively demonstrating the ability to make the company money, save them money, or both.

So whether you are an engineer, a computer programmer, a flight attendant, a reporter, a travel agent, a power plant operator, et al., you must prove that you can do the job by crafting powerful stories that illustrate that (1.) you know and have the skills required to do the job; and (2.) that you have actually performed the skills required to do the job, and performed them well.

OK, YOU CAN DO THE JOB, BUT DO YOU *WANT* TO DO IT?

Just proving to the hiring manager that you can *do* the job, that you have both the hard *and* soft skills required of the position, is very important, of course. But there still is more the hiring manager will want to learn from you. He or she will want to know if you actually *want* to do the job.

There are a variety of methods hiring managers use to elicit an answer to this question. A typical approach might go like this:

"Where do you see yourself in five years?"

While at first glance this might seem like a question upon which you can comment on your dreams, goals and long-term desires, it actually is nothing of the sort. In today's economic climate, organizations continue to be "flattened," i.e., there are fewer and fewer layers of management at all levels. That means that "upward mobility," as we once knew it, has become severely limited. So, how you answer this question is really quite important today. Let me give you an example of how a certain kind of answer, even though it was meant to demonstrate initiative and ambition, actually backfired on a candidate I was representing.

Several years ago, when a chemist I was presenting to a client company was asked the "Where do you see yourself in five years?" question, here is how he answered:

"I would like to be able to get into the company, learn this role and prove myself. Within a couple of years I would like to become an R&D team leader, and then move into the role of lab manager."

Now, one might expect the lab manager, with whom the candidate interviewed, to be quite impressed with the candidate's ambition and initiative. In fact, the feedback I got from the lab manager was anything but positive.

"Skip, this candidate's focus in on getting *my* job," the lab manager told me. **"It's *not* on developing new products for the company. I need someone who has a passion for new product development, not someone who will be gunning for my job the next five years."**

Was the lab manager a little too "insecure" himself? Perhaps, but that's hardly the point. After all, he was the one doing the hiring, and the answer the chemist candidate gave him to the "five year" question made him *instantly* see "the shadows on the wall"!

Where did this candidate go wrong? He failed to answer the question the hiring manager *really* was asking, even if the hiring manager himself may not even have been aware of it. That question? Do you *want* to do *this* job? Or, more precisely, do you *want* to do *this* job *five years down the road*?

This proved to be such a valuable lesson for both the chemist job seeker *and* me that I have since incorporated it into my coaching and list as one of the "headhunter" hiring secrets regarding the rules that the companies play by. So, when my next candidate, also a chemist, was asked the same question, by the same lab manager, she responded this way:

> "Over the next five years, I want to become known as the person who can develop new, novel surfactant technology that makes the company money. I see myself hitting the ground learning the processes and procedures that you follow, understanding the mission of the group and how it aligns with the company goals, then immersing myself in new product development, where I can apply my creativity and help the company make products that customers want so we all make money. I would love to be able to help write some technical papers, help patent some products and do anything possible to make this lab team world-renowned in what we do."

Not surprisingly, she got the job, a $95,000-a-year Research and Development chemist position, although she and the first candidate were equally qualified, in terms of their ability to "do the job." The second candidate "led the witness" in terms of proving she "*wanted* to do the job."

YOU *CAN* DO THE JOB, YOU *WANT* TO DO THE JOB, BUT *WILL* YOU DO THE JOB?

Now that you've convinced the hiring manager that you *can* do the job, and that you *want* to do the job, he or she will want to learn one additional thing: *Will* you do the job?

There are a number of ways hiring managers can ask the appropriate question(s) to learn this information, but typically, here is how the question will be phrased:

> "Tell me about a job in your career that you have liked the best."

As in the previous examples, you should begin to answer this question by telling a story, or relating an appropriate anecdote, about a position similar to the one you're applying for that you found particularly exciting and enriching. Let's say, for example, that the job you're currently applying for is that of a paint chemist. Here is how you might answer this question:

> "When I first started working for my present employer three years ago, one of the first projects I worked on was the development of a new, improved type of cement paint. As you probably know, many paints used on concrete don't perform all that well. We worked long, hard hours—even many weekends—but in the end my team developed a concrete paint that our retailers couldn't keep on their shelves. Let me tell you, that was a very exciting project, and I learned so much from it. Plus, the company had a new product that increased overall income from the paints division by ten percent the first year!"

Notice how this answer clearly communicates the joy the chemist took in the project and how the results of the project increased income 10% (made 'em money). Additionally, the concept of "team" was woven into the story. Now, here is where the "will you do the job" part comes in. Note the phrases "long, hard hours" and "even many weekends." This phraseology clearly demonstrates that one is "willing to do the job."

He is "leading the witness" in regard to proving he "*will* do the job."

So far, so good. The hiring manager may follow up with a question such as this, in order to further gauge your commitment to doing the job for which you are being considered:

> "Tell me about a time when you were working on a project that started to run behind schedule, and what you did about it?"

What the hiring manager is attempting to get at here is, again, what kind of a "work ethic" you have. Will you do the job? Can you rise to the occasion when needed? Are you willing to go the "extra mile" by working nights, weekends, maybe even putting off your vacation?

Even though you have already addressed the "work ethic" issue, at least in part, with your previous answer, you might amplify your answer in this way:

> "My job is always very important to me. I know my team and the company depend on me and I don't want to let them down. So, whatever it takes in time and extra effort to get the job done, and done right, as well as on time, is what I am committed to do."

Let me provide a couple of additional real examples from candidate-hiring manager interactions. The candidate was interviewing for a technical sales position. The product was sold to industrial facilities and technical service was part of the sale. Since most industrial plants run 24/7 there is a chance that, one or two times a year, you might get a call from a customer at night or on the weekends.

A good way to answer the 'How well do you work under pressure?' question is to relate a story or anecdote about how well you previously handled a stressful career situation.

This particular candidate interviewing for the job was asked the following question:

"If you were to get a call from one of your clients at 8 at night, what would you do?"

The candidate's answer was to prove less than thrilling to the hiring manager. It was:

"I would call them back at 7 tomorrow morning."

By now you surely know that this was an incredibly self-defeating answer. Still, somehow containing his shock and surprise at the candidate's answer, the hiring manager continued to probe. He asked the candidate:

"Why would you do that?"

As if the candidate hadn't already dug a deep enough hole for himself, he chose to add insult to injury with his answer to this question!

"I turn my cell phone off at 7 every night and I don't turn it back on until 7 the next morning."

I'm sure that you won't be surprised that the candidate was immediately rejected from further consideration. At that point the hiring manager had little doubt in his mind that the candidate would *not* do the job, or at least not do it in the manner that would be expected.

Yet another question hiring managers may ask concerns how you would perform in the job if you were under pressure. The question is usually phrased something like this:

"How well do you work under pressure?"

But do NOT fall into the trap of giving the simplified answer of, "Yes, I am able to work well under pressure." The well-coached candidate who knows the *"real rules of the game,"* along with our "headhunter" hiring secrets, will take the opportunity to relate an appropriate anecdote, or tell a brief story, about how they have handled pressure in the past, ideally in a position similar to the one they are currently seeking. In other words, "lead the witness."

Here is how you might answer the question using the concepts we have studied:

"Though we all would prefer not to have to work under pressure, there are many times when frankly, we just have to. A customer demands something, a product is delayed, and we now have to make up the time. Or, sometimes, there are so many priorities that we just find ourselves under a looming deadline. When that happens, I seem to actually be able to perform at even a higher level of intensity. The adrenaline kicks in, ideas start flowing more freely, and even though there is pressure, my performance seems to actually go to the next level."

An astute interviewer would perhaps follow up with this additional question:

"How so? Give me an example or two."

This is your opportunity to focus on your strengths. Amplify the answer you've just given by expanding on some of your *specific* strengths and give illustrations regarding how you have *applied* these strengths for the benefit of the company, citing *specific* results. But don't just focus on your *hard* skills. Mention some of the pertinent *soft* skills you have that served you (and the company) well when the "heat" was on. For example, you might mention how important it is to you to be able to deliver on your promises, always do whatever is necessary to support the entire team and make sure the job gets done, right and on time.

A skilled interviewer would have asked the question this way: "Tell me about a time when you had to work under pressure." By anticipating these types of questions and having stories prepared, you will be ready no matter how they ask the question.

271

Another question designed to evaluate how likely you are to actually *do* the job is the following:

"Why did you make the move from Company A to Company B?"

Obviously, what the hiring manager is getting at with this question is to determine if you will "up and leave" if the going gets rough. He or she must— and will!—consider the time and money the company will spend to get you "up to speed" in the position the company is trying to fill. Is there a possibility the time and money could be wasted if you are the candidate hired? Don't cast "shadows on the wall" with your answer. Be truthful, of course, but emphasize the *positive* in your answer and assiduously avoid even the hint of the *negative*. Here is a good way to respond to this question:

"I loved my job at Company A, I really did. But when I was offered a tremendous opportunity at Company B to advance my career and enhance my skill set, I didn't see how I could turn it down. I even visited with my boss at Company A to discuss the move. That's how conflicted I was at the time. She strongly encouraged me to 'go for it.' I will be forever grateful for her advice and encouragement."

The hiring manager is also looking for evidence of a logical thought pattern on your part with this question. Since career moves tend to be serious considerations, he or she wants to make sure you weren't motivated to move by emotion, or because of difficulty getting along with your boss or co-workers, or just because another company offered you more money.

HANDLING 'TOUCHY-FEELY' QUESTIONS

The types of questions just covered hardly represent an exhaustive list of all the questions you *might* be asked during a face-to-face interview. Numerous books have been written on interviewing, and many provide you with long lists of possible interview questions. But very few of them will tell you to "be aware of the 'shadows on the wall' syndrome." Or, that you need to **"lead the witness"** through stories, in order to demonstrate that . . .

> ➤ You *can* do the job.
> ➤ You *want* to do the job.
> ➤ You *will* do the job.
> ➤ You are a *cultural fit*.

Armed with this information, you can master any interview question!

Now, let's look at some additional questions.

Many interviewers seem to revel in asking "Barbara Walters" (the famous TV interviewer) type questions, in order to throw candidates off, and then to see how well they can think on their feet. While you should take such questions seriously—you can't assume, for example, that the person asking the questions is anything other than serious—you can also have a little fun with them, as long as your answers aren't outrageous in any sense. And, keep in mind the type of position you're applying for when you answer such questions. (In the table below, assume you're applying for a sales position.)

Question	Possible Answers
If you were a color, what color would you be?	**Black** – "I always want to make sure I stay "in the black" with my sales efforts, i.e., make money!" - Or - **Blue** – "Blue is a calming color and that is what I am able to do in a crisis situation with a client, help bring calmness and clear thinking into the mix."
If you were a car, what car would you be?	**A Corvette** – "I want to be able to get to as many prospects as I can, in the fastest, most efficient way." - Or - **A Prius** – "A Prius uses advanced technology to get the most miles out of a gallon of fuel as possible and that describes me as a salesperson. I want to make sure my customers get the most value out of the technology we bring them."
If you were an animal, what animal would you be?	**A Tiger** – "A tiger is known as a tenacious, skilled hunter. That's the approach I take in seeking out new business."

Of course, there are many ways in which you could answer these kinds of questions, and the specific manner in which you actually do answer them depends in large part, as I just pointed out above, on the specific position for which you are applying. The "right" answer to such "off the wall" questions is in crafting an answer that will "lead the witness." An answer that will address one or more of the four questions: Can you do the job? Do you want to do the job? Will you do the job? Are you a cultural fit?

ARE YOU A CULTURAL FIT FOR OUR COMPANY (AND FOR ME)?

Once the interviewer has exhausted questions designed to determine your suitability and desire for doing the job, chances are, they will then turn to questions about their own company, and what you know (or *don't* know) about it. If you've done your homework and research you should be able to make a very good impression when asked, "What do you know about our company?" You should be able, for example, to intelligently discuss the company's relative position within its industry ("your company is number one in 'category X' in the 'Z' industry"), its latest earnings, anything recently in the news that reflects favorably upon the company, etc.

Make sure you read recent press releases, the annual report and the CEO's "Letter to the Shareholders." In doing so, you will learn the mission, vision and values of the company. As you answer the interviewer's questions and "lead the witness," weave verbiage into your answers that aligns itself with what you have learned about the company.

If you cannot provide this kind of information in your answer, you will be perceived as not having done even the basic research about the company, and you will therefore be quickly *excluded* from further consideration. So, advice to the wise: Do your homework and do it well, in preparation for *any* personal communication with the company, e. g., telephone, email or face-to-face, because you must demonstrate that you are a cultural fit at all times.

ANTICIPATE 'PERSONALITY,' 'CONFLICT HANDLING' QUESTIONS

In an attempt to get a better handle on your particular personality type (and your cultural fit), you should anticipate that the hiring manager probably will ask you a question like this:

> "Would you describe yourself as a 'risk taker,' or do you usually 'play it safe'?"

To be sure, this is a *very* "loaded" question! Before answering, you must first determine how you "read" both the hiring manager and the company he or she represents. Are "risk takers" valued or shunned? Are employees who are considered to always "play it safe" scorned for being "drones"? Unfortunately, without knowing more—a lot more!—about both the hiring manager and the company, you may not be able to quickly make such an inference. So what to do? How to answer this question? My recommendation: Take the "middle" ground, by giving an answer along these lines:

> "In this economic environment, one has to do both simultaneously. If you play it too safe, you might find yourself falling behind your competition. By the same token, if you take foolish risks, you may find yourself losing money or making an unwise decision. So, I usually do a 'cost-benefit analysis', in order to be able to take *calculated* risks, risks where we have analyzed the possible outcomes, both positively and negatively, and feel the benefits outweigh the costs."

Then, the hiring manager may follow up that "killer" question with one that's equally challenging to your ability to think on your feet:

> "What do you do if you have a conflict with a co-worker?"

Here is a good answer to such a question:

> "Unfortunately, in life there is conflict, and that includes in the workplace. What you must not do is become offended. Everyone has a right to his or her own opinion. You respect the opinions of your co-worker, ask questions and work to iron out any differences.

> "If it is affecting the project or the goals of the company and we can't work it out, then I will take it to a trusted colleague to see if she can offer some helpful advice. It that fails, then it may be time to have a confidential conversation with my boss. I only will do that if indeed it is having a negative impact on the company's performance.

> "If it seems to be more between the other individual and me, then I respect her opinion and work to ensure that I do what I am supposed to do. We always have the right to agree to disagree."

In addition to your being a "cultural fit" for the company, each person that you interview with will consciously (or subconsciously) be evaluating your "cultural fit" with regard to himself/herself. Does she feel that you will get along with her and that she will get along with you? The next chapter, **"Pacing and Mirroring"** addresses this in depth.

WHAT IF YOU ARE UNEMPLOYED?

Ideally, being currently employed while investigating other career opportunities puts you in a stronger position than if you currently are unemployed. Still, we all know that, in the current job market particularly, more and more candidates who are seeking these opportunities are no longer employed. That means you should certainly anticipate questions dealing with the reason(s) you are currently without a job.

Hiring managers can be expected to ask you how long you have been unemployed. This will help the manager assess how "viable" a candidate you might be. That is, if you've only been without a job for, say, a month, that tells the manager one thing. If, on the other hand, you haven't been employed for the last year, that tells him or her quite another thing. So, how should you answer the **"How long have you been unemployed?"** question? Quite simply, state the facts because you're not going to be able to hide them, or at least not for long.

Without question, you definitely have to be honest in your answer. There simply is no way around this issue. After all, your dates of employment are on your résumé, and you can be assured that, if you become a serious candidate, those dates will be verified, and any "gaps" will be revealed. The "good" news in this economy, if it can be called that, is that being out of work more than six months is no longer the huge "red flag" it used to be. In today's job market, it is a "yellow flag."

Usually, the hiring manager will broaden the "probe" by turning to another sensitive—and *fully* "loaded"—question:

"How many interviews have you had since you started your job search?"

This one is tricky. If none, you have to say "none." But add to that, "I am looking for the right opportunity where my background and skill set will bring value to the company." If your answer is in the range of one to four interviews, then say the exact number and add, "What is important is finding the right opportunity in which my background and skill set can bring value to the company." And, if your answer is "more than four," just say, "several" and then use the same phraseology. You certainly don't want to say something like, "Ten"! The "shadows on the wall" will immediately appear for the hiring manager and you will immediately be out of the running! He will think to himself, *"There must be **something** wrong with this candidate. He has had ten shots at jobs and walked away empty handed each and every time."*

Let's assume you answered with "four" interviews. Alarms may be going off in the hiring manager's head, but he or she is still willing to give you the benefit of the doubt. A next question is likely to be:

"Are you currently entertaining any offers?"

While this may seem a question designed to empathize with your job search plight, it's actually nothing of the sort. The hiring manager is still trying to ignore those fleeting "shadows on the wall" that are starting to appear.

The best way to answer this question is, again, simply to tell the truth. Try this approach:

"I have not received any firm offers at this time, although I am in the interview process with another company. However, based upon what I have learned here today, I am very excited about your company and this position, *which clearly would be my first choice*."

Until you sign the offer from *any* company, it is *not* "firm." If you do have a genuine offer in hand from another company that you are considering, do

NOT say that! If you do, you will immediately be *excluded* from further consideration. You just handed the hiring manager the perfect excuse he or she was looking for to move on to the next candidate without feeling any remorse whatsoever.

And remember, you can't turn down an offer you don't have, so you are being truthful in saying "this position would be my first choice," because until you sign and return an offer and clear the contingencies (discussed in Phase Four), it has every potential of truly being your first choice.

The bottom line here: The more effective you are at "leading the witness" throughout the interview process, the easier it is to position yourself as a TOP candidate even if you are unemployed.

'MIRRORING' AND 'PACING'

Whether we're talking about the telephone interview or the much more important face-to-face interview, or virtually any type of communication, you must always, always, always project a very positive attitude and a high degree of enthusiasm for the position you are seeking, as well as for the company offering the opportunity. "Do you want the job?" is communicated equally by *what* you say and by the *way* you *say* it! Your tone of voice, the inflection of your voice, your facial and hand gestures, your overall body language—all of these things clearly demonstrate your enthusiasm, or general lack thereof. Always keep this in mind.

I've known of candidates who sometimes *reluctantly* went to job interviews. They claimed they weren't interested and decided to go just because they said they wanted the "practice"! Then, after meeting with three or four people from the company, and hearing more about the opportunity and the company offering it, they suddenly began to get excited! Too late, I'm afraid. By projecting nonchalance and a general lack of enthusiasm at the beginning of the interview, they forfeited any opportunity they might have had to become a top candidate for the position.

All along the way, each interviewer is consciously or subconsciously evaluating whether or not you and he/she will get along with each other. This section provides you the techniques for strengthening your ability to demonstrate that you are a **'cultural fit.'**

IMPORTANCE OF INFLECTION AND WORD EMPHASIS

Although English is not normally regarded as a "tonal" language, i.e., one in which the tonal range can change the meaning of spoken expressions, the emphasis placed on certain words in a *spoken* sentence can indeed completely change the meaning. Let's take a look at an example of how that works.

This innocent-looking, very short sentence could have *seven* different meanings, some intended, some unintended, depending upon which word the emphasis is placed upon.

"I think she has a good résumé."

- If the emphasis is placed on "I," as in "*I* think she has a good résumé," it implies that I really don't care if anyone else thinks she does or not.

- By placing the emphasis on the word "think," I am implying that I merely *think* she has a good résumé, but I could be wrong.

- If I place the emphasis on "she," I am suggesting that, while others' résumés might not quite be adequate, *hers* is good.

- If "has" is the word emphasized in the sentence, I am suggesting that, even though we haven't seen it, she indeed does *have* a good résumé.

- If "a" is the word emphasized, I am essentially saying that, even though she may have a lot of résumés that *aren't* good, she at least has *one* résumé that is good.

- If "good" is the word emphasized, then her résumé is good, particularly compared to other résumés.

- And, finally, if I place the emphasis on the word "résumé," I am suggesting that, whatever her other deficiencies may be, she at least has a good *résumé*.

The point of all of this, of course, is to show you that *how* you say something, the emphasis you place on your spoken words, can easily overshadow what you *meant* to say. So choose—and use!—your words carefully to avoid misunderstandings, or worse, leave an impression that you certainly never intended during various communications with prospective employers.

PRACTICE 'MIRRORING' AND 'PACING'

In sales there is this saying: "People buy from people they like." The same thing is true when it comes to the hiring process: "People *hire* people they like." But there is even more to it than that: "People *hire* people they like—*and* people who are *most like themselves*."

Let's say the job search is now down to just two people, you and one other candidate. Obviously, they like *both* you and the other candidate or neither one of you would have made it this far. So, now will it come down to which one of the two of you they like the *most*? No, it will come down to which one of the two of you they like the most *and* the one who is *most like themselves* (the cultural fit). You can improve the odds that you will be the person ultimately selected by practicing what is known as "mirroring" and "pacing."

Mirroring is a subtle technique in sales that is nonetheless very powerful. If you are speaking to someone who is soft spoken, tone it down. If you are speaking with someone who is a fast talker, speed it up. If they cross their legs, then very subtly cross *your* legs. If they lean back, you lean back. This takes some time to perfect and it must be practiced, but it's easier to do if you have prepared your stories and have followed the training in this book up to this point.

Mirroring helps a decision-maker feel that she can trust you. Another word for this technique is "subliminal" selling. Try it with family and friends. If you master it, you will find that you can get others to follow you. You mirror them, they feel good in your presence, then you subtly take the lead and subconsciously they will follow you.

How important is the concept of mirroring? It can be the difference between getting hired or getting excluded. Consider a comment we recently received from a hiring manager about one of the candidates our firm presented:

> "He was just too assertive for our culture. I don't see him fitting in here at all."

Had this candidate practiced mirroring, he would have lowered his voice, slowed his speaking pace and used body language that reflected that of the hiring manager. Chances are, the story of his candidacy would have ended on a far more positive note.

Finally, do your research on each individual person you will be interviewing with. Get an agenda up front. Know who is on the agenda. Google them! See if the are on ZoomInfo! See if you can locate them on LinkedIn. By knowing as much about the company, each person you interview with and implementing voice inflection, pacing and mirroring, you will effectively "lead the witness" in terms of answering the question, "Are you a cultural fit?"

BE PREPARED FOR DIFFERENT TYPES OF FACE-TO-FACE INTERVIEWS

Thus far, we have concentrated on the face-to-face interview that is conducted solely by the hiring manager or other professional interviewers from the company. Often, though certainly not always, the first face-to-face interview will be limited to one of these professionals. After all, the initial interviewer certainly doesn't want to take up the time of numerous other people within the company to interview each and every candidate. Only those candidates who survive the initial face-to-face interview usually are presented to, or interviewed by, other company officials, say, the hiring manager's boss, for example.

As the pool of candidates is reduced to just a few candidates remaining in consideration, subsequent face-to-face interviews most likely will consist of the candidates meeting with several company representatives, either at the same time or serially. In this section, we'll take a look at these kinds of interviews, and examine how you can adequately prepare not to be *excluded* at this late stage of the game.

SERIAL INTERVIEWS AT THE COMPANY'S LOCATION

These kinds of interviews usually involve your meeting with half a dozen or so of the company's representatives onsite. Normally, this kind of interview arrangement involves the hiring manager, usually the person who conducted your first face-to-face interview, taking you around to various people within the organization to introduce you to them. (It also gives the hiring manager a chance to "shop" you to the rest of his staff, in order to get their feedback about you following your visit.)

If at all possible—and I realize it won't always be—try to learn the names and titles of all those with whom you are scheduled to meet. Oftentimes, the hiring manager will send you an agenda prior to your actually meeting with the company representatives, and usually the names and titles of those persons will be mentioned in the agenda. If you haven't been sent one, ASK! That at least gives you a place to start. Follow the same procedures mentioned in previous sections to learn something about these people. As previously mentioned, try to find their profiles on LinkedIn and ZoomInfo. Google them. Get any and all information you can in the time you have because forewarned is forearmed!

Be sure to take enough résumés and networking business cards with you to the site. Ideally, you have assembled the "smile file" we discussed earlier and will be taking that. (And, don't forget to *get* all the business cards you can from the people you'll be meeting with.) Chances are, many of the people you'll be meeting with will *not* have seen your résumé and may not even know your name.

You should have answered virtually every question imaginable when you first visited with the hiring manager, but be prepared to answer them again—numerous times, as you meet with these half dozen or so people. Use the same "selling" points and emphasize the same strengths and accomplishments with each of the people you meet, no matter how boring and repetitious it may become for you. *You* know you've already been asked the same questions by the last three people you visited with, but the person you're next visiting with *won't* know that.

CONTINUE TO 'LEAD THE WITNESS'

Just as is usually the case with hiring managers, the people with whom you'll be meeting will normally *not* be expert interviewers, and most will not even be sure where or how to begin an interview with you (or anyone else, for that matter), so you've got to give them a little "help," you've got to continue to "lead the witness." Let's assume that the person you're meeting with starts off with this comment:

> "Kim, I was just put on the interview agenda and, to be honest about it, I haven't had time to even review your résumé. Let me take just a moment to look it over and then we'll talk, OK?"

You'll then have a choice: Either sit silently and wait (for what will seem like an eternity, under the circumstances) for the person to read completely through your résumé, or get him (and you!) "off the hook" with a comment like this:

> "Jim, I understand. If it would be more convenient for you, I can start by just telling you a little about myself. That way, you can go over my résumé at your leisure later. Would that be helpful?" (Notice you are using the sales skill of "asking questions"! Also, If they agree, you "tell them about yourself" using the structure we outlined earlier.)

One more thing: If you were unable to learn anything in your research about the person interviewing you, you could ask the following question:

> "Jim, I am certainly excited about the possibilities of working for your company. If you would be so kind as to share with me your

role, then I may be able to better share with you what I can do that aligns itself with supporting your role or department."

Not only will a statement like this allow you to begin building rapport with the person interviewing you, it will also provide you with the type of information you need to know about the person. He or she will also now start talking and you will be able to see/hear his or her style. That way you can begin to effectively "mirror" and pace yourself.

THE GROUP INTERVIEW

This kind of interview typically involves your meeting with six to eight (or more) company representatives in a conference room. There are various reasons why a company arranges a candidate meeting of this type. Perhaps it's just as simple as being the most convenient, least time-consuming method for a number of people to interview you. Quite often, however, it's also intended to see if you can be intimidated. If, in the role you're being considered for, you will be required to meet with groups of customers, or conduct meetings with clients, the company is testing you to see how well you handle yourself in group settings.

Whatever you do in this situation, make sure you don't appear "fidgety" or otherwise ill-at-ease. Work the room. Take charge when appropriate. Maintain eye contact when answering a person's question. Use your notebook to periodically jot notes, but as I previously advised, don't concentrate your entire focus on your notes! Ask for business cards from everyone present at the meeting, but don't put them all in one stack. Arrange them on the table in front of you according to how each person is seated around the table. That way, you will be better able to connect names with faces, as well as being able to address people by the word they most love to hear—their own name!

While it can be overdone, don't hesitate to repeat questions you're asked. For example, you might say something such as this, "Jim, let me review. What you are asking is . . . , correct?" Or, "To make sure I answer your question properly, what I heard was. . . ." And then on another question, you might want to ask the questioner, "Jim, did that properly answer your question?" These conversation tactics will make it quite apparent that you're *paying attention*!

THE LUNCH OR DINNER INTERVIEW

A lot of candidates make the mistake of assuming that any kind of a "meal" meeting is where you will be expected to, well, eat. Wrong! The purpose of this kind of meeting is for you to be *interviewed*, plain and simple. You can always eat later. And whatever you do, don't order something "messy" to eat, such as spaghetti (remember the "spaghetti-eating" candidate mentioned earlier), ribs, or a juicy hamburger where the juices will be running down your chin! Instead, order something "clean" and easy-to-eat. Take small bites, too, so that you won't have your mouth stuffed with food when (you'll notice I didn't say "if") you are asked a question.

A major danger zone during any kind of meal meeting is alcohol. If the meeting is at lunchtime, *never* order an alcoholic beverage—even if the interviewer does. If it's a dinner meeting, take your cue from the interviewer. If he or she orders a beer, you probably would be safe also ordering *one*, provided you even drink alcoholic beverages, that is. In no case, however, should you order "hard" liquor, even if the interviewer does. And, if you do order an alcoholic beverage, *make it just one*—regardless of how many drinks the interviewer might order. If the position for which you are applying involves driving a motor vehicle (company car, etc.), **do not order even a single drink**. This is a trap!

It's well known that alcohol can easily loosen one's tongue. Don't fall into this unnecessary trap. Don't let your guard down. Be friendly, but just remember that the interviewer is *not* your friend, so be careful what you say, as well as how you say it!

THE INTERROGATION – 'GOOD COP – BAD COP'

Sometimes interviews can turn downright ugly and confrontational, but that's hardly an accident. Actually, it's a type of "game" some employers choose to play, in order to see how you will react/respond under pressure. You may feel as though you're being *interrogated*, rather than being interviewed. And you know what? Many times that will be *precisely* what is happening and what was intended!

Oftentimes the interviewers even employ one of the classic interrogation techniques used by police agencies, the "good cop—bad cop" technique. Here is how it works:

One interviewer asks a weird, "off the wall"—or even an *illegal*—question (the "bad cop"). "I'm sorry," the other interviewer quickly adds. "He shouldn't have asked you that. You don't have to answer that question (the "good cop")." Even though most of us are familiar with the "good cop–bad cop" set up, we can still fall for it anyway! You will quickly find yourself saying something along the lines, "That is OK. I am happy to answer it." Don't you fall for it, though.

Another interrogation technique is, after the interviewers have peppered you with questions, they abruptly tell you the interview is over. Unless you are a very unusual candidate, you quite likely will leave the office totally "shell-shocked." Again, the interviewers are merely testing you to see how you handle stress, the unexpected. Not fun, and very few companies practice such interview techniques today, but it's still something you might want to be on the alert for and be prepared to handle.

HUMAN RESOURCES VERSUS HIRING MANAGER INTERVIEWS

Human Resources interviews are for totally different reasons from the hiring manager interviews. Whereas ALL of the other interviewers want to know if you *can* do the job, *want* to do the job, *will* do the job, and are a cultural fit, HR professionals will evaluate you and provide their feedback and impressions to the other team members on you in the following areas:

- Authenticity (Is your résumé truthful?).
- Stability (Reason for each career move/job change).
- Language fluency.
- Relevancy of your experience as it relates to the job.
- Your potential fit within the company culture.
- Salary expectations.
- Family background.

HR will generally ask the more traditional kinds of questions, such as, "Why did you decide to go to the University of (fill in the blank)?" "Walk me through each of your job changes." "Why are you interested in our company?" "What do you know about our company?" "What is your current salary?" or "What are your salary expectations?"

Notice the trend. Many of these areas deal with "safety." Are you a *safe* choice or do you pose a *risk?* Implement the secrets we have discussed and you will be able to exit the HR interview "safely," i.e., not be excluded.

How does HR get you to let your guard down? Simple!

At some point in the interview they often turn to telling you about various company benefits, e.g., perks, vacation, medical insurance plans and so forth. Despite this, however, this is NOT the time for *you* to start asking questions about such things! Why? Because if you ask too many questions the old "shadows" will start creeping onto the HR professional's office wall. For example, if you start asking too many questions about the dental plan, the HR professional will begin to think, "Maybe this person has some serious dental problems that could end up costing the company a LOT of money," and suddenly another candidate is a lot more attractive in their eyes.

Then you may get the grand tour. "You" will work in this office. These are "your" co-workers, this is where "you" will be able to hold meetings, this is "your" break room, etc. Don't be fooled by this approach. Again, the point is to make you feel relaxed and comfortable, so that you will let your guard down and start telling them things you shouldn't tell them. Many people mistake the "tour" to mean "they are about to make me an offer!" It does *not* mean that at all! The appropriate, safest, response for you is to tell the HR professional that you are very impressed with the company and excited about the opportunity. That's it!

THE TECHNICAL INTERVIEW

In this arrangement you are put together with someone from IT, R&D or engineering, let's say. These people may or may not have a personality. They may or may not know how to interview. In all honesty, they usually don't even care about knowing the "correct" way to conduct a candidate interview. The one thing they are seeking to learn is how well you know any technical material and/or techniques that may be required by the position for which you are applying. In other words, do you have the *technical* skills and knowledge required to do the job?

If you have misrepresented your skills and/or your background in any way, this is where you will be exposed. However, sometimes I have had candidates get caught in these types of interviews where the questions asked are so far out of line, no one could "pass" the interview. You tell the interviewer what you can, what you are familiar with and comment about the fact that you love to learn and take your skills and knowledge to the next level. If you are thrown an occasional "curve," don't try and bluff. Just say, "I'll have to research that and get back with you." Then, make sure you do, because sometimes this is a test and those who do *not* get back are the ones excluded! Those who *do* get back with the "technical interviewer" tend to move forward.

THE PRESIDENT/CEO INTERVIEW

If you get to an interview with the President or Chief Executive Officer of the company you can pretty much assume you're nearly at the "goal line." Do not, however, expect this interview to last very long or be very detailed. This top executive has subordinates upon whom he or she relies to "screen" virtually all the company's job candidates, with the sole exception of the very top executive positions. However, if the CEO or President is on the agenda to meet with you and suddenly he or she becomes "unavailable," that is generally not a good sign. Nine times out of ten it means you were *excluded* from further consideration before getting to this level for an interview.

However, some times there are legitimate reasons why the President/CEO cancelled out on his or her interview with you at the last moment. In my experience, that's the case about 10% of the time. So, be sure to send your

"Thank You" notes after you leave the company—just in case you were actually told the truth about the President/CEO's sudden "unavailability."

In all of your follow-up communications, be sure to emphasize how excited you are about the company and the position, as well as stress the value you can bring to both of them.

If you do indeed meet with the President/CEO, does that mean you are going to get an offer? Maybe, maybe not. What it does mean is that you impressed all of his or her subordinates enough that they wanted you to pass the "sniff" test with the head of the company.

THE POWER OF 'POWER WORDS, PHRASES'

By now you know how very important it is to say the right *things* during interviews, as well as to make sure you say them in the right *ways*. By inference, you probably have been able to pick up quite a few examples of how and when to use the so-called "power words," e.g., in your résumé, when presenting your skills and accomplishments, communicating the benefits you can bring to an employer, etc. I believe these power words are so very important in the job search that I have provided a list of the *most* powerful in the table below. I would strongly advise you to become familiar with such words and phrases and weave them into virtually every communication, written and verbal, during your entire job search.

SUGGESTED POWER WORDS & PHRASES

Magnetize
Rarity
Horsepower
Centrifuge
Distill
Infrequently
Turbo-Charged
Delivered
All-Star
Benchmarked
Unmatched
Unrivaled
Beyond
Have you ever stayed awaked at night thinking about . . .
Every once in awhile you come across . . .
Record-breaking
Fueled by
Creates
Instrumental in . . .
Fill needs not quotas, which has enabled me to break all sales records . . .
Breakthrough
Separate from the pack . . .
Weed out

Get in the habit of using these power words and phrases when answering interview questions. Use them to paint your "word pictures," "stories" and anecdotes. Do they work? You bet they do. At my recruiting firm we use them all the time whenever we present candidates to our various client companies, so I know they work. They will work for you too!

Closing the Deal

Since finding a new job is just like any other type of sales process, *closing* "the deal" is what will separate you from most of your competitors.

The completion of the face-to-face interview is where you begin attempting to close the deal. Chances are, you won't be able to close it *on the spot*, although in rare circumstances, you may.

The way you answer the interviewer's questions as the interview winds down, as well as the questions *you* ask at that point, however, can either quickly eliminate you from further consideration or leave the door wide open to being the candidate ultimately selected for the job.

WHAT TO ASK, WHAT NOT TO ASK AS INTERVIEW ENDS

As all things must, even interviews come to an end, although admittedly, it often seems as though they never will. Sometimes the interview ends abruptly, sometimes it just cruises to a stop. Even though you probably have answered more questions in just a few hours than you've answered during the last year, questions nonetheless remain, even as the interview is coming to an end. Some of these questions will come from the interviewers, while others will come from you. Here are some final, "winding down" questions you should anticipate from the interviewers, as well as some suggested ways to answer them:

Question: "May we contact your references?"

How to Answer: By now you know that you should have your references lined up and prepped. Have a separate sheet of paper with your references on it and make it available to hand to anyone who asks this question and, of course, the answer is "yes."

Question: "When are you available to start?"

How to Answer (if currently employed): "Since I am currently employed, out of professional courtesy to my current employer, I would like to provide a two-week notice." **(IMPORTANT:** Do NOT answer this question like this: "I would like to give my employer a two-week notice. I also have three weeks of vacation saved up. So, would five weeks from now be OK?" Remember, you still don't have an offer! If you respond in this manner you won't have to worry about having it, either!)

How to Answer (if not currently employed): "Since I am not currently employed, I am available to start immediately."

Question: "If we were to make an offer to you, is there anything that would keep you from accepting it?"

How to Answer: "I am very excited about this opportunity and I think I have a lot of value to offer you. If an offer is extended, I would be honored. How do we work this out?"

IMPORTANT: Do NOT put any preconditions on *anything* at this time. If you do, you won't be offered the job. It is a lot of work for a manager to have the company put an offer together, and they want to make sure you aren't wasting their time. At the same time, this is no guarantee of an offer, so don't press. When you ask, "How do we work this out?," they will respond along the lines of, "We've all got to put our heads together and review all the information and we will get back to you."

Now, let's examine the types of questions *you* are likely to have as the interview is ending. First, we'll address the types of questions you should avoid asking at all costs, even though I know you will be sorely tempted to do so. Maybe you feel that, at this point in the game, you're really a "shoo-in" and any question would be "fair game." Don't you believe it!

QUESTIONS TO AVOID ASKING AS INTERVIEW ENDS

Any questions that can cast a "shadow on the wall" in the hiring manager's mind should be avoided at all costs!

EXAMPLES

"Is there a training program available to bring me 'up to speed' in this job?"

> **(Now the hiring manager starts to wonder if you actually *do* have the skills necessary to do the job.)**

"How often do you have to work overtime here?"

> **(Uh-oh . . . this person apparently isn't willing to work hard.)**

"Whom did you say are your biggest competitors?"

> **(Did this guy do *any* homework on the company?)**

"What is the salary range for this position?"

> **(Well, she's obviously more interested in money than in opportunity.)**

"How well does your department get along with other departments?"

> **(Does this person have a problem getting along with other people?)**

"Is 'flex time' available? How much vacation is there?"

(Wow! This person is more interested in "playing" than working!)

QUESTIONS SUPERSTARS ASK – MOVING FROM EXCLUSION TO INCLUSION

One of the rules of the hiring game is that the majority of the people hired in a down economy are those who can have an *immediate* impact, are enthusiastic and are the *safest* choice (not a risk). Questions, as illustrated on the previous page, that are short-sighted, self-centered and lacking deep interest and concern will help ensure you are quickly eliminated.

The superstars ask questions that illustrate they are thinking of the company and their value to the company, not the other way around. Next are just a few examples of the types of questions you should ask as the face-to-face interview comes to a close. Obviously, you wouldn't use all of them, but select a few that seem most appropriate to your particular situation.

This, for the first time, can be where a hiring manager begins to possibly think in terms of *inclusion* rather than *exclusion.* If you haven't cast any "shadows on the wall," have proved to the hiring manager that you *can* do the job, *want* to do the job, *will* do the job, are a cultural fit, and you built rapport, then the single biggest differentiator at this point in the process between you and the remaining candidates will be the level and quality of questions you ask. Asking better questions than your competitors forces the hiring manager to exclude them, which, by default, means you are included.

EXAMPLES

"Would you please describe a typical day and week for a person in this role?"

"What are the top two or three issues you would like for me to get involved with on 'day one'?" **or** "Is there a particular training issue or performance challenge that you would need for me to think about and tackle on 'day one'?"

"What is your vision for the team over the next one to three years, and what do you see my role being in helping you to accomplish that vision?"

"What, in particular, did the person in this position prior to me do especially well, and what do you wish they would have done differently or better?"

"What attracted you to the company, and what do you consider are its strengths and weaknesses?" **or** "I understand that you have been with the company for 11 years. That is impressive in this day and age. What are the things that you find exciting about the company and keep you and others motivated day in and day out?"

"Could you tell me a little about the people on the team that I would be interacting with on a routine basis?" **or** "What is the background of those I would supervise?" (If a manager's position.)

"Could you please describe for me your management style and how you like for your subordinates to communicate with you?"

"I understand that XYZ and ABC are two of your largest competitors. How does the company contribute to the thought leadership in the marketplace, in order to differentiate itself from these two competitors?"

"What do you consider to be the company's 'killer' application (or product or process)? What percentage of market share does it have? How do you think we could make it even better or capture more market share?"

"In your opinion, what makes this company a great place to work?"

"When you fill this position, what are the success factors six and twelve months down the road that will tell you that bringing this person onboard was the right decision?"

"What, in your opinion, separates your most successful design engineers (or another appropriate position) from the ones that haven't been as successful?"

"What do you think would be the biggest challenge for someone with my background coming into this position?"

"Based upon our conversation, I understand the team has achieved double-digit growth every year for the past four years, which is quite impressive. What do you feel are the main contributors to that success?"

'CLOSING THE DEAL' IS *YOUR* RESPONSIBILITY

You've answered all the interview questions thrown at you, and then answered yet some more as the interview was winding down. You've asked all the questions that were appropriate (and safe!) for you to ask both during and at the end of the interview (the superstar questions), and now it is time to depart.

So, you're almost there, right? The job is practically yours, correct? Well, not quite yet. Even assuming you "nailed" the face-to-face interview, like any good salesperson you now have to "close." And by the way, it is *your* responsibility to close, not the interviewer or hiring manager.

Be sure to get a business card from *everyone* you meet with during the face-to-face interview.

Now that you're literally heading out the door, since the interview has officially ended, the best approach to use is one incorporating subtlety. "Close the sale" as salespeople are taught to do, but *don't* ask for the job. **Instead, close (ask!) for the next step:**

> "Based upon all of the candidates you have interviewed so far, as well as the people who have held this position in the past, what do you see as my strongest assets and my possible weaknesses? Do you have any concerns that I need to clear up in order to be your top candidate?"

- OR -

> "Based upon our conversation so far, is there anything that would keep us from moving forward to the next step in the process?"

- OR -

"I really appreciate your time today and I am very interested in this opportunity. What can we do together to take this to the next step"?

Then, like a good salesperson quickly learns to do—shut up! There is an old saying in sales that goes like this: After you've asked for the "order," the next person to speak loses. Keep this in mind because it's true!

The typical response you can expect from the hiring manager or interviewer usually goes something like this:

"Well, we'll have to put our heads together and see where we are in the entire process before we make our final decision."

A suitable response to this "canned" response might be the following:

"Mr. hiring manager, I certainly understand. I just want you to know how very excited I am about this career opportunity. I truly believe I can bring substantial value to you and the company. Thank you for your time."

- OR -

"I appreciate your taking the time to see me today. I believe I am well qualified for the position and that I can make an immediate contribution. I am very interested and I look forward to hearing from you soon."

BUT, in some cases, the hiring manager may actually answer your question, i.e., tell you his/her concerns. This provides you with a great opportunity to address them, on the spot.

First acknowledge the concern, i.e., "roll with it" by saying, "I understand" or "I appreciate that." Then do what we have studied—ask a question. "May I address that?" After you have addressed the concern, conclude with a question, "Did that satisfactorily address your concern?" If yes, then conclude with the question, "Are there any other areas of concern that I may address for you?" If no, use one of the statements above to conclude the interview.

Hiring Manager (Jim): "Skip, I feel you are strong in areas A, B and C but I do have a concern about D."

You: "I appreciate your concern about D. May I address that, please?" (Then address the concern.) "Did that satisfactorily address your concern, Jim?"

Jim: "Yes, it did."

You: "Are there any other areas of concern that I may address for you?"

Jim: "No, that covers it. We will put our heads together and get back to you."

You: "Jim, I appreciate you and your team taking the time to see me today. I believe I am well qualified for the position and that I can make an immediate contribution. I am very interested in this position and I look forward to hearing from you soon."

After making such a closing statement, the rest remains pretty much up to the hiring manager and the company. That is not to say, however, that you've done all you can to ultimately become the successful candidate. You will still send a timely "Thank You" note, properly timed follow-up emails, etc., once leaving the company site. The point is, you will NOT be "out of the running" unless—and until—you actually receive the dreaded "We appreciate your taking the time to apply for . . . but we've decided . . ." letter from the hiring manager or company.

The secret is: Do NOT close the interview with the typical, 'Thanks for your time. I hope to hear from you' comment! Close by asking for the *next step*.

Most job seekers simply do not realize the power of closing the interview. They simply depart having only said, "Thanks for your time and I hope to hear from you." Or, "I have enjoyed our conversation. If there are any further questions, just let me know." Or, worse yet, "Good luck in your search"! (Yes, I have known some job seekers to say just this!)

THEY DON'T CALL ... THEY DON'T WRITE ... NOW WHAT?

You just had what you considered to be one of the best interviews ever . . . but now . . . silence. What happened? What should you do next, if anything?

Most important, you don't want to get discouraged. Rejection is simply part of life; it will happen. Maybe it has happened here, and maybe it hasn't. You really don't know because you haven't heard anything further from the company since you interviewed with them.

The fact of the matter is, companies simply will *not* get back to you unless they have an interest. They seldom, if ever, will let you know where you stand in the selection process, and even less often, will they ever let you know why you weren't selected for a position.

Maybe you cast a "shadow on the wall" and positioned yourself as an "unsafe" candidate. They are not going to tell you, "We eliminated you because you had spaghetti hanging out of your mouth during lunch," or "We are concerned about your comment that you have kids resistant to your moving here."

And, sometimes, there is another reason. Most companies have hidden, secret criteria that guide their hiring decisions. Maybe there is a problem in the company. Maybe they have been running behind on production due to personnel issues. Maybe they need a person who handles conflict well, and the way you answered their questions about conflict may have resulted in your being eliminated, without you ever knowing it. There could be any number of reasons, but you'll quite likely never know what they are.

No company is going to come out in a job description and say that one of the requirements is "the ability to handle conflict among production workers."

Many times you will not hear back from a company because of 'internal' issues you have no way of knowing about. Other times, you may have been *excluded* simply because you failed to heed one (or more!) of the 'secrets' discussed in this book!

Maybe the boss is really demanding, but he has connections in the company and will never be let go. Certainly, they aren't going to tell you in the job description or in any interview that you have to be able to get along with a particularly demanding boss. However, questions will be asked along those lines to see how you deal with bosses who are demanding, or with criticism or with micromanagers, etc.

If there have been layoffs and morale is down, you will not see in the posting, "Must be able to work effectively in an organization with low morale." But questions still will be asked along these lines.

And let's discuss age again. If you see a posting that says, "5+ years of experience" and you have 30, you aren't going to get the job. The "secret" is that the number of years they are looking for is close to the number cited (in this case, "5"), *not* the "+" sign. But, by saying "5+ years of experience," there is absolutely nothing illegal about the posting. Many postings will have a range of years, 10 to 12, as an example. If you are too far on either side, you won't get the job. They are telling you not only the experience level being sought, but the pay grade as well, in that subtle communication. Someone with 18 years of experience should be making 25% to 30% more than someone with 10-12 years of experience. If they are not, then the company will question ("shadow on the wall") the skill set of that particular individual.

A lot of rejection takes place in finding a job. That is why the Daily Misogi is so critical. Don't wallow in self pity. Do not become depressed or dysfunctional. Remember that the "yes" is almost always at the end of a string of "no's," and, on average, it takes . . .

SIX First Time Face-to-Face interviews
to receive one job offer (6 1FTF ~ Offer)

In other words, control what you *can* control, i.e., your career search activities, number of daily *targeted* "connects," etc., and don't worry about what you can't control. Remember, the job search is both a "numbers" and a "skills" game!

Control what you CAN control:
Your daily number of *targeted* CONNECTS!

If you are at all typical, you probably will start analyzing why you didn't get to the next step in the hiring process (second face-to-face interview, etc.), or even why you didn't get the offer. Work to analyze not why you weren't included, but instead try to analyze why you were *excluded*.

Think back through the interview and try to assess how you answered the "key" questions asked of you? Did you "stumble" on any of the "gotcha!" questions? Did you cast any "shadows on the wall"? Did you dress professionally? Did you have a value proposition for the prospective employer, i.e., how you could either make 'em money or save 'em money, or both? In other words, did you address all of the issues and considerations we have discussed throughout *"Headhunter" Hiring Secrets* up to this point?

But the reality is this: You will probably never know the reason(s) why you were excluded. Companies have their secret hiring criteria and they are not going to tell you what those are. The best thing you can do is an analysis of why you were excluded so that you aren't *excluded* the next time out! And this is when it is powerful to have a coach, someone who can think through these things with you and help you to assess your successes and failures.

To Follow Up or Not To Follow Up . . . That is NOT the Question!

I can't overstress the vital importance of properly following up with a hiring manager after the face-to-face interview. Correctly following up after this interview can literally spell the difference between making the "final cut" and not making it.

How should you follow up? I am defining the follow-up as the next communication you send AFTER the "Thank You" note you sent immediately following the interview. The *best* way to follow up is with either *one* letter or *one* phone call to each person with whom you interviewed.

But, you might be thinking, "It has been three weeks and I haven't heard back from them. I have probably been eliminated so why should I follow up?" Good question. I have a good answer too: If you *have* been excluded, then certainly, following up won't change that. But what if you *haven't* yet been excluded?! Then, it could make all the difference in the world.

Say, for example, that the selection is down to just two or three people, and you are one of those people. You make it a point to follow up, while the other candidates, assuming they are already out of the running (or that they "have it made"), decide to forego this "nicety." Whom do you think would be most favorably looked upon as a candidate, all other things being equal?

Timing is very important when it comes to following up a face-to-face interview, however. If you were told before you left the interview that the process will take 10 days or more, and you follow up the next day, or even within several days, this actually can count against you! The employer will conclude that you just weren't listening very well.

REMEMBER
The *best* days and times to send an EMAIL are on Tuesday, Wednesday or Thursday, from 9 a.m. to 10 a.m. and from 2 p.m. to 3 p.m.

So when do you follow up? Either right after the time period the hiring manager told you a decision would probably be made regarding the "next steps" or in 10 calendar days after your face-to-face interview. (If you had a phone interview and haven't heard back in 10 days, you were most likely eliminated.) Keep moving forward with your daily connects. If they circle back to you and invite you in for another face-to-face, great but don't wait for them. Keep moving forward with your other activities.

An effective follow-up is either with:

- A letter or
- An email or
- BEST YET → A live phone conversation

If you use a follow-up letter or an email, keep them short and succinct, and reiterate two to three important points relating to the *company's* needs, as you understood them during the interview, as well as how you can *meet* those needs.

Do NOT follow up with a voice mail. Typical voice mails left are often along these lines:

"Jim, this is Skip Freeman. I am calling to follow up on the interview we had a couple of weeks ago . . ."

- OR –

"I just wanted to follow up on the meeting we had regarding the computer programming position. I am very interested in the position and . . ."

Seldom will the hiring manager call you back regarding your voice mail. If you are going to call, you must talk to the person. And when you do, the "I am calling to follow up . . ." type of call is simply ineffective. Your follow up has to provide value and solutions to their needs.

The script for the live follow-up phone conversation is simply this:

"Linda, this is Skip Freeman. I want to thank you again for considering my candidacy and I am very confident that I can bring value to your firm in this position. I know you are in the decision-making process, and wanted to know if there were any final questions I could answer for you?" (Now, STOP . . . don't say anything else. Let her respond.)

She may say, "Yes, there is one more thing" and ask you a question. Most likely, however, she will say,

"No, everything was answered."

So what do you do? Do what sales people do! Ask a question. Go back to the list of questions we suggested you consider asking toward the end of an interview. Choose one that you **didn't ask.**

"Linda, may I ask YOU a question?" (She agrees.) "I have been seriously thinking about the opportunity and position and am very interested. What, in particular, did the person in this position prior to me do especially well, and what do you wish they would have done differently or better?"

After her answer, briefly reiterate your value, based upon what she just told you, especially if you can offer a solution to one of his comments on "what she wishes that person would have done differently or better." Asking a well-thought-out question, showing you are thinking about the company, the hiring manager and her business, is the best way to follow up. It also shows initiative and the fact that you aren't afraid to PUTT! (Pick Up The Telephone.)

Thank her, reiterate your interest and that's it for ten days. Any subsequent follow up must be at a "higher level." Have you authored a paper? Have you found a press release or worthy news article on the company or the hiring manager? Future follow up must be differentiated and unique. I have known candidates who have called, written, emailed and then called again, with the same mundane "I am calling to follow up" message. The hiring manager, who had them picked as the number one choice, begins to think, *"If I hire her, is she going to be continually bugging me and everyone else in the organization? I had better not take that risk."* ("shadows on the wall"!) and now you are out of the running.

On the other hand, I have known candidates to be excluded because they *didn't* follow up, especially for sales positions. The hiring manager thinks, *"If she were truly interested, she would have reached out to us one more time. Is that also the approach we can expect her to take with our customers and prospective customers?"*

'OFFER LETTER' NOT SAME AS 'EMPLOYMENT CONTRACT'

Let's now switch to a more positive outcome following a face-to-face interview—the company likes you, you like the company, you get an "offer letter"! Hooray! Time to celebrate! Well, almost. . . .

It's vitally important that you know that an *offer of employment* (either verbal or written) is *not* the same as a "contract for employment."

Most people in the work force today will receive an offer letter if a company wants to employ them. Generally, only those employees at the very highest levels will receive an actual employment contract.

Employment contracts spell out exactly what your compensation is, your duties and responsibilities, your title, your benefits, usually to whom you report, whether or not the contract is for a set length of time and sometimes even your work environment, i.e., what office you will have and other details.

My recommendation is that if you are provided with an employment contract, pay an attorney to review it for you. It can be worth every penny you have to spend!

Well-written contracts help avoid legal issues. Both sides can review the document to determine exactly the responsibilities and duties of each party. The document itself clarifies the issues, or at least it should.

An employment contract will protect you, the candidate, from promises made by a manager that actually cannot be enforced or from misunderstandings. You interpret a certain promise one way and the manager feels he meant it another way. Without a contract, you won't be able to prove your "version" of the promise. Or, what if the manager gets promoted, fired or quits? What are you going to do? The answer? Nothing without an employment contract.

If the economy ever gets back to where it was in 2006-2007 and there is a "candidate shortage" again, you will have leverage here. You can ask for an employment contract and probably have a 50/50 shot at getting one. Until then, you can ask for one but accept the fact that you most likely aren't going to get it.

It is then your decision as to whether you wish to continue or not. Press too hard and the company moves on to the next candidate.

Counterpoint – an employment contract can also be used against you. If you have a two-year contract, for example, it can keep you from leaving if you want to. It can guarantee pay, but it doesn't necessarily guarantee completely what you will do or even where you will do it. I have known employees with a contract to be given some very unimpressive tasks to do, things the company needed done but didn't want to give to someone who might say "no" and leave the organization. I have seen people forced to relocate because of their employment contract.

Offer letters are the norm, so we will review them in the next section.

'VERBAL OFFER' USUALLY COMES FIRST

When a company decides it wants to hire you, you will receive the news from either your recruiter, a Human Resources representative from the company, or many times, from the hiring manager himself or herself. Nearly always, this initial "offer" is a *verbal* one, made over the telephone.

"Jim, we are pleased to let you know that we are interested in extending you an offer," is usually how the conversation begins.

Drum roll . . . applause . . . you must show ENTHUSIASM and EXCITEMENT! Respond with something along these lines:

"Mr. Hiring Manager, this is GREAT news! Thank you for calling!

But also, don't go over the top and keep on and on.

The caller will then outline the basics of the offer, i.e., the salary, bonus potential (if any), job title, basic duties and responsibilities and, usually, the anticipated start date.

FINALLY, THE 'BALL IS IN YOUR COURT'

Now, let's back up. Throughout the entire process you need to be doing due diligence on the company so that, by the time you have completed the final interview, you should already know, or at least have a pretty good idea, if the company is one that you would like to work for or not. Do they have a good reputation? What is their position in the marketplace? If you are working with a recruiter, and they have placed people with the company before, speak to them about the company and get their input, let them attempt to answer any lingering questions or doubts you might still harbor.

It's also very important that you feel you will enjoy working with the people at the company. You will be spending a lot of time at the job, so you want to work with people who have character, are professional and personable (based upon what is "personable" to you). Look on your social networking sites to find people who work for the company. Send them a message or give them a phone call letting them know you are thinking of going to work for the company. Ask them what they like—and dislike!—about the company.

A powerful website where you can sometimes learn what people think of a company is www.vault.com. You can also get information regarding interviews from this site. Just remember that you must filter the information. Someone may have an axe to grind, or, if they didn't do well on an interview, and try and flip it back to the company.

By the time you receive an offer, it is too late to start deciding whether or not you would like to work for that company. Your due diligence needs to have been completed *prior* to receiving an offer.

While Vault is a great tool, use it in conjunction with reaching out to people on LinkedIn and Facebook who work for the company, and again, filter *all* of this information carefully. Remember, it is easier for people to discuss the negatives over the positives at times, and you can get some tainted information. As long as you filter the information properly, you will be doing due diligence far beyond that which is done by 95% of candidates.

If, by the time you receive a verbal offer, you have decided that you probably don't want to work for the company, politely thank them and tell them that you need two days to "think it over." Then, give them a specific time and date that you will call back and then make the call! (If you are working with a recruiter, let them know immediately. Don't wait the two days. Let the recruiter tell the company that you are no longer interested. Don't keep the recruiter in limbo. Remember, they have a responsibility to fill the position.)

Is telling a company you need two days "burning bridges"? Not really. In fact, during the two days you may change your mind! As you're "thinking it over" during the two days, though, be aware that there is a possibility that the company may go ahead and make an offer to someone else, and when you call back, they will tell you they have already filled the position. So, only take this stand if you feel that you most likely will *not* accept the offer or really are not sure. But you need to make up your mind in two days—even if the company took two months.

IF YOU DECIDE YOU'D LIKE TO WORK FOR THE COMPANY

If the company is a good company, and you definitely feel that you would like to work for them, then your approach is going to be far different, of course.

If the verbal offer is **stronger** than what you imagined, say to the person making the offer,

> "Jim, I very much appreciate this and I am excited about the possibilities. I look forward to evaluating the details of the offer in writing. When do you think HR will be able to provide me with a copy?"

Another approach:

> "Jim, I can't make any commitments today, but I am very excited about the possibilities. Yes, I would like to move the process forward and get some numbers on the table. When do you think HR will be able to provide me with a copy?"

Obviously, you would like to earn as much money as possible. The fact is, however, companies want to pay as little as possible. Thus, if the offer is far better than what you could have imagined, there may be a little negotiating room, but not a lot. So be extremely careful about pressing your luck unless you already have another offer on the table.

Hiring managers look bad if a written offer is not accepted, so that's why a verbal offer is usually made first. They are 'feeling you out' to gauge your response and enthusiasm.

If you are working with a recruiter, remember we get paid a percentage of your base salary, so we are motivated to get you as much money as possible. However, we also often know the company's limits and we will so advise you. If I were working with you, and I tell you that the maximum a company will offer is $65,000 base, and that is what they offer, then you will probably squash the deal if you press for anything over $65,000. Companies have options in a down economy; most job seekers don't, unfortunately.

Unlike when you aren't sure if you will accept an offer, here you are *not* giving a hiring manager a timeframe by asking, "When will HR be able to provide me with a copy of the offer?" This prevents them from making an offer to someone else and gets them excited about the fact that you will probably accept the offer. By asking this question, you are putting the ball back in their court.

Now, what about the situation in which the verbal salary offer is *less* than you planned or hoped for? First, make sure your expectations were realistic in today's job market. How long did it take them to make you an offer, i.e., what was the timeframe between the final interview and the verbal offer? If it has been over a week and the offer is lower than you had hoped, that suggests filling the position is either not urgent and/or they have other options. That probably means you don't have a lot of room to negotiate. You also have to weigh their offer against how many offers you currently have, how long you have been searching for a new opportunity and other personal factors. Also, "salary compression" is very real in a down economy. Do not forget that.

Many job seekers also forget that cost-of-living is an additional factor. You can do a cost-of-living comparison at several sites on the Web. If the cost of living in the area where you will possibly be relocating is less, that will be reflected in the salary offer. If the cost of living is 10% less than where you currently live, then the salary may be 10% less. However, the converse is not always true. If the cost of living is 30% higher, don't expect a 30% increase in salary. For cost-of-living comparisons, this is the website we use:

<u>www.fasrelo.com</u> → Relocation Tools → Salary Comparison

You also need to consider benefits that come with the job. Bottom line: It is important to analyze the *total* package. So, **if the offer isn't what you expected**, set the stage in this manner:

> "Jim, I certainly appreciate this and I am excited about the possibilities. I need to evaluate the offer in writing, as there are a couple of areas of concern that I need to study. When do you think HR will be able to provide me a copy?"

(Again, say this *only* if the verbal offer is *less* than what you had hoped for or expected!)

With that, the hiring manager will probably ask, "What are the areas of concern?" This is where you prepare the ground work for negotiations. If, for example, the salary is low, you should say,

> "Jim, the salary is a little lower than I had hoped. However, I realize that it is the total package that is the most important, which is why I look forward to evaluating the total offer in writing."

At this juncture, the Hiring Manager will either let you know the offer will be on its way from HR or will ask you what your expectations are. Do not ask for anything higher than 15% more than what they are telling you. If the offer is significantly lower than 15% of your expectation, then, long term you may be disappointed. (Example: Salary is 25% less than your expectation. If you are fortunate enough to get the 15% back, you are still 10% lower than your expectation. Is that acceptable? Only you can compare and contrast and know what you can and cannot live with.)

If you ask for something higher than 15%, you may receive a call back stating that they can't do that and they have actually selected another candidate. Fifteen percent is generally the tipping point.

Example 1: Let's say the hiring manager calls you, extends the verbal offer and the salary portion is $70,000. You really feel you should be making $78,000, so you tell the hiring manager,

> "Jim, I certainly appreciate this and I am excited about the possibilities. I need to evaluate the offer in writing, as there are a couple of areas of concern that I need to study. When do you think HR will be able to provide me with a copy?"

The hiring manager responds as expected:

> "What are the areas of concern?"

You respond with:

> "Jim, with my proven track record of (and restate your economic value, which you have discussed on your résumé and in your face-to-face interviews), an $80,000 salary is, I believe, fair for both of us."

Notice that you stated $2,000 higher ($80,000) than what you actually feel you need ($78,000). Also, notice that by using the suggested phraseology, you are not attempting to be a "hardball" negotiator. NEVER attempt to be a hardball negotiator. Yes, it is important to negotiate. In fact, it is *critical* that you negotiate, but if you become a hardball negotiator, they may feel that they have made a mistake and suddenly are not so sure they want you on their team after all. You are no longer the "safest" candidate.

One more extremely critical point: You only have room to negotiate within the parameters of what the company feels the position is worth. For example, let's say the range for a position is $60K to $80K and you are offered $70K. That is a fair offer right in the middle of the range. Remember, the upper limit of the range is $80K so you will have a high degree of probability of knocking yourself out of the running if you ask for anything over $80K. The realistic expectation is that the absolute highest amount they will offer you is the top of the third quartile, i.e., $75K. Thus, if you feel you should be making $78K and ask for $80K, the realistic adjustment to the offer will most likely be between $70K and $75K. Mentally plan your expectations accordingly.

Example 2: If the range for your new position is, say, $90,000 to $100,000, and the highest paid person is currently at $92,000, you probably aren't going to get anything above $91,500—no matter what. If you were paid more than the highest paid person who has tenure and that ever leaked out, it could cause disruption and discontent in the organization.

Recognizing these realities, what could you expect the hiring manager's response to be (in **Example 1**) to your request for $80,000 when the company's offer was $70,000? Here are some possibilities:

"I will see what I can do."

"$70K is the best I can do."

"I think you will find the total package to be quite satisfactory."

"I certainly can't go to $80K, but, if I talk to my boss, I might be able to get it up $2K."

Regardless of what is said at this point, STOP! **Do *not* negotiate further!**

Your two objectives up to this point are:

- Getting the offer in writing.
- Setting the stage for negotiations, not actually negotiating.

Thank them and tell them that you look forward to receiving the offer in writing.

YOU CAN'T TURN DOWN OFFER YOU DON'T HAVE

The important step at this point is to get the offer in writing and see, specifically, what the company comes back with. You can't turn down an offer you don't have so that is why you don't cast any "shadows on the wall" and why you don't do any "hard" negotiating, which will reposition you as a risky choice.

You **must** get the offer in *writing*. A verbal offer means nothing.

So, let's assume now that you indeed do have the "offer letter" in hand (either via email or overnight). You begin reading and evaluating the contents. Chances are, unless you have a background in Human Resources, or another area where you became familiar and at ease with employment jargon and concepts, some of the language and terms can be confusing. Let's examine some of the more common verbiage used in the typical offer letter today.

'AT WILL' EMPLOYMENT

Do not be concerned about "at will" statements in an offer letter. That is standard and means that the company can let you go at any time for any reason. But in turn, it also means that you also can leave at any time for any reason. In fact, most states are "at will" employment states, so this language must be in the offer letter in these states.

BENEFITS

For the most part, benefits are set by company policy and are *not* negotiable. Vacation is possibly the one exception and we will discuss that in a moment.

The health benefits (to include dental, vision, mental health and others) are set. Often, you will have choices of benefits, based upon the plan you select and the premium you agree to have deducted from your salary each month. The one area of advice: Make sure you understand how *dependents* are covered. This can often be significantly different among companies and have an impact on your final income.

Other benefits that are often fixed are disability income, life insurance (you may be able to buy various levels), retirement, 401(k) (including the company "match"), tuition reimbursement, charitable gift-matching, stock purchase plan, paid holidays and paid sick leave. You have the right to ask for a copy of the benefits book so that you can read it over. Your request for a copy of the benefits book (package) is fair and there shouldn't be a problem here.

VACATION

There may be some room for negotiation here. If you have one week or two weeks with your current company, or have been unemployed, you may be pushing it if you go for anything over two weeks. If you are interviewing for a higher level position and/or have a number of years of experience, going for three weeks is fair. On rare occasions, four weeks can sometimes be obtained. However, remember the question employers will quietly be asking themselves, "Are you coming to work or coming to play?" "Do you want a new career opportunity or are you just looking for how much time off you can get?"

Remember, in interviewing we discussed that one of the points you must prove is, "Are you willing to do the job?" All three factors still apply here. An offer at anytime can be withdrawn if you aren't careful.

MOVING EXPENSES

It is fair to request to see the moving policy so that you can understand it. Unless you are interviewing for a higher level position, movement of household goods and 60 to 90 days of temporary living expenses are pretty standard, along with one (sometimes two) house-hunting trips.

In today's marketplace, companies rarely buy someone's home (unless, again, it is a high-level position). If you aren't at that level, then there is nothing here that you can negotiate.

Seldom is anything paid toward closing costs, points, release from a lease, shipment of boats, RVs, etc. Sometimes an item or two can be negotiated here but you have to be careful in these negotiations.

Find out if the company pays for the expenses directly or if they give you the money. Do they "gross up" any taxable portion of the moving expenses? If not, this is another area for possible negotiations.

[**Note:** As I write this section of *"Headhunter" Hiring Secrets,* I am seeing yet another sign of these economic times. One of our candidates has just been made an offer. He is currently employed and has a track record of success. The company making the offer is a $4 billion company with a stellar reputation, excellent product line and a history of innovation. The salary is an increase in pay and the commission plan is more lucrative. Up until this year, the company paid for the shipment of household goods and 60 days of temporary living. Their new policy is to provide a flat fee of $5,000 toward moving. We are going into negotiations with the company on the candidate's behalf and I am confident we will be able to get some additional relocation money. However, we will not get the full amount required for shipping all of his household goods. Thus, the candidate will ultimately have to make a decision based upon all of the merits of the offer, the company and which job (his current one or this one) offers the greatest long term growth and opportunity.]

COMMUNITY

Contact the Chamber of Commerce and get information on the community prior to getting an offer. As we have already discussed, after the interviews, you must determine if the company is a place you would love to work. Do the same for the community. There is nothing worse than a great opportunity in a community where you feel less than safe or don't want to raise your children. Know this *before* you get to the offer stage, or you may not have time to study and understand it completely.

Also, use, for example, Google Maps. Google Maps enables you to see satellite views of the area. Depending upon the age of the image for that area, you can see malls, schools, parks, restaurants and sometimes you can even get a sense of the neighborhoods, i.e., their layout, their proximity to the job, etc.

TIMELY DECISIONS

Let's review for a moment. As previously stated, you need to have, for the most part, completed your due diligence after the final interview and before the written offer. If you are not sure you want to take the offer, you have two days. If it is a fair offer and you want to take it (assuming the proverbial "i's" can be dotted and "t's" crossed), then again, you have two days *maximum* to get back with the company once you have received the written offer. At this point a company is evaluating you on your ability to make timely decisions. Asking for a week to "think about it" is unprofessional and impolite. It doesn't matter how long the company has taken to put the offer together, you are now the one who needs to step up, take charge, make a decision and move forward with negotiations, if it is going to be a "yes," and professionally turn them down if it is going to be a "no."

Your timeliness and professionalism at this stage go a long way toward ensuring that you get off on the right foot with your new company. Your new career starts now. Not the day you show up for work, but now.

NEGOTIATIONS

Now, let's address key components of the negotiation process. The key to powerful negotiations is having taken good notes during your interviews. You have listened carefully to their needs. You know what is important to the company, you have demonstrated your value and this empowers you to negotiate from a position of strength, not weakness.

If you "wing it" during the negotiation phase, you will not be successful. If you know how you specifically deliver value, you sell your value as solutions to their needs as you ask for concessions.

Once you have the offer in writing, make sure you understand the exact title, scope of responsibilities, your authority, performance requirements, etc. You and your employer must agree on exactly what it is you will be doing before you can really negotiate. By making sure you understand this completely, and by knowing the needs because of the notes you took during the interviews, you can now negotiate.

Most importantly, negotiations must NOT be via email. Email conveys factual information but cannot communicate emotional information, such as tone of voice and inflection (which, we have seen, can change the meaning of a sentence).

The ideal scenario for the follow-up negotiations, after you have received the written offer, is face-to-face. The next best is voice-to-voice, i.e., the phone.

Do not negotiate via email. Face-to-face is best and voice-to-voice is second best.

Start with the non-salary items first. But, you may be thinking, when they made the verbal, you said to comment on salary.

Let's review the earlier hypothetical discussion you had on the telephone when the hiring manger made you the verbal order.

The verbal offer was $70,000, and you told the hiring manager that, with your "proven track record," as well as the demonstrated value you could bring to the company, you believed an $80,000 salary would be "fair for both of us."

As I advised, you stopped negotiating over the phone about salary at that point, waiting until you had the offer in hand before continuing. Now that you have that offer, let's say that the salary is still at $70,000. Where do you go from here?

Since it is obvious from the written offer that the company didn't budge at all on the salary issue, your first "next step" is to work on negotiating and getting concessions on the little things, i.e., get the company to start saying "yes," then move to the bigger things, such as salary and bonus opportunities. If they ultimately do not budge at all on the salary, and you have achieved some of the smaller things, it may still be an excellent opportunity for you.

START DEVELOPING YOUR LIST OF QUESTIONS, CONCERNS FOR FURTHER NEGOTIATIONS

You have received the verbal offer and now you have the offer in writing. Prepare your list of questions and concerns for the *final* negotiation phase and call the hiring manager and schedule a time to discuss the offer.

If you don't reach him or her live, leave a voice mail and send a follow-up email in the following manner:

Voice mail:

> "Jim, I received the written offer. Thank you. I am very interested in the position and would like to set up a time when we can review the items in detail. My number is 678-123-4567."

Then follow up with this email:

> **Jim,**
>
> **I received the written offer letter. Thank you. I am very interested in the position and would like to set up a time when we can review the items in detail. Out of professional courtesy I also left you a voice mail, not knowing which one of these you might receive first.**
>
> **If you could please let me know a time when we can discuss the offer, I would appreciate it.**
>
> **Regards,**

Note: If you have established a solid relationship with the hiring manager and know that he does they do text messaging, then sending a text to schedule the follow up is also acceptable.

> **Text: Rec'd offer. Thank you. Very interested. Pls advise time when we can discuss and I will call you.**

It is now time to have the "live" conversation. Here are some examples of ways to address various concerns and issues after you have received the written offer:

Start off with a "safe" comment and question:

> "Jim, thanks again for the offer regarding the position of _____
> I am very interested in this opportunity. May we review the duties and responsibilities, please?"

After that portion of the conversation, reiterate the value you bring to the company followed by moving into your negotiation phase:

> "Jim, I would like to discuss a few questions and concerns I have and I truly hope that we can iron them out. Is that OK with you?"

Then bring up any concerns/questions from your list with salary being last. As an example, let's say that the company is offering you $5,000 less than what you were making and you also have to pay more on health benefits. You could address it along these lines:

> "Jim, based upon the benefits brochure, it appears that I will have to pay $100 more a month for health insurance than with my current company. That is $1,200 a year extra."

> "What flexibility do you have to enable us to address this issue?"

Now obviously, if they are offering you $10,000 *more* than what you currently are making, then this wouldn't be much of a problem, would it?

The key is NOT to be confrontational. Address the issues one at a time and ask leading questions, such as what was illustrated, "What flexibility do you have to enable US to address this issue?" Note the word "us." Make it a "team" effort. It is you and the hiring manager now working together to solve the issue.

Do not give ultimatums. Do not adopt a "take it or leave it attitude." Do not attempt to renegotiate any point that has already been agreed to. Don't let them attempt to renegotiate a point unless you get a concession in return.

And, if you are working with a recruiter, let us do our job here. We are good at this. As stated above, let us, or if you are doing it on your own, let the hiring manager know that you want the job and "hope that things can be worked out."

Putting an offer together involves a great deal of work. If the company has gotten to this point they want you. You have a little bit of power. The key here is that you have a *little* bit of power. Not a lot. They have the ultimate power to decide if they want to retract the offer and proceed with their second choice or even "keep looking." And if you attempt to "push" them, that's what you can expect them to do!

Many job seekers get way too hung up on salary. The key to successful job negotiations is to consider the entire package, not just salary. Sometimes, for example, a "signing bonus" can be a great way to wrap everything up in one package without having to address every single point individually.

> "Mr. Hiring manger, in essence, to cover the a, b, c, d and e we have discussed, and to keep it simple and easy for both of us, a $6,000 'signing bonus' will enable us to close the gap. What can we do to make that happen?"

- OR -

> "Is there anything we can do here?"

Notice the way the question is asked—the word "we" is used. Again, you are suggesting that you and the hiring manager are working together. The question is respectful and upbeat. It keeps things open and moving forward.

Another approach that is successful is to comment on what is positive about the offer as a way to open up conversation and negotiations:

> "Jim, I am very excited about this offer and I am looking forward to working with you and MNO Company. The 401(k) matching is very solid, the health insurance plan is better than what I currently have and the bonus plan is very motivational. But I do have a comment and a concern. My comment is that I was really hoping for $80,000 versus the $70,000 in the offer, and the 60 days of temporary living expenses in this market is a concern, with the housing situation the way it is. Is there anything we can do here to address these two points?"

CAUTION: Statements such as, "Is that all you can do?" or "I have to have 'X' dollars to even consider this . . . ," anything that is the slightest bit "hardball" or "in your face," will shut down conversation and make the company move on. And I have heard candidates actually use such phrases during negotiations!

On the other hand, some people are actually afraid to negotiate. They are afraid that it will "ruffle feathers" and the offer will be rescinded. That only happens if you are unprofessional, demanding, threatening or unreasonable in your requests. And even if you are thrilled with the offer, negotiate. If you don't, then you have immediately eroded confidence in your abilities. Ask for the benefits package and find a couple of things to negotiate. The company may concede or they may not. They may have been throwing a "low ball" offer to you to test you. Or, they may in fact have given you their very best shot out of the gate. You won't know until you ask, and they want you to ask. Candidates who bring value never have to accept an offer without negotiations.

Just to recap, then. The key considerations regarding negotiations are the following:

- They *must* be done in a **timely manner** (within two days).
- They *must* be done **face-to-face** or **voice-to-voice**, *never* by email.
- They *must* be **professionally conducted**.
- The concessions asked for *must* be **reasonable** and within the boundaries discussed previously.

You're *expected* to negotiate when made an offer

I will be going into negotiations a little more deeply in the next section because this phase is so critical to your career search.

NON-COMPETE AGREEMENTS

If you have a signed non-compete agreement with your current company, make sure you know that you can actually accept an offer with the new company without any encumbrances or restrictions. If you were laid off, then, in most cases, it shouldn't be an issue. However, the only way to know for sure is to have an attorney review it. The worst thing for both you and your new company is to suddenly find yourselves in a crisis situation because of a previous non-compete agreement or arrangement. Often, the company you are negotiating with will have its legal counsel review the non-compete before finalizing anything.

In return, you have the right to review any non-compete arrangement that your new company would like you to sign prior to accepting a final offer. The way to ask is by using the "Oh, by the way...." question. "Oh, by the way, when I start, is there a non-compete document that MNO Company has new employees sign?" If the answer is, "Yes, there is," ask for a copy to study. The company should not have a problem forwarding you a copy. You need to know what you are agreeing to when you start.

DON'T GO BACK TO THE 'WELL' MORE THAN TWICE!

As discussed in the previous section, you are *expected* to negotiate when a company makes you an offer, but, in negotiations, don't go back to the "well" more than twice. Anything beyond that is going to wear them out. As already illustrated, maybe you commented on the salary during the verbal offer. By now, you have outlined all of the details in the main negotiation. They sent you a revised offer letter. Thank them. If things have moved in a positive direction, thank them and accept. If they are close, tell them just that. This is your second and *final* "trip to the well."

"Mr. Hiring Manager, thank you. We are close. Everything is great but one point."

- OR-

"Everything is great but two minor details."

After these are discussed and addressed, don't negotiate further. I have heard more than one hiring manager comment,

"Does he want the job or not? If he asks for one more thing we are moving on."

The person with whom you are negotiating may wait a few days before getting back to you to "make you sweat." Don't worry. If you were respectful, professional and aren't being unreasonable, you are fine. If they decide to move on, then you didn't want to work there anyway. If they come back with something in the middle and you haven't been to the well twice, ask one more time. If you have been to the well twice, now it is time to make a decision.

If they come back after round one with *part* of what you asked for, thank them. Tell them that you really appreciate them going to bat for you and that you are thrilled with X, Y and Z. On point Q, however, you were still hoping for . . . and then ask them in a manner such as this:

"Is there any flexibility at all here?"

Show enthusiasm and a genuine desire to do the job and you will be fine. If they say,

"This is really the best we can do . . ."

Then conclude with,

> "Thanks so much again for going to bat for me. This is something that I really want to do and I need to review everything thoroughly. May I get back with you to let you know my decision at 3 p.m. tomorrow afternoon?"

Now make them sweat just a little, but just a little—not a lot!

And if you have a good recruiter, don't play games with them. They are on your side. Remember, we get paid more when *you* get paid more!

Finally, once you have signed the written offer and sent it back in, negotiations are *over*. Do NOT attempt to do any further negotiations at this point. You will now appear to be unprofessional and will be getting your future career off on the wrong foot, or worse, the offer may be rescinded. Yes, that can still happen.

Also, and this is **critical** . . . be sure to clear *all* contingencies before resigning.

CLEAR ALL CONTINGENCIES
BEFORE RESIGNING

After receiving just the verbal offer, some candidates are ready to draft their resignation letter and hand it in to their current employer. Don't even consider doing this! Remember, a verbal offer means nothing. It is just the catalyst to get the written offer going. Although it's rare, sometimes a company will not want to provide a written offer. If that happens, my advice is to move on. So, if you are currently employed, do absolutely *nothing* regarding resigning from your current employer until *all* the details of any offer are "nailed down" *in writing*.

After you have reviewed the written offer, negotiated and now have a final offer in hand, it never hurts to have a lawyer review it. Of course, that will cost you some money, so that is totally up to you. If you do have it reviewed, my recommendation is not to communicate that to the new company. That can create another, unnecessary "shadow on the wall." Why is he doing that? the new employer may wonder. Doesn't he trust us? Is he the litigious type? In fact, at no time during your contacts with the new company (interviews, letters, etc.) should you ever bring up *anything* of a litigious nature—unless you are a lawyer and are interviewing for a legal position.

No matter what, do *not* resign from your current position until *all* contingencies are lifted in regard to the offer, and you have something *in writing* from the company (an email is sufficient) telling you that all contingencies are lifted.

What types of offer contingencies are we talking about? The most universal one is the drug screen. A statement such as, "This offer is contingent upon. . . ." is quite typical. For some positions, a physical examination is required. The majority of companies will do a background check to verify education, employment history and many will do a criminal background check. If you will be driving a company vehicle, there most likely will be a Department of Motor Vehicle check regarding your driving record. If professional licensing is involved, companies will verify your license (Example: Professional Engineer, etc.). If you are being offered a position that involves the handling of money, a credit check might also be performed. And I have seen this happen—out of the blue, the company asks for a copy of last year's W-2! Do you have to provide it? Only if you want the job.

Once you have a statement, again, *in writing*, that *all* contingencies are lifted, and a start date has been established, then and only then should you resign from your current position!

To recap, then, **never, never, never resign because** . . .

- You feel an interview went well.
- You have a verbal offer.
- You have a written offer.
- You dislike your current company, your boss or co-worker et al.

The easiest time to find a job is when you already have a job. Companies will have a tendency to hire an employed person over an unemployed person time after time, regardless of one's credentials.

Things don't always work out, either, despite the fact that they may seem to be sailing along quite smoothly. Let me give you an example.

My firm recently had five candidates in the final interview stage for five different positions. After the final interviews, the five companies told us that they wanted to make the candidates offers. All five candidates said they would accept a "fair" offer. When the economy started going south, though, all five companies put all five positions either "on hold," or they cancelled them!

This can—and does!—happen, particularly in a down economy, so make absolutely certain that all the "i's" are "dotted" and all the "t's" are "crossed" before even considering resigning from your current position! Make sure *everything* is *in writing* and that *all* contingencies are lifted!

Sad to say, though, even at that point the offer can still be rescinded. (See the later section on **"The Finish Line—You Have the Job"** for more details on this kind of development.)

ALWAYS RESIGN PROFESSIONALLY AND WITH 'CLASS'

If you are human—and I am assuming, of course, that you are!—you may have a very strong desire to "show" your current company, boss, or even current co-workers, that, while they may not have fully appreciated you and your efforts, you have found another company that sees your *real* value.

My earlier advice about "spewing venom" still holds. Resist the temptation!

On the other hand, you may actually *love* your current company, boss *and* co-workers and the thought of having to tell them you're leaving suddenly seems like the worst possible thing you could ever do.

If you suddenly find yourself having "buyer's remorse". . . wondering how you are going to tell your boss and everyone else that you will be leaving . . . now might be a good time for you to review the reasons why you were looking for a new opportunity in the first place.

Making a career move strictly for more money, as we have discussed, usually is not a wise idea. If you are moving because of career opportunity (promotion, more responsibility, bigger or better company, or even a smaller, more nimble, entrepreneurial firm), geography, reducing travel, changing industries and the like, then you are making a career move for the right reasons. If you are just "kicking tires"—playing a job offer against your current company, in an attempt to get more money through a counter-offer—then you are simply playing with fire.

After reviewing your reasons for seeking new career opportunities, and if you are completely satisfied that you are making the right decision, then you must "suck it up" and resign from your current employer. Just make sure you do it *professionally* and with a tremendous amount of "class." Taking any other approach usually will come back to haunt you in your career, even years down the road. Believe that.

THE RESIGNATION PROCESS – GIVING NOTICE, RESIGNATION LETTER

A *two-week notice* is considered the professional norm. Don't, however, tell your new company that you will start with them in *three* weeks—unless you have one week of scheduled vacation that you *absolutely* have to take, e.g., for a pre-arranged honeymoon, tenth wedding anniversary, etc. Unless your scheduled vacation is for something along these lines, my recommendation is to *cancel* your vacation!

Under no circumstances whatsoever should you tell a new employer that you can't start with them for, say, *four* weeks or even more! (Maybe you're awaiting a huge bonus and need to still be employed by your current company, in order to receive it.) That will just give the company reason to seriously consider "candidate number two." The company quite likely will think that you should have thought of that before you started your job search and timed things accordingly.

What if your current company asks you to stay onboard for, say, another three or four weeks? Politely decline. Two weeks is the professional norm, and if you try to tell your new company that you need to provide more than a two-week notice, they will begin to question where your loyalties lie—with your new company or your current one, and they may well retract the offer!

Keep in mind, if you were going to be downsized, your current company would not hesitate to give you a "pink slip" at 2 p.m. on a Friday afternoon and give you one to two hours to pack up your desk and leave! Happens every Friday. Certainly, they won't give *you* a "two-week notice." Unless there is an employment contract in place, you have the right to resign anytime you want. Likewise, they can let you go anytime they want.

How do you resign? First, you prepare a **letter of resignation**, using a format and approach such as that shown in the sample resignation letter on the next page.

[Your Name]
[Street • City • State • Zip Code]
[Phone # • Fax phone # • Messages phone # • Email]

[Today's Date]

[Recipient's name]
[Company name]
[Address]
[Address]
[Address]

Dear [Recipient's name]:

Please accept this letter as my formal notice of resignation from [Company name], effective [date, two weeks from date above]. The associations I've made during my employment here will truly be memorable for years to come.

I hope a two-week notice is sufficient for you to find a replacement for me. If I can help to train my replacement, or tie up any loose ends, please let me know.

Thank you very much for the opportunity to work here.

Sincerely,

[Sign here]

[Your name, title]

cc [Names for copies]

Keep this in mind: A resignation letter is merely a statement of fact. That is all. The only reason for the letter is so that the employer will have it to show the State Unemployment Agency, in the event you should try to collect unemployment. Other than that, it goes into your personnel file. Too many people spend countless sentences telling the company about how much they "loved it here" and are "sorry to go" (then why are they resigning?!), or they will use the letter as a "pressure relief valve" and "spew venom" all over the company. A letter like that can someday come back to haunt you.

One more thing, if the company thinks later that you stole company information, or are violating a non-compete agreement, *anything* you have put in writing can be—and will be!—used against you! (Remember how we discussed in the "interviewing" section how *anything* you say can and will be used against you? That always holds true! Even after you have left.)

DELIVERING YOUR LETTER OF RESIGNATION

Unless your boss is traveling, or just totally unavailable, ask to see him or her *face-to-face*. Don't resign over the telephone, or through email, unless your boss just can't see you. But, do *not* let your boss's unavailability prevent you from resigning. If you simply can't meet personally with the boss, then meet with his or her boss. As a last resort, you will have to meet with a representative from the Human Resources department.

Here is how we advise all of our candidates to handle the face-to-face resignation with their boss:

- The objective of giving notice is **informational**. It is *not* an exit interview. It is *not* the time for emotion. Just present the facts. Present your letter. You are leaving. A transition needs to be planned. And one more thing: A resignation is NOT another part of your decision-making process. You aren't judging whether you are going to actually go to work for the new company based upon how people react when you tell them you are going to resign. Your decision-making should have been completed *before* you accepted and sent back the signed offer letter from your new company.

- What is your relationship with your boss? (If it is good and longstanding, reassure her that you will help with the transition. Don't mislead her and suggest that you will stay, when you know that you will not. That ultimately puts her in a very bad situation.)

- Get to the point! Within the first 30 seconds, the words, "I am leaving" (with absolutely *no* qualifiers) should be clearly stated, and stated with confidence. Don't "mince" words.

- Tell your boss that you are "not at liberty" to discuss either the salary you've been offered or the name of the company you will be working for. Remember, in most companies, when you sign the "welcome aboard" documents on day one, you agree to keep your salary information confidential. You most likely did it with the company you resigned from, and the new company you are going to will most likely require it as well. I have known situations in which an offer was rescinded because word got out that the person disclosed his salary and it got back to the hiring company.

- Tell your boss your start date at the new company, and say that you are prepared to give *two weeks* notice, no more. Remember, two weeks notice is the professional norm and is considered quite adequate.

- Stay *positive*! If your current company is a bad company, or if the boss is a bad boss, resist the urge to say so! It's almost over! Remember, the best revenge is living well!

- Don't put off this meeting with your boss. Do it now! The longer you put it off, the more difficult it becomes. Remember, this may be an uncomfortable 10 minutes, but you are making a *career* decision that could last a lifetime. Don't let 10 minutes of discomfort keep you from a lifetime of opportunity.

- If you have gotten this far in your search and the new opportunity is what you are looking for, don't let not having the courage to say good-bye stop you. Remember, they will give you a pink slip without hesitation and without shedding a single tear.

RESPONSES/REACTIONS TO EXPECT WHEN YOU RESIGN

What responses/reactions can you expect to receive when you do deliver your letter of resignation to the boss? In my experience, they pretty much run along the lines of those shown in the table on the next page.

Response/Reaction	Percentage of time to expect this response/reaction	How this reaction/response manifests itself
ANGER!!!!!!	10%	Outrage! How could you do this to us?! After all we've done for you! You ungrateful wretch!
Largely Unfazed	10%	Good luck and good bye! We wish you the best. Go ahead and clean out your desk and turn your keys in on your way out the door.
Truly Happy for You!	20%	Congratulations! Good luck! Let's plan the two-week transition. Your boss is truly, genuinely happy for you. Everyone is sad to see you go and will even throw a "going-away" party for you. Beware, however, for this "joy" could easily "bleed into" the next reaction, "setting you up for the counter-offer."
SETTING YOU UP FOR THE COUNTER-OFFER!	60%	Your boss may say something along these lines: "You haven't told anyone else, have you?" "I appreciate this information. What I would like for us to do is to discuss this further this afternoon." "WOW! This sure is unexpected. I just got you the promotion I promised you. And the pay raise." "I really don't know what to say. Let me see what we can do to make you change your mind." **BEWARE!** Accepting a counter-offer is almost always career "suicide"!

ACCEPTING A COUNTER-OFFER IS CAREER 'SUICIDE'

About sixty percent of the time the reaction to your resignation will be one of what appears to be genuine disappointment and surprise. Even though the boss will feign shock—"I really don't know what to say . . . You really caught me completely 'off guard,'" etc.—the fact of the matter is, the boss may really be thinking, "What rotten timing! If he quits now, then I and the rest of the team will have to pick up the slack until we find someone to take her place. Or, worse, in this economy, the company may not allow us to hire anyone to replace her. Let's see what I can do to talk her into staying . . . until we can get rid of the disloyal wretch later on, on *our* terms, not hers."

Enter the counter-offer!

The boss is going to try to keep you until he or she is ready to let you go, so they will attempt to convince you to stay by offering a salary increase, perhaps a new, expanded position, more authority, etc., etc., etc. And, while you may be tempted to seriously consider such a counter-offer, if you do accept it, you are going to be committing career "suicide" 80% of the time!

Why? First and foremost, once you have submitted your resignation, from that point on you will be marked as "disloyal," a "traitor," even to have *considered* leaving the company. That salary increase you were "promised" in the counter-offer might suddenly get "hung up" because of "unexpected budgetary constraints." The promised promotion could just as easily get "side-tracked." And, as just mentioned above, the principal thing the boss is trying to "buy" with a counter-offer is more *time*, time that will allow her to deal with you on her own terms, when *she* is ready to deal with you.

COUNTER-OFFER TACTICS

Be aware that there are some companies that are very good at playing the counter-offer game. The last week of your two-week notice, the "big boss" might suddenly be in town and ask to take you and your spouse to dinner.

Suddenly you are invited to a "high level" meeting that you have never been privy to before.

You get the document with your promotion and pay raise in it. (**CAUTION**: Most of the time it is your regular raise *in advance* and you won't get one the next time around.)

Know that all of these tactics are games. Don't fall for them. Still, remain courteous, polite, respectful and professional throughout the process.

HOW TO HANDLE THE COUNTER-OFFER

The best way to handle a counter-offer is to instantly take command of the situation when you go in to resign. Remind your boss, in a cordial, professional, yet firm manner, that your mind is already made up. Reassure your boss that you will do all you can to assist in a smooth transition during your remaining two weeks with the company. Assuming that the company even wants you to stay for another two weeks—some companies will want you "out of there" once they know your decision is final—continue to act very professionally in all that you do during the transition. Sure, it might be awkward for you during the last two weeks, but that's just human nature. By exiting in a graceful manner, you will have left behind some solid references as well as some friends.

If you would like some additional information on the counter-offer, the strategies employed, the pitfalls involved, I strongly recommend the two links featured below:

Counteroffer Article from *Today's Engineer*

(http://www.todaysengineer.org/2007/Jan-Feb/conundrum.asp)

Counteroffer Article from Insurance Industry

(http://www.ceinsurance.com/counteroffer_suggestions.htm)

A TRUE STORY ABOUT THE 'COUNTER-OFFER' CONCEPT

As recruiters, we work to identify passive talent, i.e., people "buried in excellence doing a good job in their current position." We had identified one such individual who was a sales representative with a chemical company, had a stellar track record of sales success, had been with his company for five years and had been promoted twice. His next promotion would be to a District Sales Manager position, where he would have had the opportunity to manage 12 to 15 sales professionals. The only hold up on the promotion? The current company had an unwritten "time in service" policy. In other words, no one ever got promoted to District Sales Manager with less than eight years of service with the company—no matter how good they were!

The company we were representing needed a District Sales Manager and we knew this candidate was ready to move forward in his career. He went on to interview with the new potential company and was very impressed with everything he saw and heard. He did his due diligence and confirmed that the potential company's reputation was rock solid. The company was one of the top three in the industry of about 45 competitors. By now, this individual had been on two interviews and felt things were moving in a positive direction, so he "tested" his position with his current company in the following manner.

His boss's boss was coming into town and he was having dinner with him. At dinner the candidate asked if he had any advice on what he needed to do to earn the right to become a District Sales Manager. The boss's boss said, "Keep on doing what you're doing and you will get there. But you have to remember that no one gets to be a District Sales Manager until they have been with us for at least eight years, so hang in there and you will make it."

So the candidate now unequivocally knew that if he received the offer with the new company he could be a District Sales Manager *now* versus having to wait three more years if he stayed with his current company (assuming nothing happened that would get in the way or derail his career).

Our candidate was successful in his final interview, received an excellent offer and, after the contingencies were lifted, went in to resign. That is when it started. The guilt trip. "You are being groomed," our candidate was told. "We have great plans for you." He was asked to fly to corporate headquarters and meet with the Division President (which he did, against our advice). There he was offered a four percent raise and given the full "red carpet" treatment. Lunch with a group of executives. Comments about how he was "the future of the company," but the candidate held firm and did not accept the counter-offer. Throughout, though, he remained polite and respectful.

Within two months of starting with the new company, he received a certified letter in the mail from his former employer accusing him of violating a non-compete agreement by calling on one of his old accounts. The fact was that he hadn't been within 400 miles of that account, as verified by the sales representative with whom he was traveling that day. To the old company, the "groomed candidate," with the "great potential" was now a threat to them. They were now trying tactics to cast some doubt in the new employer's mind about the individual's honesty and integrity.

What do we glean from this? The old company was never the candidate's friend. As soon as the candidate left, even though they had flown him to corporate headquarters and told him all of those wonderful things, they went on the offensive!

Moral of the story: Remember, a company—any company—is only interested in its own well-being, not yours. You have to make your career decisions based upon *your* needs, not the company's. Still, always, always, always take "the high road."

THE FINISH LINE—YOU HAVE THE JOB!

At last, you've reached the Finish Line! You've received the offer, successfully negotiated any and all "sticking points" that may have existed, and you resigned from your current position with a high degree of professionalism and "class." You successfully—and professionally—resisted the counter-offer (if one was made) and are finally ready to begin your career with the new company. Now what?

Until you actually start with your new company, don't cancel *any* pending interviews or terminate discussions with other potential employers. Don't, however, continue to "shop," either. What you want to do is simply make sure the plug isn't going to get pulled on you and everything go down the drain.

Even though you have successfully 'landed' your new position, until you actually *start* with the new company, do NOT cancel pending interviews or terminate discussions with potential employers.

Yes, that happens—even at this point!

After 30 days in your new position, take your résumé off any job boards to which you posted it. Remember your notebook mentioned in the **Preliminary Planning & Preparation** section? If you were diligent about keeping your notebook current, you can easily and quickly delete most of your online résumés after securing your new position. The reason I say "most" is that some résumés get "spidered" out onto the Web and you can never retrieve them. (Once again, this is why you must always create a résumé that follows the guidelines established in the **Marketing** section.)

Thinking about keeping your résumé on at least some of the job boards, just to "dangle the carrot," i.e., to see what opportunities might pop up down the line? My recommendation? Forget it! Remember, some Human Resources departments of major corporations continually monitor "The BIG Three" job boards (Monster, CareerBuilder and Yahoo HotJobs). What if your name came up in a search? Your boss would have good reason to confront you.

What would you say? Even if it truly is a résumé that is still "out there" from your most recent job search, you could lose credibility by not having removed it from the job boards. Why risk it?

You could always say something such as, "I didn't remove it because I forgot my UserID and password," but that could easily backfire on you as well. Now the hiring manager may wonder about your organizational skills and your ability to pay attention to detail. Just don't put yourself in this unnecessary situation in today's economy.

It is perfectly acceptable, however, to retain your profile on LinkedIn and ZoomInfo, and to keep your Facebook page updated. And, of course, you should keep your current résumé updated, just not posted. Continue to network, blog and write articles for your industry, if you have the skills and talent. That way, you become—and remain!—the "rag man," and will be the one others want to know and hire. In this economy, and arguably, in *any* economy, it pays to *always* be prepared!

CONTRACT STAFFING COULD BE YOUR 'ACE-IN-THE-HOLE'

With career searches today taking sometimes as long as six months or longer, it might be worth your while to seriously consider consulting or contract staffing positions. Also, as the economy regains steam, contract staffing is the first area where new hiring can be expected to occur.

If you truly have skills in demand within your industry, consulting no longer has the stigma it used to. Not all that long ago, if you had "consulting" on your résumé, hiring managers and recruiters often would think, "Why can't this person find a *real* job?" Today, that is not necessarily the case.

If you have something to offer, make a case for it. Sell your services. It enables you to continue to gain experience, make new networking contacts, earn money, and in many cases, advance your career.

An alternative way is to become a "contract staffer" for one of the contract staffing firms in the marketplace, such as Adecco, Kelly, Manpower, CDI, et al. Many professional positions can be filled with someone willing to work contract staffing. Examples include project management, engineering design, marketing, R&D, product launches, advertising and the list goes on.

Contract staffing is the term often used for positions that could be considered exempt and "temp" is often the term used for the positions normally considered non-exempt.

If you become a consultant, you may need to incorporate, obtain a Federal Tax ID number, file company taxes, develop a pricing structure, market/sell your services and so forth.

Contract staffing eliminates all of the steps dealing with incorporating, filing taxes and the like. You would become an employee of the contract staffing firm and work for their client. You are usually paid an hourly rate and provided a W-2. To compensate for the fact that there are often few, if any, benefits, your equivalent pay rate is generally 25% higher than if you were salaried. For example, if you were an engineer making $60,000 per year, your contract staffing pay rate would be calculated as follows: $60,000/2080 (the number of work hours in the year) * 1.25 = $36.06.hour (equivalent to $75,000 per year). The $15,000 extra is for you to buy health insurance,

335

compensate you for not having paid sick days, holidays, vacation and no matching 401(k).

Anytime we come out of a recession, contract staffing/temporary staffing is the first area to ramp up. Companies want to make sure that the rebound is "for real." Many times, these positions can be converted to "direct hire" positions, once the company is confident we won't backslide into another recession.

The term "direct hire" is the preferred term used by businesses today, rather than the term "permanent" placement, although you will still hear the terms used interchangeably. However, many companies try to avoid the use of the word "permanent," as a lawsuit a few years ago awarded someone years of pay when they were hired into a "permanent" placement position and then were let go.

In this economy, companies also want to do their best *not* to make a hiring mistake. Thus, many often "try before they buy," i.e., they will hire someone in a 60- to 120-day contract role to make sure it is working out before making a final decision.

Also, companies still need the work done. Projects must be completed, new products need to be rolled out, markets still need to be studied, new roads must be designed and built, and companies can often bring on contract staffing professionals because those funds usually come out of an operating budget that is different from the regular payroll budget.

Keep these options in mind. Most hiring managers will not view "consulting" or "contract staffing" on your résumé as anything but positive if you can quantify the work done during the period (developed a new product, designed a road, took a new product to market, etc.). In fact, there are even some sales positions that are contract staffing. This enables you to prove to a company that you can sell, take business from the competition or break open a new territory. You can be creative in these areas.

Finally, "Why can't a company pay you directly on a 1099?" you may ask. "Why do you have to incorporate or go through a company that does contract staffing?" Two words—tax laws. If you are paid on a 1099, then the company doesn't pay its side of Social Security or Medicare/Medicaid withholding taxes, they don't pay unemployment taxes and they don't pay worker's compensation. Because of the lack of payment of unemployment taxes, many states have made the mischaracterization of a person as a 1099 employee versus a W-2 a criminal offense.

So, if a company clearly has work that needs to be done but seems hesitant to hire you (or anyone) one area for negotiations is to suggest to the company that they hire you on a temporary basis, then you can contact staffing firms and find one that will represent you. (**The HTW Group** will consider doing this for you if you are a degreed professional. If you have a company that will consider hiring you in a contract staffing role, get in touch with us online at http://www.hiretowin.com, and we can work out the arrangements and do the paperwork.)

IF YOU ACCEPT CONTRACT STAFFING

If you take a contract staffing position, do *not* stop networking. If the assignment is not extended, or does not turn into a direct hire role, you don't want to have lost all momentum in your career search. However, one thing you don't want to do is quit a contract position before the assignment is over. If they gave you a position for four months and you quit after just two months, leaving them "high and dry," word will get out. With social media and the power of networking, word can spread and you can damage your future. So make sure that if you take a contract staffing position, you are doing it for the right reasons, i.e., you can commit to the timeframe, you can pour yourself into the assignment, and you can still network. Do not accept a contract staffing position because you are tired of a job hunt, or frustrated with how much time it might be taking, and you think this might be "an easy way out." If you desperately need money, for example, that is a "correct reason" to take a contract staffing position. Just be committed to it.

SHOULD YOU TAKE A LESSER JOB IN A DOWN ECONOMY?

This is a tough question. First, you have to be mentally ready and psychologically able to do that. Some people simply can't make it work. After a few weeks of lower pay, reduced responsibilities, a lower title, reduced perks, they become a liability for both themselves and the company they work for. Companies will also be afraid that you will "jump ship" at the first chance. It is hard to be excluded from the type of meeting that you actually once were in charge of, just to give you one example of what a "reduced" position could mean.

Because of the fear employers have that you will "jump ship," they may not offer you a lower position. You will have to do a good job of selling them on the fact that you are looking for career growth and opportunity, and that you are willing to do what it takes to prove yourself, which again, is often easier said than done.

If you are on a severance, you don't have to take the first thing that comes along. If you are running out of money, suggesting that you do the work for them on a contract staffing basis often makes perfect sense for both parties.

AFTERWORD

My recruiting firm, **The HTW Group**, has helped hundreds of people in the last seven years move their careers forward. **Our candidates** have a **50-60% greater probability of obtaining a position** in a shorter period of time than the job seeker who does not have the advantage of our coaching and mentoring.

The purpose of this book is to be able to reach out to more people and help them know the rules of the game that companies play by when hiring. If we can help just one more person land their next career sooner rather than later, we will have done our job. We hope that person is you!

The job market is competitive and, I strongly suspect, will become even more brutally competitive in the years ahead. Since not every company and every hiring manager situation will be the same, please send us your stories. Tell us what works for you and what doesn't.

Help us to build a virtual network of advice to share with all who wish to participate. By the way, that is the power of networking. Join our LinkedIn group, **Job Hunting Power**.

Send your stories and comments to skip@headhunterhiringsecrets.com.

I am not going to say "good luck" because I don't believe in luck.

Do not tell yourself, "I hope I find a new job," because you can let yourself be poisoned by hope.

Instead, each day analyze your successes and failures. Only then can you replicate success and apply new lessons gleaned from the failures. **Spend some time thinking,** and whether you call it a Misogi, meditation or quiet time . . . recall what Steve Jobs said to the 2005 graduating class at Stanford, "Remembering that you are going to die is the best way I know to avoid the trap of thinking that you have something to lose."

About the Author

Skip Freeman has successfully completed more than 300 executive search assignments in just seven years. Specializing in the placement of sales, engineering, manufacturing and R&D professionals in industry, he has developed powerful techniques that help companies hire the best and help the best get hired.

Skip, a distinguished graduate of the United States Military Academy, West Point, is a lifelong student of leadership, people and the principles of success. While serving in the U.S. Army Corps of Engineers and Chemical Corps, he also earned a Master of Science degree in Organic Chemistry from The Georgia Institute of Technology and a Master of Business Administration degree in Marketing from Long Island University.

As a platoon leader, he led one of the military units responsible for removing highly radioactive debris and contamination from Enewetak Atoll, a site in the Pacific used for nuclear weapons testing. Honing his engineering platoon into a well-functioning unit, he kept his project ahead of schedule and under budget. Their success was due to **effective processes** coupled with the **right people**. Following a tour of duty as an instructor at West Point, Skip moved into industry. As a field sales representative for a major chemical company, he achieved the company's highest level of recognition by his third year. With this proven track record of success, he further progressed into various sales management roles and was Vice President of Sales and Marketing for an industrial filtration company before starting his own executive search firm to help companies "hire to win."

Skip points out that today's job seekers face three major hurdles when looking for new opportunities:

- First—Flawed hiring processes. Every company, whether or not they have an effective hiring process in place, believes that they do. **Flawed hiring processes hurt excellent job seekers.**
- Second—Most job seekers look for a new opportunity only five or six times in their life, which puts them at a significant disadvantage when they **"go up against companies"** that hire people every month or every week.
- Third—The **rules of the hiring game have changed forever.**

Skip, a veteran "headhunter," knows the "secrets" that help job seekers overcome all three hurdles and get HIRED! In fact, his "secrets"-coached candidates have a 50-60% greater probability of being hired versus candidates who "go it alone," which is why he wrote this book.

You can contact Skip via email at skip.freeman@hiretowin.com. His website is www.headhunterhiringsecrets.com. For continued, up-to-the-minute, powerful "secrets" regarding how to play by the new rules of the hiring game and WIN, join Skip's **LinkedIn** Group, **"Job Hunting Power."**

INDEX

Made in the USA
Lexington, KY
29 January 2013